Property of

Matthew Thomas

HU B21

semantic priming

ESSAYS IN COGNITIVE PSYCHOLOGY

North American Editors:
Henry L. Roediger, III, *Washington University in St. Louis*
James R. Pomerantz, *Rice University*

European Editors:
Alan D. Baddeley, *University of York*
Vicki Bruce, *University of Edinburgh*
Jonathan Grainger, *Université de Provence*

Essays in Cognitive Psychology is designed to meet the need for rapid publication of brief volumes in cognitive psychology. Primary topics will include perception, movement and action, attention, memory, mental representation, language, and problem solving. Furthermore, the series seeks to define cognitive psychology in its broadest sense, encompassing all topics either informed by or informing the study of mental processes. As such, it covers a wide range of subjects including computational approaches to cognition, cognitive neuroscience, social cognition, and cognitive development, as well as areas more traditionally defined as cognitive psychology. Each volume in the series will make a conceptual contribution to the topic by reviewing and synthesizing the existing research literature, by advancing theory in the area, or by some combination of these missions. The principal aim is that authors will provide an overview of their own highly successful research program in an area. It is also expected that volumes will, to some extent, include an assessment of current knowledge and identification of possible future trends in research. Each book will be a self-contained unit supplying the advanced reader with a well-structured review of the work described and evaluated.

Titles in preparation

Gallo: *Associative Illusions of Memory*
Gernsbacher: *Suppression and Enhancement in Language Comprehension*
Park: *Cognition and Aging*
Cowan: *Limits to Working Memory Capacity*
Mulligan: *Implicit Memory*

Recently published
McNamara, *Semantic Priming*
Brown: *The Déjà Vu Experience*
Coventry & Garrod: *Seeing, Saying and Acting: The Psychological Semantics of Spatial Prepositions*
Robertson, *Space, Objects, Minds, & Brains*
Cornoldi & Vecchi, *Visuo-Spatial Representation: An Individual Differences Approach*
Sternberg et al., *The Creativity Conundrum: A Propulsion Model of Kinds of Creative Contributions*
Poletiek, *Hypothesis Testing Behaviour*
Garnham, *Mental Models and the Interpretation of Anaphora*
Engelkamp, *Memory for Actions*

For continually updated information about published and forthcoming titles in the Essays in Cognitive Psychology series, please visit: **www.psypress.com/essays**

semantic priming

perspectives from memory and word recognition

TIMOTHY P. McNAMARA

PSYCHOLOGY PRESS
NEW YORK AND HOVE

Published in 2005 by
Psychology Press
Taylor & Francis Group
270 Madison Avenue
New York, NY 10016

Published in Great Britain by
Psychology Press
Taylor & Francis Group
27 Church Road
Hove, East Sussex BN3 2FA

© 2005 by Taylor & Francis Group, LLC
Psychology Press is an imprint of Taylor & Francis Group

Printed in the United States of America on acid-free paper
10 9 8 7 6 5 4 3 2 1

International Standard Book Number-10: 1-84169-079-1 (Hardcover)
International Standard Book Number-13: 978-1-84169-079-7 (Hardcover)
Library of Congress Card Number 2005001559

Library of Congress Cataloging-in-Publication Data

McNamara, Timothy P.
    Semantic priming : perspectives from memory and word recognition / Timothy P. McNamara.
        p. cm. -- (Essays in cognitive psychology)
    Includes bibliographical references.
    ISBN 1-84169-079-1 (alk. paper)
    1. Semantics--Psychological aspects. 2. Priming (Psychology) I. Title. II. Series.

P325.5.P78M38 2005
401'.43'019--dc22   2005001559

Taylor & Francis Group
is the Academic Division of T&F Informa plc.

Visit the Taylor & Francis Web site at
http://www.taylorandfrancis.com

and the Psychology Press Web site at
http://www.psypress.com

To my parents,

Harold Joseph McNamara and Coleta Rose Eck McNamara,

who "primed" me for a career in psychology.

CONTENTS

ACKNOWLEDGMENTS

I am deeply indebted to Jim Neely, who read and commented on the book's manuscript twice. Jim raised issues I had not thought of, pointed me to articles I had overlooked, and improved the writing in several places. His comments improved the book immeasurably. I am grateful to the following individuals who read portions of the book or introduced me to key articles in new areas of research: Derek Besner, Christine Chiarello, Dorothea Chwilla, Daniel Holender, David Huber, Michael Kahana, Mika Koivisto, David Noelle, Richard Pastore, and David Plaut. I must thank Alice Healy, who invited me to collaborate on my first semantic priming experiment when I was a first-year graduate student. I also want to thank my editor, Paul Dukes, who was always encouraging and did not nag me unnecessarily. My daughters, Alexandra Hoblitzelle and Kalen McNamara, constructed most of the author index and I greatly appreciate their help. Finally, I am immensely grateful to my wife, Wendy Hoblitzelle, and daughters for their patience, support, and love.

SECTION

I

Introduction

What Is Semantic Priming and Why Should Anyone Care About It?

In 1971, David E. Meyer and Roger W. Schvaneveldt published an article in the *Journal of Experimental Psychology* entitled "Facilitation in Recognizing Pairs of Words: Evidence of a Dependence Between Retrieval Operations." This article would become one of the most influential articles published in cognitive psychology. In the first experiment, 12 high-school students were asked to decide whether two simultaneously presented strings of letters were both words (e.g., *table-grass*) or not (e.g., *marb-bread*). Of the word-word pairs, half were semantically related (e.g., *nurse-doctor*) and half were not (e.g., *bread-door*). On the average, responses were 85 milliseconds (ms) faster to related pairs than to unrelated pairs. This phenomenon came to be known as "semantic priming." As evidence of the impact of this discovery, consider that this article, the published version of James Neely's dissertation (Neely, 1977), and Neely's 1991 review chapter (Neely, 1991) had received, collectively, more than 2,500 citations as of November of 2004 (*ISI Web of Science*).

Priming is an improvement in performance in a perceptual or cognitive task, relative to an appropriate baseline, produced by context or prior experience. Semantic priming refers to the improvement in speed or accuracy to respond to a stimulus, such as a word or a picture, when it is preceded by a semantically related stimulus (e.g., *cat-dog*) relative to when

3

it is preceded by a semantically unrelated stimulus (e.g., *table-dog*). The stimulus to which responses are made (e.g., *dog*) is the *target* and the preceding stimulus (e.g., *cat* or *table*) is the *prime*. The classical task for investigating semantic priming is the *lexical decision task*. The stimuli consist of correctly spelled words and meaningless strings of letters called "nonwords" (e.g., *blit*). On each trial of the experiment, a prime and a target are displayed on a computer screen. Participants are instructed to read the prime silently and then to decide whether the target is a word or a nonword. The standard finding is that lexical decision responses are faster and more accurate when the target is semantically related to the prime (e.g., *cat-dog*) than when the target is semantically unrelated to the prime (e.g., *table-dog*). Another commonly used task is *naming* or *pronunciation*. In this task, people are asked to read the target word aloud as rapidly as possible (nonwords are typically not presented). Again, the common finding is that people can name the target word faster when it is primed by a semantically related word than when it is primed by a semantically unrelated word.

The *semantic* in *semantic priming* implies that priming is produced by true relations of meaning, as exist, for instance, between the concepts *dog* and *goat* (both are mammals, are domesticated, have fur, etc.). In fact, the term *semantic priming* typically refers to priming caused by a mixture of semantic and associative relations, as exist between the concepts *dog* and *cat*. These concepts are semantically related but in addition, if people are asked to list the first words that come to mind in response to *dog*, they list *cat* with high frequency (and vice versa). By way of contrast, *goat* is rarely listed as an associate of *dog*. Consistent with usage in the field, I shall use semantic priming to refer to both kinds of priming unless I need to distinguish the two. The difference between priming caused by purely semantic relations and priming caused by semantic and associative relations is explored in Chapter 10.

Why has semantic priming captured the attention of several generations of cognitive scientists? I am not a social historian of psychology, but I can hazard a few guesses. One likely answer is that semantic priming occurs in many cognitive tasks, including lexical decision, naming, and semantic categorization. The ubiquity of semantic priming suggests that it is caused by fundamental mechanisms of retrieval from memory (e.g., McNamara, 1992a; Ratcliff & McKoon, 1988).

Another equally important answer is that semantic priming came to be used as a tool to investigate other aspects of perception and cognition, such as word recognition, sentence and discourse comprehension, and knowledge representations. Most of the research reviewed in Chapters 15 and 17 is of this type. As another example, Swinney (1979) used semantic priming to investigate the effects of sentence context on the retrieval of meanings of ambiguous words (e.g., *bank*). Participants listened to sentences similar to the following one through headphones:

> For several weeks after the exterminator's visit they did not find a single bug in the apartment.

Immediately or shortly after the presentation of the ambiguous word (*bug*), a target stimulus was visually presented for lexical decision. Word targets could be related to the contextually appropriate meaning (e.g., *insect*), a contextually inappropriate meaning (e.g., *spy*), or to none of the meanings (e.g., *sew*) of the critical word. The intriguing finding was that when targets were presented immediately after the ambiguous word, lexical decision responses were faster for targets related to any meaning of the critical word (*insect* or *spy*) than for targets related to none of the meanings of the critical word (*sew*). However, when testing was delayed, responses only to the contextually appropriate target were facilitated; for instance, responses to *insect* were faster than responses to *spy* or to *sew*, which did not differ. These findings suggested that the initial retrieval of a word's meanings was not sensitive to the context provided by a sentence but that only the contextually appropriate meaning was incorporated into the mental representation of the sentence's meaning (see Simpson, 1994, for qualifications).

A third factor that may contribute to semantic priming's enduring influence is that when people participate in semantic priming tasks, they are often not aware that semantic priming is occurring. This is especially true when the prime is presented so briefly that people claim not to have seen it! (See Chapter 14 for details.) Even the most jaded of experimental psychologists can become unnerved when his or her behavior is affected by events that occur outside conscious awareness.

This book was written for a scientifically sophisticated audience. It will be of most use to faculty researchers, graduate students, and advanced undergraduates in the cognitive sciences and neurosciences. My goal is to review theoretical and empirical advancements in the scientific understanding of semantic priming. Neely (1991) provided an outstanding review of the field as it existed prior to 1991. My book uses Neely's chapter as a starting point and focuses primarily (although not exclusively) on theoretical and empirical developments subsequent to the publication of his chapter. In addition, I try to focus on empirical issues and findings that have turned out to be especially important for testing models of semantic priming.

This book is organized into four sections. The first section, which contains only the present chapter, is introductory.

The second section reviews models of semantic priming. This section of the book contains six chapters, which review, in turn, Spreading

Activation Models (Chapter 2), Becker's Verification Model (Chapter 3), Compound-Cue Models (Chapter 4), Distributed Network Models (Chapter 5), Multistage Activation Models (Chapter 6), and a collection of other models (Chapter 7).

The third section, which contains 11 chapters, reviews some of the major issues and findings in semantic priming research. Chapter 8 examines several important methodological issues that arise in semantic priming experiments. Chapter 9 looks at automatic and strategic priming processes. Chapter 10 examines whether priming can be produced by purely semantic relations (e.g., *goat-dog*) or also requires associative relations (e.g., *cat-dog*). Chapter 11 reviews work on mediated priming, which is defined as priming between words that share an associate but are not themselves associated (e.g., *lion-stripes*; the mediator is *tiger*). Chapter 12 looks at research on priming across intervening unrelated items (e.g., *lion, table, tiger*). Chapter 13 reviews research on backward priming, which refers to the situation in which the associative relations from the prime to the target are weak but the associative relations from the target to the prime are strong (e.g., *baby-stork*). Chapter 14 investigates subliminal priming. The question I attempt to answer is whether semantic priming occurs when the prime is presented outside conscious awareness. Chapter 15 reviews research on the prime-task effect, which refers to the finding that the occurrence of semantic priming depends on how the prime is processed. Chapter 16 examines studies that have shown that semantic priming depends on the overall context in which prime-target pairs appear. Chapter 17 looks at interactions among semantic context, word frequency, stimulus quality, and stimulus repetition. These complex findings are important because they provide strong constraints on models of priming and word recognition. Chapter 18, which is the final chapter in the third section, reviews findings on hemispheric asymmetries in semantic priming, from electrophysiological measures of semantic priming, and from functional neuroimaging investigations of semantic priming.

The fourth and final section of the book contains a single chapter in which I summarize the findings from the previous chapters and speculate on future directions for research on semantic priming.

The editors of this series told me that this book did not have to be a comprehensive review and I took this promise to heart. Several important areas of research have been omitted. I am most embarrassed about not reviewing the important findings on semantic priming in the fields of cognitive and clinical neuropsychology. I have minimal familiarity with these literatures, and writing a chapter on them would have required more time and space than I could afford. To make the project manageable, I limited the review to studies of semantic priming in which semantic context was defined by a small number of words (usually a single prime word). This constraint carves out most of the important work on lexical ambiguity resolution (e.g., Simpson, 1994). I also have not reviewed research on the Stroop effect (Stroop, 1935), even though it can be viewed as a type of semantic priming. The literature on the Stroop effect is enormous and an entire book could be devoted to that one phenomenon (see e.g., MacLeod, 1991). Finally, unlike some authors, I devote little attention to differences between tasks, such as lexical decision and naming, and I do not view the naming task as the "gold standard" for investigating semantic priming. My reading of the semantic priming literature is that these two tasks usually produce quite similar patterns of performance, and when they do not, the differences seem to be produced by easy-to-understand task demands, not by fundamental differences in the mechanisms of semantic priming. My hope is that despite these limitations and idiosyncrasies, this short book will be useful to those who want to know more about the models and the properties of semantic priming.

II

SECTION

Models

Spreading Activation Models

Spreading activation can be considered the canonical model of semantic priming. It was first incorporated into a model of memory by Quillian (1967); this model was elaborated and extended by Collins and Loftus (1975). Spreading activation models also were proposed by Anderson (Anderson, 1976, 1983a, 1993), and spreading activation mechanisms were discussed by Posner and Snyder (1975a). Although these models differ in several important ways, they share three fundamental assumptions: (a) retrieving an item from memory amounts to activating its internal representation, (b) activation spreads from a concept to related concepts, and (c) residual activation accumulating at concepts facilitates their subsequent retrieval. For example, the visual presentation of word, such as *lion*, activates its internal representation. This activation spreads to related concepts, such as *tiger*. If the word *tiger* appears soon after the word *lion*, it can be identified more quickly than normally because it is already partially activated.

The process of spreading activation has historically been incorporated into network models of memory. There are many notational schemes for constructing such networks (e.g., Anderson, 1976; Collins & Loftus, 1975; Norman & Rumelhart, 1975; Quillian, 1967). They have in common the idea that memory is conceptualized as a network of *nodes* interconnected by *links*. The nodes correspond to concepts and the links correspond to various types of relations between concepts. An example of a piece of semantic network can be found in Figure 2.1. In this network, ellipses are

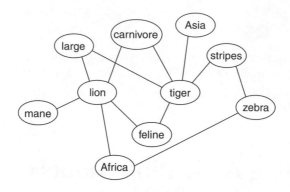

FIGURE 2.1. Example of semantic network. Concepts are represented by nodes. Relations between concepts are represented by links between the nodes.

the nodes representing concepts, and the lines connecting them are the links representing the relations between the concepts.

This network represents facts such as lions are large, lions live in Africa, lions are feline, tigers live in Asia, tigers are feline, tigers have stripes, and so forth.[1] For this network to support cognitive activities, such as language comprehension, categorization, and problem solving, the links would need to be labeled to distinguish different types of relations (e.g., lions *are a kind of* feline, lions *live in* Africa), but for current purposes, this highly schematic version suffices. The only spatial relation of importance in this network is connectedness. One can think of a semantic network as a bunch of marbles attached by strings. The marbles and strings can be arranged in an infinite number of ways, and as long as the strings do not break, the structure is unchanged.

□ Collins and Loftus's Model

Collins and Loftus's (1975) model of semantic processing distinguishes knowledge of the meanings of concepts from knowledge of their names. The conceptual network is organized according to semantic similarity, as in Figure 2.1. The names of concepts are stored in a lexical network organized according to phonemic similarity. In the lexical network, for instance, several links would exist between the nodes for *car* and *bar*, but no links would exist between the nodes for *car* and *bus*. Each node in the lexical network is connected to at least one node in the conceptual network.

The following assumptions were made about the spreading activation process:

1. Activation begins to be released from a concept at a constant rate when it is processed, and the longer it is continuously processed, the longer it continues to release activation (eventually, the release of activation must cease).[2] Processing a concept would include (but is not limited to) reading its written form, understanding its spoken form, or just thinking about the concept.

2. Only one concept can be actively processed at any one time, but once activation is released, it spreads in parallel though the links and nodes in the network. Using Figure 2.1, if a person started thinking about lions, activation would spread in parallel from the *lion* node through links to all of the associates of *lion* (i.e., *mane, large, carnivore, Africa, feline*) and would spread in parallel from those nodes to all of their associates, and so on. The restriction on the number of actively processed concepts followed from Collins and Loftus's assumption that executive control of attention was serial.

3. Activation arriving at a given node from multiple sources summates at that node. For instance, if someone were thinking about lions and then started thinking about zebras, activation from these two sources would spread through the network and add together at a node such as *tiger*. The node for *tiger* would be more active with two sources than with only one.

4. Activation takes more time to spread greater distances, with distance measured in the number of links traversed. Returning to Figure 2.1, activation would take more time to spread from *mane* to *Asia* than from *mane* to *lion*.

5. Activation decays with distance, and the rate of decay is a function of link strength. The farther a node is from the source of activation, the less activation will reach it, and the weaker the links are on the path, the less activation will get there.[3] For example, in Figure 2.1, if we assume that all of the links are of equal strength, then if *mane* were a source of activation, more activation would arrive at *lion* than at *Asia*. In addition, if the strength of the link from *lion* to *carnivore* were stronger than the strength of the link from *lion* to *Africa*, then more activation would spread to *carnivore* than to *Africa*.

6. Activation decays with time or intervening mental activities. This assumption just ensures that activation goes away eventually by some mechanism.

The feature of Collins and Loftus's model that accounts for its enduring influence is that it provides an easy-to-understand explanation of semantic priming. Consider a lexical decision task in which a prime word and a target word are displayed on each trial. Subjects are instructed to read the prime silently and then to decide whether the target word is a correctly spelled word in English (assuming English-speaking subjects). Start with a trial in which the prime and the target are unrelated, such as *table-tiger*. Reading the word "table" would cause activation to spread from the concept *table* to all of its associates, and to all of their associates, and so on. The node corresponding to *chair* would therefore be active, but very little if any activation would get to *tiger* because *table* and *tiger* are presumably very distant in the network. When the word "tiger" appeared, its node would be in a state of baseline activation. Lexical decision time would depend on the normal duration of the perceptual and the cognitive processes needed to decide whether or not the string of letters on the computer screen constituted a correctly spelled word in English. Now consider a related trial, such as *lion-tiger*. In this case, activation from the prime, *lion*, would spread to *tiger* because they are relatively close in the network and connected by several paths. When the word "tiger" appeared, the node for *tiger* would be more active than baseline. This heightened level of activation could facilitate any of a number of cognitive processes, including identifying the letters, retrieving the meaning of the word, and subsequent decision processes. The point is that the raised activation level of *tiger* facilitates processing of *tiger* when it follows *lion* relative to when it follows *table*.

Two lines of evidence are problematical for the Collins and Loftus model. Ratcliff and McKoon (1981) showed that priming in item recognition was statistically reliable when the SOA (stimulus onset asynchrony) between the prime and the target was as short as 100 ms (no priming occurred at an SOA of 50 ms). This result indicates that activation spreads very rapidly. In addition, the magnitudes of priming at an SOA of 100 ms were the same for prime-target pairs close in network distance and pairs far in network distance. The effects of network distance appeared in the sizes of priming effects at the longer SOAs: more priming eventually occurred for close pairs than for far pairs. Lorch (1982) obtained similar results for semantic priming in a naming task. In another line of research, Ratcliff and McKoon (1988, Exp. 2) showed that the decay of priming could be very rapid, within 500 ms in some circumstances. These findings contradict basic assumptions of the Collins and Loftus model (as well as Anderson's, 1976, model) but are quite consistent with Anderson's (1983a) ACT*.

□ ACT*

The spreading activation mechanisms in Anderson's models (Anderson, 1976, 1983a, 1993) have gone through several stages of development over the years. I focus on the ACT* model (Anderson, 1983a) because, as just discussed, the earliest version (ACT, Anderson, 1976) has been empirically disconfirmed, and more recent versions (ACT-R, Anderson, 1993) are similar to many compound-cue models (discussed in Chapter 4), in that only direct associations between concepts are behaviorally relevant.

ACT* provides an elegant mathematical model of spreading activation. The essential assumptions are these:

1. Activation flows from a source and spreads throughout the semantic network. A node will be a source of activation if the stimulus it represents is present perceptually or if it is the goal of a cognitive activity.
2. The activation emanating from a node is divided among its immediate neighbors according to their relative strengths. For example, in Figure 2.1, if *lion* were a source and each of the five nodes directly connected to *lion* were of equal strength, then each node would receive one fifth of the activation released from *lion*. The strength of connection between nodes is defined in terms of node strength; link strength is not defined in the model.
3. Activation spreads extremely quickly. The rate of spread is a parameter of the model. Rates on the order of 1 ms per link have typically been used. Effects of network distance are attributed to differences in asymptotic activation levels. For example, in Figure 2.1, activation spreading from *lion* as a prime would reach *carnivore* and *stripes* within a few milliseconds of each other. However, the maximum activation level reached by *carnivore* would be higher than the maximum reached by *stripes*.
4. The nodes in the network reach their asymptotic activation levels very quickly. The rate of this process depends on parameters of the model. Typical parameter values cause the entire network to reach asymptotic activation in fewer than 50 ms.
5. Activation decays with the distance it travels. The proportion of a node's activation that is maintained in the spread to its neighboring nodes is a parameter of the model. Values in the range of 0.8 are typically used.

6. The period of time that a node will remain a source of activation in the absence of attention (the stimulus the node represents is not perceived, the node is not the goal of a task, etc.) is a parameter of the model. Values on the order of 400–500 ms are often used. Because the rate of decay of activation is high, the network will decay to baseline activation levels within a few hundred milliseconds once all sources of activation have been removed.

Because nodes in the network reach their asymptotic activation levels so quickly, most priming phenomena can be modeled by examining properties of the network at asymptote (e.g., Anderson, 1983b; McNamara, 1986; McNamara & Diwadkar, 1996). Asymptotic activation is given by the following equation:

$$a_i = c_i + m \sum_k s_{ik} a_k$$

where a_i is the activation level of node i; c_i is proportional to the strength of node i if i is a source of activation and is 0 otherwise; m is the maintenance factor; s_{ik} is the strength of the association from k to i and is defined as the strength of node i divided by the sum of the strengths of all nodes connected to k; and a_k is the activation of node k. This relation produces a system of n equations in n unknowns that has a unique solution provided m is less than 1.0 and s_{ik} is defined as stated (Protter & Morrey, 1964).

As an example, consider the network in Figure 2.1. Assume all nodes have strength = 1.0 and that $m = 0.8$. Consider, first, making *tiger* the only source of activation. This case corresponds to an unrelated-prime condition in which the prime is very distant in the network. The activation of *tiger* is 1.89. By comparison, the activation of *lion* is 0.65 and the activation of *mane* is only 0.10. The related-prime condition can be modeled by making *lion* and *tiger* both sources of activation. In this case, the activation of *tiger* jumps to 2.54. The difference between 1.89 and 2.54 constitutes the semantic priming effect.

The account of semantic priming in ACT* is quite different from that provided by the Collins and Loftus model. In the Collins and Loftus model, the prime sends activation to the target, and the target can be in a preactivated state even though the prime is no longer being processed. In ACT*, however, both the prime and the target must be sources of activation—both must be objects of attention—for the association between them to produce heightened activation of the target. Priming occurs in ACT* because the prime is still a source of activation when the target appears.

Based on the near absence of citations in the word recognition literature (but see Neely, 1991), I must assume that most researchers are unaware that Anderson (1983a, pp. 96–106) proposed a model of lexical decision using a production system. This model generalizes to naming. The distinction between declarative and procedural knowledge is fundamental to ACT* (e.g., Anderson, 1976; Ryle, 1949; Squire, 1987). In brief, declarative knowledge can be verbalized, visualized, or declared in some manner; procedural knowledge consists of skills, cognitive operations, and knowledge of how to do things. In ACT*, declarative knowledge is modeled in networks of propositions (e.g., as in Figure 2.1), images, and temporal strings. Procedural knowledge is modeled by production systems (e.g., Newell, 1973; Newell & Simon, 1972). A production is a condition-action rule. The condition specifies a pattern of information that must hold in working memory. If the pattern exists, the production applies and the action is performed. An action could consist of adding information to working memory, executing an external behavior, or both.

Anderson's model of the lexical decision task relies on three sets of productions. One type of production automatically labels alphabetic stimuli as words. The assumption is that accomplished readers have one such production for every word in their reading vocabulary. For example, such a production for the word *lion* might be

IF the stimulus is spelled L-I-O-N
THEN assert that the stimulus is similar to lion.

Because the pattern matching processes are imperfect, this production may also label near words (e.g., *lian*) with the closest matching word (*lion*). It cannot, therefore, be used as the basis of the lexical decision. The spelling of the similar word must be checked against the visual stimulus. The naming task would use only the productions that identify similar words (i.e., no spelling check is involved) and whatever productions would be needed to pronounce the word.

The second set of productions performs the spelling check when the subject is not expecting any particular word to be present. These productions classify the stimulus as a nonword if the similar word and the stimulus mismatch in spelling and as a word if a mismatch cannot be found. These productions cannot be employed unless a similar word has first been identified. A counterintuitive implication of these assumptions is that subjects go through a state of identifying each nonword with some word in the lexicon. Presumably, other mechanisms would be needed to handle unpronounceable nonwords (e.g., *xzqpyt*).

The third set of productions performs the spelling check when the subject is expecting a particular word. These productions do not depend on the identification of a similar word; instead, the stimulus is compared to the anticipated word. If they match, an immediate "word" response can be made. A mismatch, however, does not justify a "nonword" response. The subject might have expected *tiger* but been presented with *table*. If there is a mismatch between the stimulus and the expected word, processing reverts to the second set of productions described previously. It is assumed that a similar word is identified by the labeling productions while the third set of productions is executing.

The basic semantic priming effect is explained as follows. Presenting a prime will activate related words in the semantic network, including their orthographic features. This activation will facilitate pattern matching in the productions that compare the spelling of the stimulus to the similar word. If the target is unrelated to the prime, these various productions will proceed at their normal rate. Hence, the model predicts facilitation but not inhibition in paradigms in which subjects do not have expectations for particular words.

Expectation can benefit processing in two ways. First, the production that identifies a word similar to the visual stimulus is skipped. Second, an expected word's representations will be active, and this activation will facilitate comparing it to the visual stimulus. However, if the expected word does not appear as the target, there is a cost to switching the goal to determining whether the visual stimulus matches the similar word. The model therefore predicts both facilitation and inhibition in paradigms in which subjects use expectations.

To be more specific, if the subject is expecting a particular target to follow the prime, the expected word's representations will be active (more than one target can be expected; this situation is discussed in Chapter 9). If the expected word appears as the target, and it is semantically related to the prime (e.g., the subject expects *tiger* to follow *lion*, and it does), it will benefit from activation from the expectation, skipping identification of the similar word, and automatic spread of activation through the semantic network. If the expected word appears as the target, but it is not semantically related to the prime (e.g., the subject expects *robin* to follow *lion*, and it does), it will benefit from the expectation and skipping identification of the similar word but not automatic spread of activation. If the expected word is not the target but the target is related to the prime (e.g., the subject expects *robin* to follow *lion* but *tiger* appears instead), there will be a cost incurred from violation of the expectation but facilitation from automatic spread of activation. Finally, if the expected word is not the target and the target is not related to the prime (e.g., the subject expects *tiger* to follow *lion* but *chair* appears instead), only costs will be incurred from violation of the expectation. Data relevant to these predictions will be discussed in Chapter 9.

Becker's Verification Model

Becker's verification model of word recognition (Becker, 1976, 1979, 1980, 1985; Becker & Killion, 1977; see also Paap, Newsome, McDonald, & Schvaneveldt, 1982) is commonly understood to explain semantic priming solely in terms of strategic processes (e.g., McNamara & Holbrook, 2003; Neely, 1991). The seeds of this interpretation are easy to identify. The model's name, its use of serial comparison processes, and Becker's comprehensive discussions of the role of attention in word recognition at time when attention was equated with strategies and consciousness have all contributed to the view that the verification model can only account for strategic semantic priming. I now believe that this interpretation is incorrect. In the light of research demonstrating the role of attention in semantic priming and the apparent dissociation of attention from conscious strategies (see Chapters 9, 15, and 17), Becker's model has a surprisingly youthful countenance.

According to Becker's model, a visually presented word is stored in visual sensory memory (e.g., Sperling, 1960). Processes responsible for sensory feature analysis then extract "primitive" visual features from the representation in sensory memory and feed this information to word detectors in the lexicon (e.g., Morton, 1969). These features consist of line segments, curves, angles, and so forth, but not the "relational" features needed to recognize a word definitively. For example, the primitive features in the letter R might consist of two line segments and an arc, whereas the relational features might specify that the endpoints of the arc

19

are attached to the top of the vertical line segment, that the 315° line segment is attached to the bottom of the arc, and so on. Because many words in the lexicon will share primitive features with the stimulus, many word detectors will be activated initially. The purpose of this stage of processing is to limit the number of possibilities for a subsequent analytic search. The set of such activated word detectors is referred to as the "sensory-feature defined set" or "sensory set."

A verification process is responsible for completing the identification of the word. The verification process samples one word from the sensory set and constructs a complete visual representation of the word using its stored primitive and relational features. This representation is compared to the representation in visual sensory memory. If these representations match sufficiently well, the stimulus is identified as the candidate word currently being considered. If the match is not sufficiently close, another candidate is sampled from the sensory set and the verification process is repeated. Sampling, construction, and comparison continue until a match is found or the sensory set is exhausted.

Semantic priming is explained as follows. When the prime is recognized, semantic information about the word becomes available and word detectors in lexical memory are activated according to their semantic similarity to the prime (e.g., Morton, 1969). Word detectors that exceed their criteria for activation are included as members of a semantic-feature defined set, or "semantic set." The semantic set is used by the verification process in much the same way as the sensory set. The semantic set is available as soon as the prime is recognized, typically prior to the presentation of the target. It can therefore be used by the verification process to facilitate recognition of the target. The verification process samples the semantic set while the sensory set for the target is being created and processed. If the target is semantically related to the prime, it can be recognized by successful verification of a word selected from the semantic set. If the target is not semantically related to the prime, the semantic set will be exhaustively sampled, and verification will proceed to sample the sensory set. On the average, then, recognition time will be less for targets preceded by related primes than for targets preceded by unrelated primes. According to this model, semantic priming occurs because the feature analysis processes are bypassed.

Although Becker himself referred to the semantic set as the "expectancy set" and discussed at length various strategies in word recognition, such as the "specific prediction strategy" and the "general expectancy strategy" (Becker, 1980), the model does not require that the generation of the semantic set be conscious or that these processes be slow acting (see esp. Becker, 1976; Becker & Killion, 1977). Indeed, the mechanism of activation of the semantic set could be fast acting (as suggested by

Becker, 1979, p. 253), and the verification process must be fast acting, at least on the sensory set, to explain the rapidity with which words can be recognized and identified out of context.

Becker's verification model shares many features with Anderson's (1983a) model of semantic priming in lexical decision (of course, Becker's model preceded Anderson's model historically). Generation of the sensory set is similar to the identification of the similar word, except that the sensory set contains many candidates, whereas only one similar word is identified. Both models employ a verification process in which candidates are compared to the visual stimulus. The major differences exist in the explanation of facilitation in semantic priming. In Becker's model, semantic priming occurs because generation and examination of the sensory set are bypassed if the visual stimulus matches a candidate in the semantic set. These processes are analogous to expectation-based priming in Anderson's model; however, Anderson's model also includes a priming mechanism based on spread of activation through the semantic network.

CHAPTER

Compound-Cue Models

Compound-cue models of priming were proposed independently by Ratcliff and McKoon (1988) and by Dosher and Rosedale (1989). The compound-cue model is simply a statement about the content of retrieval cues. The claim is that the cue to memory contains the target item and elements of the surrounding context. In a lexical decision task, for example, this context could include the prime, or even words occurring before the prime.

The compound-cue model must be combined with a model of memory to make predictions about performance in a task. Models that have figured prominently are Search of Associative Memory (SAM, Gillund & Shiffrin, 1984), Theory of Distributed Associative Memory (TODAM, Murdock, 1982), and MINERVA 2 (Hintzman, 1986). In all of these models, the familiarity of a cue containing two associated words will be higher than the familiarity of a cue containing two unassociated words. In a lexical decision task, if the cue contains the target and the prime, familiarity will be higher for a target related to its prime than for a target unrelated to its prime (e.g., *lion-tiger* vs. *table-tiger*, respectively). If familiarity is inversely related to response time, basic priming effects can be explained (e.g., Balota & Chumbley, 1984; Ratcliff & McKoon, 1988).

To make these ideas clearer, I will walk through an example using SAM as the model of memory (for similar examples, see McNamara, 1992a, 1992b; McNamara & Diwadkar, 1996; Ratcliff & McKoon, 1988). SAM is a model of recognition and recall. The elements of long-term memory are unitized sets of features, called *images*. Images in an episodic task contain information about the item (e.g., its name), the context in which it appeared (e.g., list A vs. list B), and its associations with other items. During retrieval, cues are assembled in a short-term store, or *probe set*, and used to activate associated information in long-term memory. Recognition decisions are made on the basis of a global index of the level of activation created by the probe set. Recall involves sampling images one at a time from the set of activated images and evaluating them based on contextual and item information.

Memory is formalized as a matrix of associations between cues and images. A simplified matrix of retrieval strengths is illustrated in Figure 4.1. This matrix represents the associations among 12 items organized into three associative chains, A–B–C–D–E–F, G–H–I, and J–K–L. The cue N corresponds to an item that has no representation in memory, such as a nonword. SAM assumes that all cues are associated with all images to some degree; even a novel nonword will have some residual similarity with words in memory. In this example, the associative strength between a cue and its own image in memory (e.g., B–B′) is stronger than the associative strength between a cue and one of its immediate neighbors in a chain (B–A′), which in turn is stronger than the associative strength between a cue and an image in a different chain (e.g., B–H′). The weakest associations are those between the cue N and concepts in memory.

The familiarity of a set of cues is defined as the total activation in long-term memory in response to the cues. Familiarity is computed mathematically by taking the product of the associative strengths between each element of the cue and an image in memory and then summing these values across all images in memory. The equation for computing familiarity is

						Images						
Cues	A′	B′	C′	D′	E′	F′	G′	H′	I′	J′	K′	L′
A	1.0	.7	.2	.2	.2	.2	.2	.2	.2	.2	.2	.2
B	.7	1.0	.7	.2	.2	.2	.2	.2	.2	.2	.2	.2
C	.2	.7	1.0	.7	.2	.2	.2	.2	.2	.2	.2	.2
D	.2	.2	.7	1.0	.7	.2	.2	.2	.2	.2	.2	.2
E	.2	.2	.2	.7	1.0	.7	.2	.2	.2	.2	.2	.2
F	.2	.2	.2	.2	.7	1.0	.2	.2	.2	.2	.2	.2
G	.2	.2	.2	.2	.2	.2	1.0	.7	.2	.2	.2	.2
H	.2	.2	.2	.2	.2	.2	.7	1.0	.7	.2	.2	.2
I	.2	.2	.2	.2	.2	.2	.2	.7	1.0	.2	.2	.2
J	.2	.2	.2	.2	.2	.2	.2	.2	.2	1.0	.7	.2
K	.2	.2	.2	.2	.2	.2	.2	.2	.2	.7	1.0	.7
L	.2	.2	.2	.2	.2	.2	.2	.2	.2	.2	.7	1.0
N	.1	.1	.1	.1	.1	.1	.1	.1	.1	.1	.1	.1

FIGURE 4.1. Matrix of associations between retrieval cues and images in memory for SAM.

$$F(\{Q_1, Q_2, \ldots, Q_M\}) = \sum_{k=1}^{N} \prod_{j=1}^{M} S(Q_j, I_k)^{w_j}$$

where Q_1, Q_2, . . . , Q_M are the elements of the cue, $S(Q_j, I_k)$ is the associative strength between cue j and image k, and w_j are weights applied to the strengths. A common assumption in applications of SAM is that a limited capacity attentional mechanism is distributed across cues; this is implemented by having the weights sum to 1.0. More weight is typically assigned to the target than to other elements of the cue because it is the object of the decision.

For example, the familiarity of a cue containing a directly associated prime and target, such as {C,D}, assuming weights of 0.3 on the prime and 0.7 on the target, would be:

$$F(\{C, D\}) = (0.2^{0.3})(0.2^{0.7}) + (0.7^{0.3})(0.2^{0.7}) + (1.0^{0.3})(0.7^{0.7})$$

$$+ (0.7^{0.3})(1.0^{0.7}) + \ldots + (0.2^{0.3})(0.2^{0.7})$$

$$F(\{C, D\}) = 4.05.$$

By comparison, the familiarity of a cue containing a prime and a target from different associative chains, such as {H,D}, is $F(\{H, D\}) = 3.69$. This difference in familiarity, 4.05 vs. 3.69, is the basis of the priming effect. Primes and targets do not need to be directly associated in SAM to produce a boost in familiarity; they only need to share an associate. For example, using the matrix in Figure 4.1 and the same weights as used above, the familiarities of cues separated by one, two, and three associative steps are:

$$F(\{D, E\}) = 4.05,$$

$$F(\{C, E\}) = 3.81,$$

$$F(\{B, E\}) = 3.69.$$

Notice that the familiarity of the three-step cue, {B,E}, is no greater than the familiarity of a cue containing a prime and a target from different associative chains, such as {H,D}. SAM can therefore predict priming between items separated by two associative steps but not between items separated by three or more associative steps. Other base models produce different predictions. TODAM, for example, can account for priming between direct associates but not between items separated by more than one associative step (McNamara, 1992b). Data relevant to these predictions are reviewed in Chapter 11.

The matrix in Figure 4.1 was constructed for illustrative purposes and therefore has several unrealistic properties. For instance, the associative strengths have zero variability, which implies, among other things, that items in memory can be perfectly discriminated from items not in memory and that associated items can be perfectly discriminated from unassociated items. A more realistic matrix would have variable associative strengths, such that residual associations (e.g., H–B') would sometimes exceed direct associations (e.g., C–B'), and so forth (e.g., Gillund & Shiffrin, 1984).

There is a fair amount of uncertainty in the literature about how compound-cue models should be interpreted. For example, these models have been categorized as "post-lexical" priming models (e.g., Neely, 1991), meaning that they account for priming with processes that occur after lexical access. Compound-cue models have also been criticized because they cannot explain priming in naming tasks (e.g., Neely, 1991).

One source of confusion may stem from particular implementations used to illustrate compound-cue models. For example, in the present example, using SAM, there may be uncertainty about how to interpret the cues and the images in the context of a standard semantic priming paradigm, such as lexical decision. Are the cues low-level visual representations of words and the images their meanings? If so, what sense does it make to have the visual representation of, say, *tiger* associated with the meaning of *lion?* Alternatively, perhaps the cues correspond to word meanings and the retrieval matrix represents associations among them. This interpretation is not satisfying because it implies that the lexical decision is made after the meanings of the prime and the target have been processed completely and, presumably, after the lexical status of the target has been evaluated.

According to compound-cue models, memory retrieval is a process that unfolds over time and involves many component subprocesses (e.g., Ratcliff, 1978). The formation of the compound cue and its interactions with memory are dynamic processes. A better way to conceive of the cues and the images is that the cues are time-evolving sets of features, ranging from low-level sensory features to higher-level semantic features, and the images are bundles of features corresponding to orthographic, morphological, semantic, and syntactic aspects of words. Associative strengths in the retrieval matrix represent the overall level of match between cues and images, collapsing across types of features and processing time. The relative contributions of various types of features to the overall match will depend on the task, the stimuli, and how long processing has taken place. For example, in a task involving sequential lexical decisions on items presented one at a time, the cue may contain a relatively complete representation of the prime, including its semantic features, because it is processed up to the point of recognition. However, in a task in which no response is made to the prime, lower-level visual features of the prime may predominate. Either way, the cue contains only visual features of the target initially. As the retrieval process progresses, the relative mix of low-level and high-level features will change. Early in retrieval, all of the features of the prime's representation in the cue will match its image in memory, and high-level features will match those of the prime's associates, including the target, but only the low-level features of the target's representation in the cue will match the target's image in memory. As retrieval evolves, more high-level features of the target will become available, increasing the level of match with its own representation, the prime's image, and other associates' images.

A related problem may be that the general theory is identified with the implementations used to illustrate the theory. The compound-cue model has typically been combined with models of episodic memory, such as SAM and TODAM, to explain semantic priming phenomena. These models of recognition and recall do not apply in any natural way to the naming task. However, by taking a broader view, one can see how compound-cue processes could account for semantic priming in naming. The existence of semantic priming in naming implies that naming is an exemplar of a category of tasks that involve mapping written words to their meanings (e.g., Plaut, 1995). The computation of these mappings, and of mappings from orthography to phonology and from phonology to meaning, may be affected by the context established by compound-cues, with the relative influence of orthographic, phonological, and semantic features changing over time (e.g., Plaut, McClelland, Seidenberg, & Patterson, 1996; Seidenberg & McClelland, 1989).

Many processing details remain to be worked out in compound-cue models, especially as applied to lexical decision and naming tasks. Even so, these models provide a useful conceptual framework for understanding semantic priming phenomena. An important contribution of compound-cue models is that they place many priming phenomena within the purview of general models of memory.

5
CHAPTER

Distributed Network Models

Distributed network models have a long history (e.g., Hebb, 1949; Rosenblatt, 1962) but they did not become influential in cognitive psychology until the mid-1980s (e.g., McClelland & Rumelhart, 1986; Rumelhart & McClelland, 1986). To provide background for the discussion of distributed network models of semantic priming, I begin this chapter with a brief overview of distributed network models of knowledge representation. The development and investigation of distributed network models have become a gigantic enterprise. My modest goal is to summarize a few of the most important characteristics of these models, especially as they may help the reader to understand the models of priming.

According to distributed network models, concepts are represented as patterns of activation across a network of densely interconnected units. Similar concepts are represented by similar patterns of activation. The units can be thought of as representing aspects of the object or event being represented. These aspects, however, need not be nameable or correspond in any obvious way to the features people might list in a description of the entity. Indeed, a traditional feature, such as *has wings*, might itself be a pattern of activation over a collection of units.

Units are typically organized into modules, which correspond to sets of units designed to represent a particular kind of information (e.g., verbal vs. visual) or to accomplish a particular information-processing goal (e.g., input vs. output). For example, Farah and McClelland's (1991) model of semantic memory impairment has three modules corresponding to verbal inputs, visual inputs, and semantic representations (which are further subdivided into visual units and functional units). Units within a module are richly interconnected with each other, and units in different modules may or may not be connected, depending on the architecture of the model. For example, in Farah and McClelland's model, visual input units and verbal input units are connected to semantic representation units but not to each other.

Presenting a stimulus to the network causes an initial pattern of activation across the units, with some units more active than others. This pattern changes as each unit receives activation from the other units to which it is connected. A stable pattern of activation eventually appears across the units. The particular pattern instantiated across a set of units in response to an input, such as seeing an object or hearing a word, is determined by the weights on the connections between the units. Knowledge is therefore encoded in the weights, which constitute the long-term memory of the network.

The feature of distributed network models that may explain more than any other their continuing influence is that they learn. A network can be trained to produce a particular output, such as the meaning of a word, in response to a particular input, such as the orthographic pattern of the word. Training involves incrementally adjusting the weights between units so as to improve the ability of the network to produce the appropriate output in response to an input.

Another important characteristic of distributed network models is that their performance can decay gracefully with damage to the network. This characteristic is a result of having knowledge distributed across many connection weights in the network. For example, even with up to 40% of its visual semantic memory units destroyed, Farah and McClelland's model was able to correctly associate names and pictures more than 85% of the time.

Recently, several distributed network models of semantic priming have been proposed. These models fall into two broad categories.

In one category of models, which I refer to as "proximity models," priming occurs because related primes and targets are closer to each other in a high-dimensional semantic space than are unrelated primes and targets (e.g., Cree, McRae, & McNorgan, 1999; Masson, 1991, 1995; McRae, de Sa, & Seidenberg, 1997; Plaut, 1995; Plaut & Booth, 2000). A fundamental assumption in these models is that concepts are represented by patterns of activity over a large number of interconnected units. Related concepts have similar patterns of activity. Semantic priming occurs because in processing a target word the network begins from the pattern created by processing of the prime; this pattern is more similar to the target's representation when the prime is related than when it is unrelated to the target. In effect, the network gets a head start in processing the target when it is preceded by a related prime. Plaut's model (e.g., Plaut, 1995; Plaut and Booth, 2000) distinguishes semantic priming, which is attributed to overlapping semantic features, from associative priming. Associative priming occurs in this model because the network learns to make efficient transitions from primes to targets that co-occur frequently during training.

The other category of distributed models, which I refer to as "learning models," attributes semantic priming to learning that occurs when a word is recognized or is the object of a decision of some kind (e.g., Becker, Moscovitch, Behrmann, & Joordens, 1997; Joordens & Becker, 1997). These models also assume that concepts are represented by patterns of activity over a network of units and that semantically similar concepts have similar patterns of activity. However, in these models, semantic priming is caused by incremental learning. Each presentation of a word causes all of the network connections participating in recognition to be altered, so as to increase the probability of producing the same response to the same input. This learning facilitates processing of the word if it reappears but also facilitates processing of words with similar representations (e.g., a semantically related target). Learning decays very slowly and is permanent unless undone by additional learning. This class of models, unlike all other models of priming, predicts that semantic priming should occur over very long lags between presentation of the prime and the target. Data relevant to this prediction are reviewed in Chapter 12. Proximity also may play a role in these models, especially in explaining priming at short lags.

Dalrymple-Alford and Marmurek (1999b; Dalrymple-Alford & Marmurek, 1999a) have identified a possible limitation of fully recurrent distributed network models of semantic priming, at least as they have been applied to naming (e.g., Masson, 1991, 1995). This category of models includes Hopfield nets (e.g., Hopfield, 1982; Hopfield & Tank, 1986) and, in the current classification, is an example of proximity models. In fully recurrent models, each processing unit is connected to all other units, and activation of the units changes until the entire network reaches a stable state. A principal application of fully recurrent networks is pattern completion. An entire pattern of activation across all units can be recovered by setting a subset of the units to their appropriate values.

For the purposes of modeling word recognition, the units can be grouped into modules corresponding to orthographic, phonological, and semantic features of words (Masson, 1995). Word recognition is simulated by assigning appropriate values to the orthographic units and then updating phonological and semantic units until they reach stable states.

The meaning of a word is considered to be accessed when the semantic units settle on their appropriate values. This process is facilitated by the prior presentation of a semantically related word because those units corresponding to shared semantic features between the prime and the target have values appropriate for the target when its orthographic units are clamped on. These models can account for semantic priming in tasks in which the response requires access to the meaning of the word; presumably, lexical decision is such a task (e.g., Dalrymple-Alford & Marmurek, 1999b; Masson, 1991).

Word naming requires access to a word's pronunciation, which in the model is available when phonological units settle on values appropriate to the word. Masson (1995) conjectured that because phonological units receive input from all other units, including semantic units, they too would settle faster on appropriate values for a target word if the target were preceded by a semantically related word than if it were preceded by a semantically unrelated word. Masson showed that this effect occurred in his model. However, Dalrymple and Marmurek (1999b) presented evidence that this relatedness effect was primarily caused by interference from an unrelated prime, not by facilitation from a related prime. Based on the results of a series of simulations, they concluded that facilitation only occurs along direct links in fully recurrent models (e.g., semantic-semantic, phonological-phonological) and that Masson's model, in particular, could not account for semantic priming in naming if the naming response depends only on when the phonological units settle on the correct values.

Masson (1999) was able to identify circumstances under which settling of phonological units was facilitated by the prior presentation of a semantically related word. For example, if the semantic units were partially instantiated with the pattern corresponding to the prime and stochastic updating was used, the target's phonological units settled faster in the related prime condition than in the target-alone baseline condition. Even so, in many natural implementations of fully recurrent models, including Masson's (1995) original one, facilitation of this kind does not occur. One must keep in mind, however, that fully recurrent models readily account for priming along direct paths. Hence, to the extent that naming depends on settling of semantic units, in addition to phonological units, fully recurrent models will be able to explain semantic priming in the naming task.

Because Plaut's proximity model (Plaut, 1995; Plaut & Booth, 2000) plays a prominent role in subsequent chapters, I want to explore it in greater detail. This network learns to associate written words with their meanings. The written form of each word is represented by a pattern of activation over a set of orthographic units, and the meaning of each word is represented by a pattern of activation over a set of semantic units. The model implements both "pure" semantic relatedness (similarity of meaning in the absence of association, e.g., *dog-goat*) and associative relatedness (e.g., *dog-cat*). The only type of semantic relation currently instantiated in the model is shared category membership (e.g., dogs and goats are both mammals). The categorical relatedness between two words is encoded by the degree of feature overlap between their semantic representations. Within categories, words differ in how typical they are of the category, such that typical members share many features with the prototype of the category (e.g., *collie*) and atypical members share fewer features with the prototype (e.g., *dachshund*). Associative relatedness is determined by the frequency with which one word follows another during learning. Words can also differ in their frequency of presentation during learning.

A schematic illustration of the architecture of the model can be found in Figure 5.1. The orthographic units are fully connected to the hidden units, which facilitate learning of the mapping from the orthographic units to the semantic units. The hidden units are fully connected to the semantic units, and vice versa, and the semantic units are fully connected to themselves. Orthographic representations are randomly assigned to semantic representations, ensuring that similarity in orthographic form is not predictive of similarity in meaning. The activation of each unit at any point in time is a weighted average of its current activation and the input it is receiving from all other units to which it is connected.[1]

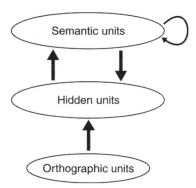

FIGURE 5.1. Architecture of Plaut's distributed network model of semantic priming. Ellipses represent groups of units with a common function; arrows represent full connectivity between groups (e.g., each orthographic unit is connected to all hidden units).

To train the network, a word is presented to the network by providing each orthographic unit with external input that is positive if the corresponding feature is present and negative if the feature is absent in the word's orthographic representation. While the external input is held constant, all of the units in the network update their activation levels. The weights on the connections between units are then modified so as to improve the match between the actual activations of the semantic units and the assigned semantic representation for the word.

Selection of the next word for training can be random or determined by such variables as word frequency and associative relatedness. For instance, in the application discussed by Plaut (1995), each word was assigned, before training, one associate, which was semantically *unre*lated. Associations were unidirectional; that is, no two words were each other's associate. The next word selected for training was the just-trained word's associate 20% of the time. On the remaining trials, the probability that a word was selected depended on its assigned frequency, with high-frequency words selected twice as often as low-frequency words. In Plaut and Booth's (2000) application, word pairs that were semantically related also were made associatively related. The next word selected for training was twice as likely to come from the same category as the just-trained word as from another category. In addition, high-frequency words were selected for training twice as often as low-frequency words. Repeated presentation of one word following another allows the network to learn to make efficient transitions from the meaning of the first word to the meaning of the second word, independently of semantic overlap.

The network is tested by presenting stimuli in prime-target pairs. The prime's orthographic representation is used as input to the orthographic units, and activation levels are updated for a period of time corresponding to the SOA. The target's orthographic representation then replaces the prime's, and activation levels are updated until the activation of each semantic unit changes minimally. At this point, the network is considered to have responded, and the elapsed time since presentation of the target is interpreted as the response time.

Lexical decisions can be based on a measure of the familiarity of the semantic pattern, *semantic stress* (Plaut, 1997). This measure reflects the degree to which the semantic activations are binary. The stress of a unit is 0 when its activation is 0.5 and approaches 1 as its activation approaches 0 or 1. The semantic patterns produced by the network in response to words closely approximate the appropriate binary target patterns; hence, the average semantic stress for words is near 1.0. Nonwords, however, are unfamiliar stimuli that do not drive the semantic units as strongly as words do. As a consequence, the average semantic stress for nonwords is lower. By choosing an appropriate decision criterion, words and nonwords can be distinguished based on their stress values. Words that yield stress values below the criterion and nonwords that yield stress values above the criterion can be considered errors of classification by the network. The model therefore predicts both response times and error rates.

Distributed network models have been applied to many human behaviors that depend on information traditionally represented in semantic memory, including acquisition of generic knowledge from specific experiences (e.g., McClelland & Rumelhart, 1985), word naming and lexical decision (e.g., Kawamoto, Farrar, & Kello, 1994; Seidenberg & McClelland, 1989), impairments in reading and the use of meaning after brain damage (e.g., Farah & McClelland, 1991; Hinton & Shallice, 1991; Plaut, McClelland, Seidenberg, & Patterson, 1996), and semantic priming. Although these models have had their critics (e.g., Besner, Twilley, McCann, & Seergobin, 1990; Fodor & Pylyshyn, 1988), their influence on the science of memory and word recognition has been, and promises to remain, enormous.

6
CHAPTER

Multistage Activation Models

The category of multistage activation models includes models descended from the logogen model of word recognition (e.g., Morton, 1969) and from the interactive-activation model of letter perception (e.g., McClelland & Rumelhart, 1981; Rumelhart & McClelland, 1982). Although multistage activation models differ in many important ways, they share three characteristics: (a) the models posit the existence of multiple levels of lexical-semantic representation, such as visual features, letters, words, and semantic representations; (b) the models employ excitatory feedforward and feedback connections between successive levels; and (c) each level of representation corresponds to a stage of processing. These properties may be needed to explain some of the more complex findings on semantic priming (see, e.g., Chapters 15 and 17).

☐ Logogen-Based Models

According to Morton's (1969) model of word recognition, words are mentally represented by feature counters, called *logogens*. Perception of a word stimulus causes information to accumulate in the logogens for all words that share features with that stimulus. A word is recognized when the amount of information accumulated in its logogen exceeds its recognition threshold. Semantic priming is explained by assuming that recognition of

37

a word feeds semantic features to other logogens, which accumulate semantic features in the same way as perceptual features (e.g., Meyer & Schvaneveldt, 1976). The effect of semantic context is to raise the feature count above resting level for those logogens sharing semantic features with the context. Fewer stimulus features are therefore needed to recognize a word when it appears in a semantically related context than when it appears in a semantically unrelated context.

The basic logogen model is challenged by many findings on word recognition (e.g., Besner & Smith, 1992; Wilding, 1986). For example, the model cannot account for the joint effects of semantic context, word frequency, and stimulus quality. If semantic context and word frequency both affect the thresholds or resting activation levels of logogens, as is commonly assumed, then these variables should both interact with stimulus quality or both combine additively with stimulus quality (e.g., Besner and Smith, 1992). In fact, semantic context and stimulus quality interact but word frequency and stimulus quality combine additively (see Chapter 17).

To account for these and related findings, Besner and his colleagues (e.g., Besner & Smith, 1992; Borowsky & Besner, 1993; Stolz & Neely, 1995) proposed an extended version of the logogen model. This model contains several subsystems (orthographic input lexicon, semantic system, phonological output lexicon, spelling-sound correspondence rules), but for the purposes of explaining semantic priming effects, the most important subsystems are the orthographic input lexicon and the semantic system (see Figure 6.1). The processing of a visually presented word begins with activation of that word's representation in the orthographic input lexicon. Activation of this representation feeds forward to the semantic system via pathway A. Activation of the semantic representation of the word spreads within the semantic system to the representations of related concepts, and activation of these representations feeds back to the orthographic input lexicon via pathway B. Semantic priming occurs at both levels. The presentation of the prime activates its representations in the orthographic input lexicon and the semantic system. Activation spreads in the semantic system to the prime's associates, and this activation feeds back to their representations in the orthographic input lexicon. When the target appears, it can be processed more efficiently because its representations in the orthographic input lexicon and in the semantic system are partially active.

My interpretation of descriptions of this model (especially, Borowsky & Besner, 1993) is that representations at each level function like logogens, accumulating information until a threshold is reached, at which point activation is passed to the next level. The model's account of semantic priming, however, implies that partially active representations

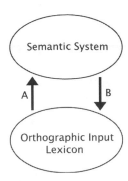

FIGURE 6.1. Architecture of simplified version of Besner and Smith's (1992) model of word recognition. Pathway A feeds activation from the orthographic input lexicon to the semantic system, and pathway B feeds activation back from the semantic system to the orthographic input lexicon.

in the semantic level can feed activation back to the orthographic input lexicon prior to reaching threshold. The model therefore seems to have both discrete and continuous processing features.

□ Interactive-Activation Model

The Interactive-Activation (IA) model was originally proposed by McClelland and Rumelhart (McClelland & Rumelhart, 1981; Rumelhart & McClelland, 1982) to explain the effects of context on letter perception. Recent progeny of the IA model include Coltheart, Rastle, Perry, Langdon, and Ziegler's (2001) dual route cascaded model and Grainger and Jacob's (1996) multiple read-out model. The IA model was not designed to explain semantic priming effects; indeed, there were sound reasons to believe that it was structurally incapable of explaining priming. The problem was that the model used only inhibitory connections within the same level of the system. If all of the connections between nodes within the semantic system are mutually inhibitory, there does not seem to be any way to account for the facilitation in processing that occurs when a word is preceded by a semantically related word.

Stolz and Besner (1996; Stolz & Besner, 1998) have proposed a generalization of the IA model that can explain semantic priming. Stolz and Besner distinguish between several levels of representation and processing, although they restrict discussion to the letter level, lexical level, and semantic level (see Figure 6.2).

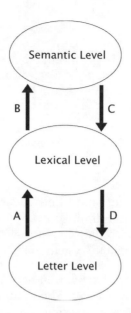

FIGURE 6.2. Schematic illustration of levels of representation and of processing pathways in an interactive-activation model of semantic priming. Pathways A and B feed activation from lower to higher levels; pathways C and D feed activation back from higher to lower levels. Adapted from Stolz and Besner (1996).

Connections between representations in the same level are inhibitory, whereas connections between different levels are excitatory (e.g., McClelland, 1987). When a written word is presented, the representations of letters are activated in the letter level, activation feeds forward to the lexical level (pathway A), and continues to the semantic level (pathway B). Inhibitory connections within each level create competition in which the letters, the word, and the semantic representation most consistent with all of the available information inhibit weaker candidates ("rich get richer; poor get poorer"). Simultaneously, activation feeds back from higher to lower levels (pathways C and D), providing top-down support for the activation of a particular word and the letters within that word.

Stolz and Besner make two crucial suppositions to explain semantic priming. First, they propose that feedforward activation from lexical-level representations to corresponding semantic-level representations (pathway B) also spreads to representations of semantically related words. For example, activation of the word *nurse* in the lexical level would primarily spread to the semantic representation of *nurse* in the semantic level, but some activation would also spread to the semantic representations of related words, such as *doctor*. The second crucial assumption is that within-level competition does not drive the activation of weaker candidates to zero. The network needs to converge on the appropriate representations while simultaneously leaving less appropriate representations partially active. Both assumptions are necessary to explain semantic priming in an IA model.

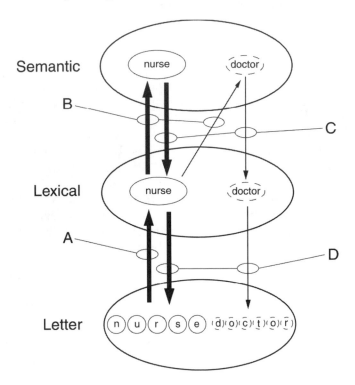

FIGURE 6.3. An interactive-activation model of semantic priming. Presentation of *nurse* activates letter representations in the letter level. Activation feeds forward to the lexical level (pathway A) and to the semantic level (pathway B). Activation of *nurse* in the lexical level partially spreads to representations of semantically related words (*doctor*) in the semantic level (pathway B). Activation feeds back from the semantic level to the lexical level (pathway C) and from the lexical level to the letter level (pathway D). Bottom-up support and within-level competition ensure that representations of *nurse* will be most active at all levels of the system, but other representations will be partially active. If *doctor* appears soon after *nurse*, it can be processed more efficiently because its letter, word, and semantic representations are partially active.

Semantic priming is explained as follows (see Figure 6.3). Presentation of a prime word, such as *nurse*, activates letter representations in the letter level, and this activation feeds forward to the lexical level via pathway A. Activation continues to feed forward via pathway B to the semantic level, activating the semantic representation of *nurse* and, to a lesser extent, the semantic representations of related words, such as *doctor*. At the same time, activation feeds back from the semantic level to the lexical level via pathway C and from the lexical level to the letter level via pathway D. In particular, the lexical-level representation of *doctor* will receive some activation via pathway C from its partially active semantic representation, and the letter representations for *doctor* will receive some activation via pathway D from the partially active lexical representation. Because of bottom-up support and within-level competition, the representations corresponding to *nurse* should be the most active representations at all levels of the system, but other representations will remain partially active. If the word *doctor* appears soon after *nurse*, it can be processed more efficiently because its letter, word, and semantic representations are partially active. Semantic priming, therefore, occurs at all three levels of the system.[1]

An important feature of this instantiation of the IA model is that semantic priming depends on connections between the lexical representation of the prime and the semantic representation of the target. I am not aware of any experimental results that bear directly on this assumption, but it does seem to imply that semantic priming between pictures or between pictures and words (e.g., Carr, McCauley, Sperber, & Parmelee, 1982; Kroll & Potter, 1984) is lexically mediated or produced by a parallel system for pictures (e.g., Smith, Meiran, & Besner, 2000).

The virtues of multistage activation models are that they explicitly identify multiple levels of representation and multiple pathways of information transmission. As we shall see in subsequent chapters, both features turn out to be important in explaining some of the more complex patterns of results in the semantic priming literature.

Other Models

The five models examined in the preceding five chapters were chosen because their authors were particularly concerned about explaining semantic priming phenomena and because they have been especially influential or promise to be. They do not, however, constitute an exhaustive list of models of priming. In this chapter, I want to provide brief overviews of several other models of semantic priming that have been proposed over the past 40 years.

☐ Forster's Models

Forster has developed several important models of language processing, including word recognition (e.g., Forster, 1976, 1979). Although these models can account for some of the basic phenomena of semantic priming, their primary aim has been to characterize the cognitive architecture of language processing. Forster's models of priming effects (e.g., Forster, 1999) have been developed primarily to explain various types of form priming (e.g., morphological priming), not semantic priming.

☐ Norris's Context-Checking Model

Norris's (1986; Norris, 1995) context-checking model includes features of Becker's verification model and Morton's logogen model. Perceptual analysis is used to establish a candidate set of lexical entries. When this candidate set is of "manageable size," a context checking process begins. This process operates in parallel with the perceptual analysis processes and occurs before conscious recognition. The context checking process assesses the plausibility with respect to the context of each member of the candidate set. Recognition criteria are reduced for plausible candidates and increased for implausible candidates. Conscious recognition of a word occurs when the combination of perceptual evidence and word frequency information exceeds the word's recognition criterion. All else equal, high frequency words will exceed their criteria sooner than low frequency words.[1] Context checking only occurs before conscious recognition. Any factor that serves to delay conscious recognition will provide greater opportunity for context checking to affect performance. Information flow in the model is entirely bottom-up; no stage of processing receives input from higher stages. However, all processes operate in parallel; for instance, perceptual analysis continues as context checking takes place.

Neely (1991) provides a thorough analysis of the strengths and weaknesses of the context-checking model. The greatest weakness, to my mind, is that the model does not have a principled way to explain why semantic priming shows facilitation but not inhibition at short SOAs (see Chapter 9). Indeed, Norris argues that a major strength of the model is its ability to account for Antos's (1979) finding of inhibition in the absence of facilitation at an SOA of 200 ms. However, as I have argued in Chapter 9, Antos's results are probably more informative about decision processes than about semantic priming. Another problem with the context-checking model is that it predicts a stimulus quality by word frequency interaction. This interaction is not typically observed in word recognition studies (see chapter 17).

☐ Neely and Keefe's Hybrid Model

Neely and Keefe (1989) proposed a hybrid model of semantic priming which contains three independent processes: spreading activation, expectancy, and semantic matching. The spreading activation process is similar to that in Collins and Loftus's (1975) model. Following Posner and Snyder (1975a), Neely and Keefe propose that activation spreads rapidly, occurs unconsciously and is not under strategic control, and produces facilitation in the processing of semantically related items but not inhibition in the processing of semantically unrelated items. The expectancy process operates when related primes and targets frequently occur together within an experimental session. Subjects use the prime (e.g., *dog*) to generate candidates for the target (e.g., *cat, puppy, animal*). Neely and Keefe assume that the expectancy process is relatively slow acting, is consciously controlled, and produces facilitation in the processing of expected items and inhibition in the processing of unexpected items. Finally, a semantic-matching process occurs in the lexical decision task (but not in the naming task). After lexical access has occurred, subjects check for a relation between the target and the prime. The presence of a relation biases a "word" response, whereas the absence of a relation biases a "nonword" response. (Expectancy and semantic matching are discussed in much greater depth in Chapter 9.)

Not surprisingly, Neely and Keefe's (1989) model can account for a greater variety of findings than any one mechanism alone can (see Neely, 1991). The important contribution of this model is that it combines a model of automatic, attention-free priming with strategic, attention-laden processes. Viewed in this way, one can see that several of the models of priming outlined in previous chapters may be combined with expectancy and semantic matching processes.

☐ ROUSE

ROUSE (responding optimally with unknown sources of evidence) is a new model developed by Huber, Shiffrin, Lyle, and Ruys (2001) to explain lexical priming effects that last on the order of seconds, including certain forms of repetition and semantic priming. The model was developed to account for a complex pattern of facilitative and inhibitory priming effects obtained in a primed perceptual-identification task.

In the standard task used by Huber and his colleagues (e.g., Huber, Shiffrin, Lyle, & Ruys, 2001; Huber, Shiffrin, Lyle, & Quach, 2002; Huber, Shiffrin, Quach, & Lyle, 2002), subjects see a prime display containing two words (e.g., *guest shade*), a briefly flashed target (e.g., *shade*), a backward mask, and a display containing the target word and a foil (e.g., *guest shade*). Subjects are required to choose the word in the final display that matches the briefly flashed target. Both choices are primed (as in the example), or just one is primed (the target or the foil), or neither is primed. This sequence of events describes the "passive" priming task. In the "active" priming task, the prime display is presented twice, and the first time, subjects are asked to make a decision about the words in the display (e.g., do the words match in animacy?). Two findings have been particularly significant. First, in the passive task, there was a preference to choose the repeated word, whereas in the active task, there was a preference against choosing the repeated word. Second, priming of both choices produced performance deficits relative to the neither-primed condition; these deficits occurred in both the passive and the active priming conditions.

This pattern of results indicates that priming in this paradigm is not determined by the enhancement of perceptual processes applied to the target; instead, priming effects seem to be determined by nonperceptual "preferences," such as biases in decision making. These preferences may be implicit and automatic. For example, the model predicts, and experiments confirm, that as target duration decreases in the active priming task, the preference against prime-related words reverses to a preference for prime-related words (Huber, Shiffrin, Lyle, & Quach, 2002). It is difficult to envision how such a pattern could be produced by conscious strategies.

Huber et al. (2001) developed ROUSE to explain preference effects in priming. Words are represented as vectors of features. Presentation of the prime activates the features of the prime words. Some of these features remain active up to and beyond the time the target is presented. By the time the choices appear, features from the primes, the target, and noise (e.g., produced by the pattern mask) are all active. Although the identities of active features are known, the sources of activation are not. A preference for prime-related words arises because of a failure to distinguish the sources of activation. The model attempts to correct for source confusion by discounting evidence associated with prime words. Evidence for a choice word provided by an activated feature is discounted when that feature is also in one of the prime words. If the effect of the prime is underestimated, say because participants do not attend closely to it (e.g., passive priming conditions), prime-related words tend to be chosen. However, if the effect of the prime is overestimated, because participants process the prime words deeply and are quite aware of their presence (e.g., active priming conditions), prime-related words tend to be avoided. In this manner, the model accounts for the preference reversal in the passive and active priming conditions. Variability in prime activation causes the deficits in the both-primed condition. Target and foil choices in the both-primed condition contain the same number of prime-activated features on the average, but there is variability from trial to trial, with the target sometimes containing more and the foil sometimes containing more prime-activated features. This variability adds noise to the decision process, reducing performance relative to the neither-primed condition.

ROUSE was designed to account for preferential effects in priming and does not have mechanisms to account for other causes of priming. In particular, the model cannot account for facilitation in the both-primed condition relative to the neither-primed condition. An example of a semantic both-primed condition might be as follows: prime = *smile*, target = *happy*, choices = *happy frown*. Priming benefits in this condition are not easily attributed to biases in decision making, as both answer options are semantically related to the prime. Both-primed benefits were observed by Huber et al. (2001, Exp. 4); similar results were obtained by Rhodes, Parkin, and Tremewan (1993) and by Masson and Borowsky (1998).

Huber and O'Reilly (2003) have developed a neural-network version of ROUSE, called "nROUSE," that predicts both-primed benefits. The property of nROUSE that enables it to predict such benefits is the organization of units into a perceptual hierarchy of low-level visual features, intermediate-level orthographic features, and high-level lexical-semantic features. The overall architecture of this model is very similar to the IA model: The visual-feature level has excitatory bottom-up projections to the orthographic level, and the orthographic level has excitatory bottom-up projections to the lexical-semantic level. The lexical-semantic level has excitatory top-down projections to the orthographic level; unlike the IA model, however, the orthographic level does not feed back to the visual-feature level. Between-level connections are excitatory but within-level connections are inhibitory. The convergence of nROUSE and the IA model on similar processing architectures suggests that such architectures may be essential for explaining word recognition and semantic priming.

In summary, although ROUSE has been applied to a relatively limited set of paradigms so far, it is a particularly promising theoretical development and is likely to be quite influential in the future.

SECTION III

Major Issues and Findings

CHAPTER

8

Methodological Issues

As in most domains of psychological inquiry, research on semantic priming has advanced on two fronts. One line of research has focused on understanding the phenomenon itself; the other has focused on how best to measure the phenomenon. In this chapter, I review research of the second type and examine several important methodological issues that should be considered when designing semantic priming experiments. Although one might expect to find discussions of prime-target SOA, the relatedness proportion, and the nonword ratio in this chapter, I have postponed discussion of these variables until Chapter 9 because they are crucially involved in the theoretical distinction between automatic and strategic priming.

☐ Counterbalancing of Materials

The measurement of semantic priming requires that performance in two experimental conditions be compared. Typically, performance on words preceded by semantically related primes (e.g., *lion-tiger*) is compared to performance on words preceded by semantically unrelated primes (e.g., *table-tiger*). Sound experimental design dictates that these experimental conditions should differ in as few ways as possible other than the semantic relations between the primes and the targets. In the context of a

51

semantic priming experiment, this means that the same items (words, pictures, etc.) should be used in the semantically related condition and in the semantically unrelated condition.

In principle, this goal should be easy to achieve: use the same items in the related and the unrelated conditions for each subject. This solution is not attractive because stimulus repetition may interact with semantic relatedness in unpredictable ways. Although the results of studies that have jointly manipulated semantic relatedness and target repetition indicate that these variables have additive effects (den Heyer, Goring, & Dannenbring, 1985; Durgunoglu, 1988; Wilding, 1986), those studies have not presented items more than three times. An interaction between semantic relatedness and repetition might occur if decisions on repeated items were made using episodic memory rather than semantic memory. If the response to a stimulus is made on the basis of memories of previous responses to the same stimulus, semantic priming may be weak or nonexistent. Target repetition becomes even less attractive as the number of experimental conditions, and hence possible repetitions, increases.

The standard solution to the materials confound is to counterbalance stimuli through experimental conditions across subjects. Consider the simplest case in which related prime and unrelated prime conditions are compared. A given target would appear in the related prime condition for one subject (e.g., *fail-pass*) and in the unrelated prime condition for another subject (e.g., *vacation-pass*); similarly, a second target would appear in the related prime condition for the second subject (e.g., *day-night*) and in the unrelated prime condition for the first subject (e.g., *sell-night*). In this manner, each subject sees each target once, but across subjects, each target appears in each condition.

The same counterbalancing manipulation should be performed for primes so that they, too, are not confounded with experimental conditions. To this end, the set of related prime-target pairs can be randomly divided into two subsets of equal size (A and B). Two subsets of unrelated prime-target pairs (A' and B') are generated by re-pairing primes and targets within each subset of related pairs. The related and unrelated pairs for one test list are selected by choosing a subset of related pairs and a subset of unrelated pairs, such that no prime or target is repeated (e.g., A–B'). A second test list is created by making the complementary choices (e.g., B–A'). Half of the subjects will see the materials in one test list and half will see the materials in the other test list. An example can be found in Table 8.1.

This approach generalizes to any number of experimental conditions. Suppose, for example, that an investigator wanted to investigate semantic priming for intact and perceptually degraded words. The design would have four experimental conditions: Related versus Unrelated X

TABLE 8.1. Example of counterbalancing targets and primes through related and unrelated prime conditions.

Target	List 1	List 2
1	fail-pass	vacation-pass
2	vacation-trip	fail-trip
3	sweep-broom	knight-broom
4	knight-armor	sweep-armor
5	sell-night	day-night
6	day-buy	sell-buy
7	eggs-ball	bat-ball
8	bat-bacon	eggs-bacon

Intact versus Degraded. The set of related prime-target pairs would be divided randomly into four subsets, and each subset would be used to generate a subset of unrelated prime-target pairs. Four test lists would then be created by assigning subsets of prime-target pairs to the four experimental conditions such that each target item would appear in each of the four conditions across lists but no item would be repeated within a list (see Figure 8.1). One fourth of the subjects would see each test list. Other designs can also be used (e.g., Pollatsek & Well, 1995).

In general, for p experimental conditions, at least p test lists are needed, and each test list is seen by N/p subjects. If the experimenter wants to collect n observations per condition per subject, then np unique, semantically related prime-target pairs are needed. The advantage of this type of design is that the manipulation of semantic relatedness is not confounded with irrelevant differences in materials. This feature is especially crucial when one has *a priori* reasons to believe that priming may be small (e.g., subliminal priming; see Chapter 14) or uses a dependent measure that is known to be highly sensitive to structural properties of stimuli (e.g., ERPs; see Chapter 18).

Designing an experiment to meet this high standard is tiresome, especially when the experiment contains a large number of experimental conditions. It is therefore tempting to use different stimuli in the experimental conditions and to try to equate the stimuli in the various conditions on features known to affect decision performance, such as word frequency, word length, and part of speech. The fundamental problem with this approach is that stimuli are equated only on those variables that the experimenter happens to think of. Effects due to differences between items are inextricably confounded with effects due to the experimental manipulation of semantic relatedness. Another tempting strategy is to assign materials to the related and the unrelated prime conditions

	List 1		List 2		List 3		List 4	
	I	D	I	D	I	D	I	D
Related prime	A	B	B	D	D	C	C	A
Unrelated prime	C'	D'	A'	C'	B'	A'	D'	B'

FIGURE 8.1. Example of counterbalancing materials through four experimental conditions formed by the factorial combination of semantic relatedness (related prime versus unrelated prime) and stimulus quality (intact versus degraded targets). A, B, C, and D are equal-sized subsets of related prime-target pairs. A', B', C', and D' are corresponding subsets of unrelated prime-target pairs formed by re-pairing related primes and targets. I = intact; D = degraded.

randomly. This approach is probably acceptable if each subject-condition combination receives a unique sample of stimuli. The problem with such a design is that it may require an enormous number of stimuli. In many studies, materials are a precious resource because they are difficult to construct, because they must satisfy many constraints created by the experimental conditions or because subjects have limited time in the experiment. More commonly, the same random assignment of stimuli to experimental conditions is used for all subjects. This approach may be acceptable if large numbers of stimuli and subjects are used. In general, a counterbalanced design is the design of choice in investigations of semantic priming.

Of course, if the materials themselves constitute a factor in the design (e.g., semantic priming for nouns vs. verbs), then stimuli cannot be counterbalanced across conditions defined by that factor. However, even in this case, one can counterbalance targets and primes across the semantic relatedness manipulation and guarantee that semantic priming within a type of material is not confounded with differences between items. When type of materials is a factor in the design, utmost care should be taken to match the stimuli in the various materials conditions on those variables known to affect semantic priming. Such variables include associative strength (e.g., Canas, 1990), semantic relatedness (e.g., McRae & Boisvert, 1998), type of semantic relation (e.g., Moss, Ostrin, Tyler, & Marslen-Wilson, 1995), and word frequency (e.g., Becker, 1979). Recent experiments have shown that naming and lexical decision responses are faster for words that do not have a common synonym than for words that do (e.g., *milk* vs. *jail*, Pecher, 2001) and that item recognition and cued-recall performance are influenced by several features of prior knowledge, including the number of connections among the associates of a target word (e.g., Nelson, McEvoy, & Pointer, 2003; Nelson & Zhang, 2000; Nelson, Zhang, & McKinney, 2001). To my knowledge, it is unknown whether or not these variables influence semantic priming, but prudence would call for controlling these variables, as well, in experiments in which stimulus type was a factor.

Because of missing data (e.g., errors, apparatus failures), the statistical analysis of the results of a semantic priming experiment is typically based on summary statistics, such as the mean or the median, computed for each subject and each experimental condition. The analysis of such data obtained from a counterbalanced design should include counter-balancing list as a grouping variable. That is, subjects who see the same counterbalancing list are treated as a level of a grouping variable in a mixed-model analysis of variance. I refer the reader to the excellent articles by Pollatsek and Well (1995) and Raaijmakers (Raaijmakers, 2003; Raaijmakers, Schrijnemakers, & Gremmen, 1999) for thorough discussions of this topic. Although the analyses recommended by these authors differ in certain details, they share the goal of isolating variance introduced by having different subjects respond to the same items in different conditions.[1] Moreover, as discussed subsequently, these analyses eliminate the need for conducting a separate analysis over items. To reduce test list X experimental condition interactions, target stimuli can be matched across lists on item characteristics (e.g., word frequency, word length) or on normative data (e.g., mean decision latency in neutral or unrelated prime conditions).

☐ Subject Versus Item Analyses and Fixed Versus Random Effects

The data obtained in a counterbalanced design can be analyzed with subjects or items as the unit of analysis. In the subject analysis, data within each cell are collapsed over items using the mean, median, or some other measure of central tendency; in the item analysis, data are collapsed over subjects. The F ratios from these analyses are typically identified as F_1 and F_2, respectively. It has become common practice since the publication of Clark's (1973) influential article to report both analyses and to reject the null hypothesis if both analyses reveal statistically significant F values. There is widespread belief that F_1 assesses the extent to which the treatment effect generalizes over subjects and that F_2 assesses the extent to which the treatment effect generalizes over items.

In fact, these beliefs are incorrect (Raaijmakers, 2003; Raaijmakers, Schrijnemakers, & Gremmen, 1999). The F ratio for a treatment effect tests whether the condition means are equal in the population, taking into account an appropriate measure of variability. It does not test the extent to which the treatment effect is similar across subjects, in the case of F_1, or items, in the case of F_2. An F ratio can be statistically significant even when a small proportion of subjects or items shows the effect (see Raaijmakers, 2003, for examples). This feature of F tests is not a problem or limitation; it is an essential consequence of what the analysis of variance is designed to accomplish.

F_1 and F_2 were introduced by Clark (1973) as a means of computing *minF'*. This statistic is an approximation of the quasi-F ratio that can be used to correct for the bias introduced into F_1 in many experimental designs when stimuli are treated as a random effect (Winer, 1971). However, *minF'* is not needed in designs in which stimuli are matched on various characteristics across experimental conditions or in counterbalanced designs, regardless of whether stimuli are treated as fixed or as random (Raaijmakers, 2003; Raaijmakers, Schrijnemakers, & Gremmen, 1999). In the case of the matched design, bias in F_1 is greatly reduced by matching of items and the use of *minF'* leads to a substantial reduction in power (Wickens & Keppel, 1983). If counterbalanced designs are analyzed properly (as described previously), then correct error terms can be found for all treatment effects and quasi-F ratios are not needed, even when stimuli are a random effect (Pollatsek & Well, 1995; Raaijmakers, 2003; Raaijmakers, Schrijnemakers, & Gremmen, 1999). Joint reporting of F_1 and F_2 is never correct; one should report either F_1 or the appropriate quasi-F ratio (or its approximation, *minF'*). Because that statement contradicts an entrenched practice in the field, I repeat it, in its own paragraph, to ensure that there is no misunderstanding:

> Joint reporting of F_1 and F_2 is never correct; one should report either F_1 or the appropriate quasi-F ratio (or its approximation, minF').

Although the analysis of matched and counterbalanced designs is not influenced by whether stimuli are a fixed or a random effect, the analysis of many other designs is affected by the status of the stimuli (e.g., a design in which the same random assignment of stimuli to experimental conditions is used for all subjects). How does one decide whether stimuli are fixed or random? The answer to this question is not as simple as one might like.

Several criteria distinguish fixed and random effects in experimental design (e.g., Kirk, 1995). In this context, "effect" refers to a variable or factor in the design (e.g., subjects, stimuli, experimental conditions). Fixed effects have the following three properties:

1. A fixed effect includes all of the levels of interest. For example, if an experimenter wanted to know whether priming was affected by associative relations between primes and targets, he or she might include prime-target pairs that were semantically related and associatively related (e.g., *cat-dog*), semantically related but not associatively related (e.g., *goat-dog*), and unrelated on both measures (e.g., *table-dog;* see Chapter 10).

2. A replication of the experiment would include the same levels. Hence, a replication of the just-described semantic priming experiment would include—at the bare minimum—the same three prime conditions.

3. Conclusions drawn from the experiment only apply to the levels of the effect that were included. Returning to the example, the design would justify conclusions about the associative and the semantic relations manipulated in the experiment but not about other kinds of prime-target relations (e.g., syntactic relations).

Random effects are the complement of fixed effects: The levels included in the experiment are a random sample from a larger population of possible levels. A replication of the experiment would include a new random sample of levels, not the same levels. Because the levels included in the experiment are a random sample from a larger population, the experimenter can generalize conclusions to the population from which the sample was drawn.

Most treatment effects in psychology are fixed effects. It is indeed rare that experimental conditions are randomly selected from a population of possible conditions. The effect of subjects, however, is usually considered a random effect. In a good experiment, subjects are randomly selected from a well-defined population, and a replication of the experiment would include a new random sample of subjects, not the same subjects. It is important to appreciate that the word "random" is not used idly in the definition of a random effect. The fixed or random status of an effect is determined by how levels of the variable were selected, not by the wishes of the experimenter (Cohen, 1976; Smith, 1976). An experimenter may want an effect to be random, but unless levels have been randomly selected, it is not random. Cohen's (1976) title is apt: Random means random.

In my experience as a producer and consumer of semantic priming experiments, the materials are never randomly selected—or even pseudorandomly selected—from a population of possible items; in fact, they are usually selected or constructed to meet peculiar demands of the experiment or to maximize the strength of the experimental manipulation. Thus, although an experimenter may wish that his or her materials could be treated as a random effect, they almost always will be a fixed effect.

A natural response to this statement might be to say that the same is probably true of subjects: subjects aren't randomly selected, so the same problem exists there too. Perhaps, but even if this is true, the fact that an approach is bad in two cases does not somehow make it right for both. Selection of subjects in a well-designed experiment can be random, and it often approximates random selection from a well-defined population, usually introductory psychology students. People can argue about whether that population is a reasonable one, but for most of us in cognitive psychology who make our livings worrying about how undergraduates think, it is probably as good as any. Moreover, there is no reason to believe that subjects are selected (or select themselves, in situations in which subjects sign up for experiments) in a way that relates to the independent variables. In contrast, as was noted earlier, items are typically selected in such a way as to maximize the effects of the independent variable. In sum, one can quibble about whether the effect of subjects is really random, but there is no doubt that in most well-designed experiments, the effect of subjects will be much closer to a random effect than will the effect of items.

The two goals of wanting to generalize one's conclusions to items other than those used in a particular experiment and of wanting to ensure that a treatment effect is not caused by a few idiosyncratic stimuli are both good ones. However, a statistical test over items is not the way to achieve these goals. The use of inferential statistics is a shortcut for repeating experiments. If an experimenter is concerned about the generality of his or her findings, then by far the best strategy is to replicate the experiment with new subjects and new materials. Given that cognitive psychology is a laboratory science, a replication is not too much to ask for; it is usually quite easy to repeat important conditions of Experiment *n* in Experiment *n+1*.

☐ Baselines

Semantic priming is a relative measure. Typically, performance on target words preceded by related primes (e.g., *lion-tiger*) is compared to performance on target words preceded by unrelated primes (e.g., *table-tiger*). A problem with this comparison is that one cannot determine whether related primes facilitate performance or unrelated primes inhibit performance or both (e.g., Posner & Snyder, 1975b). To determine the relative contributions of such facilitative and inhibitory effects to semantic priming, one needs a baseline condition that is "neutral" in the sense of being neither related nor unrelated to the target. In this context, facilitation is defined as the difference between the neutral prime condition and the related prime condition, and inhibition is defined as the difference between the neutral prime condition and the unrelated prime condition (e.g., Posner & Snyder, 1975b).

Neely (1976) was the first investigator to attempt to measure facilitation and inhibition separately in a semantic priming paradigm. He did so by including a neutral prime condition consisting of a row of Xs (e.g., Posner & Snyder, 1975b). Neely found that the overall priming effect of 54 ms (unrelated-related) was composed of 38 ms of facilitation (neutral-related) and 16 ms of inhibition (neutral-unrelated). Neely interpreted his findings in the context of Posner and Snyder's (1975a) theory of attention and concluded that semantic priming was caused by automatic spreading activation, which produced facilitation but not inhibition, and limited-capacity attention, which produced both facilitation and inhibition (these ideas will be explored in greater detail in Chapter 9).

Neely's (1976) introduction of the neutral prime condition to semantic priming paradigms was important methodologically and theoretically. A possible problem with Neely's neutral prime is that a row of Xs is not a word and therefore may not have the same alerting properties as a word prime and may not engage the linguistic system in the same manner as a word prime. To deal with these problems, investigators have, over the years, introduced several other types of neutral conditions, including using a particular word repeatedly, such as *blank, neutral,* or *ready* (e.g., Antos, 1979; de Groot, Thomassen, & Hudson, 1982), and using pronounceable nonwords (e.g., Borowsky & Besner, 1993). One possible problem with the use of a repeated word is that repetition priming may serve to decrease the time needed to encode the neutral prime, relative to related and to unrelated word primes, which typically are not repeated. Hence, facilitation would be underestimated and inhibition would be overestimated. Another possible problem is that a repeated neutral prime may lose its alerting qualities as the experiment progresses. Subjects would be less prepared for the target in the neutral prime condition than in the related-word and the unrelated-word prime conditions and might, therefore, be slower and less accurate. In this case, facilitation would be overestimated and inhibition would be underestimated. The use of pronounceable nonwords solves these problems (as long as they are never repeated) but introduces another: unfamiliar nonwords may take longer to encode than words and, therefore, processing of the nonword prime may spill over into processing of the target, artificially increasing latencies to respond in the neutral condition. Use of nonwords as neutral primes may therefore overestimate facilitation and underestimate inhibition.

To make matters worse, any of these effects might very well interact with SOA (e.g., Neely, 1991).

In a thoughtful analysis of the problem of measuring facilitation and inhibition, Jonides and Mack (1984) made two general recommendations. First, they counseled against including a neutral prime condition. They recommended that researchers focus instead on examining performance for valid and invalid cues (e.g., related and unrelated primes) as a function of other theoretically important variables, such as SOA, cue validity, and stimulus quality. Of course, Jonides and Mack recognized that some theoretical questions could be answered only by attempting to measure facilitation and inhibition. Their second recommendation was that researchers strive to create neutral prime conditions that match informative cue conditions as closely as possible, including physical properties, ease of encoding, and effectiveness as alerting signals. In addition, they recommended that researchers employ converging operations to assess the status of their neutral condition (Garner, Hake, & Eriksen, 1956). Use of converging operations might include using more than one type of neutral prime and parametrically manipulating variables thought to influence those mental processes responsible for the facilitative and inhibitory effects. An excellent example of the latter approach is Neely's (1977) joint manipulation of SOA and explicit strategies in a lexical decision task.

Borowsky and Besner (1993) have suggested that for the purpose of investigating word recognition processes, orthographically regular, pronounceable nonwords are the best choice for neutral primes. If nonword primes are not repeated, they will maintain their alerting qualities and not be susceptible to repetition priming. The major downside to the use of nonwords as neutral primes is potential encoding spillover effects: encoding of such primes may be slowed by their relative unfamiliarity and, at short SOAs, encoding of the nonword prime may not be completed by the time the target is presented. Evidence indicates, however, that such effects are very small, even at SOAs as short as 200 ms (e.g., Borowsky & Besner, 1993; McNamara, 1994). For example, in McNamara's experiments (1994, Exps. 1 and 2), which used SOAs of 350 ms, the average difference between unrelated-word prime conditions and nonword-prime conditions was +1 ms in latencies and –1.5% in error rates.

Ratcliff and McKoon (1995), however, obtained substantial nonword-prime inhibition. Across three experiments, the effect averaged –36 ms. In a series of five unpublished experiments (cited in McNamara and Diwadkar, 1996), we tried to obtain nonword-prime inhibition in lexical decisions by manipulating several aspects of the procedures. The average inhibition effect in latencies was –5.0 ms (SED = 4.5 ms, n = 2512). An important feature of Ratcliff and McKoon's results—albeit not one that we recognized at the time we were conducting our experiments—was that the absolute magnitude of nonword prime inhibition increased with SOA, from –10 ms at an SOA of 150 ms (Exp. 1) to –44 ms at an SOA of 350 ms (Exps. 2 and 3). This pattern is important because it is not consistent with an explanation based on encoding differences between nonword and word primes. Moreover, it suggests that nonword-prime inhibition might have been caused by strategic processes that take time to become operative.

This paradox seems to have been resolved by Zeelenberg, Pecher, de Kok, and Raaijmakers (1998). They showed that nonword-prime inhibition occurred when subjects were told that primes and targets would be related on some trials and that this information might help them to make the lexical decision (Ratcliff and McKoon's instructions) but did not occur when the relation between the prime and the target was not mentioned (McNamara's instructions). The overall magnitude of semantic priming was not affected by instructions; indeed, if anything, it was slightly larger for McNamara's instructions than for Ratcliff and McKoon's. Zeelenberg et al. speculated that nonword-prime inhibition may occur because of competing response tendencies produced by the nonword prime and the word target and that response competition may be exacerbated by attending more to the prime.[2]

Despite the complexities created by these findings on nonword prime inhibition, I am inclined to agree with Borowsky and Besner (1993) that orthographically regular, pronounceable nonwords may be the best choice for neutral primes in situations in which the assessment of facilitation and inhibition is theoretically important. Of particular interest to me are the results of a recently published meta-analysis of the functional neuroimaging literature on word recognition (Jobard, Crivello, & Tzourio-Mazoyer, 2003). The authors were unable to find any areas of cortex that were differentially activated by words and by pronounceable nonwords. This finding indicates that pronounceable nonwords engage the word recognition system as well as words.

Along these lines, Bourassa and Besner (1998) presented behavioral evidence that nonwords activate semantics to some extent. Briefly presented (40 ms), masked nonword primes facilitated lexical decision responses to "semantically related" targets (e.g., *sproy-paint*); semantic priming did not occur when the primes were presented for longer durations (300 ms). Semantic priming from nonword primes was about one third as large as semantic priming from word primes. Perea and Lupker (2003) presented evidence that transposed-letter nonwords (e.g., *spary*) were more effective than replacement-letter nonwords (e.g., *sproy*) as primes; indeed, in contrast to Bourassa and Besner, Perea and Lupker did not obtain reliable priming for replacement-letter nonword primes.

Although results on semantic priming from nonword primes are not entirely consistent, they nevertheless imply that care should be taken in choosing nonword primes if one wants to use the nonword prime condition as a neutral baseline. Moreover, they raise the question of whether strategic processes (see Chapter 9) might be engaged by nonword primes. To my knowledge, this question has not been investigated.

□ Sensitivity or Bias?

In tasks such as lexical decision, in which subjects must choose a response from a set of alternatives (e.g., word vs. nonword) based on evidence (e.g., a stimulus presented in a particular context), performance can be described in terms of signal detection theory (SDT) measures of *sensitivity* and *bias*. Measures of sensitivity, such as d', assess the statistical separability of evidence for the alternative decisions, and measures of bias, such as β reflect the rule used to choose among the alternative decisions (e.g., Macmillan & Creelman, 2005; Pastore, Crawley, Berens, & Skelly, 2003). Semantic context could influence sensitivity, bias, or both. An effect on sensitivity would be indicated if the benefit conferred by related primes on responses to word targets (e.g., *lion-tiger*) exceeded the cost conferred by "related" primes on responses to nonword targets (e.g., *lion-tigar*), where benefits and costs are measured in each case relative to an appropriate baseline. By contrast, if performance benefits for word targets were perfectly offset by performance costs for nonword targets, an effect on bias would be indicated (e.g., Ratcliff & McKoon, 1996).

The results of several early investigations suggested that semantic context might influence bias but not sensitivity (for a review, see Farah, 1989). More recent studies have shown that semantically related primes increase sensitivity and produce a bias to respond "word" (e.g., Huber, Shiffrin, Lyle, & Ruys, 2001; Masson and Borowsky, 1998; Rhodes, Parkin, & Tremewan, 1993). Researchers sometimes assume that effects on sensitivity are only produced by sensory-perceptual processes and effects on bias are only produced by postperceptual cognitive processes (e.g., Rhodes, Parkin, & Tremewan, 1993). This assumption is incorrect. The statistical separation of evidence distributions can be affected by any mental process involved in the acquisition and evaluation of information about the decision alternatives, including sensory, perceptual, and cognitive processes; and the rule that is applied to evidence distributions to select a response can be imposed early or late in the time course of processing. The crucial distinction from the perspective of SDT is between distributions of evidence and decision processes used to evaluate evidence, not between perceptual and postperceptual processes. (For excellent discussions of this important topic, see Pastore, Crawley, Berens, & Skelly, 2003; Pastore, Crawley, Skelly, & Berens, 2003.)

CHAPTER

Automatic Versus Strategic Priming

Automatic processes are traditionally defined as those having a quick onset, proceeding without intention or awareness, and producing benefits but not costs.[1] Strategic processes are slower acting, require intention, are conscious, and produce both benefits and costs (e.g., Posner & Snyder, 1975a; Schneider & Shiffrin, 1977; Shiffrin & Schneider, 1977). A question of long-standing interest in the semantic priming literature is the extent to which semantic priming is determined by automatic versus strategic mechanisms (e.g., Neely, 1976, 1977). Findings reviewed subsequently indicate that this distinction, as it has traditionally been defined, may need to be reevaluated. Even so, an understanding of this issue is essential because so much of the research on semantic priming has been conducted with the goal of isolating automatic and strategic components of priming.

Semantic priming almost certainly is not caused solely by strategic processes. Semantic priming occurs even when a single related prime-target pair is presented after a long series of unrelated pairs (Fischler, 1977a). It is difficult to envision how a strategic mechanism could produce priming if the subject had no knowledge that related pairs would ever appear. Semantic priming occurs when primes are presented parafoveally and subjects are instructed not to attend to them (Fuentes & Tudela, 1992). Performing a secondary task has little effect on the magnitude of priming under such conditions but reduces priming from foveally presented primes by approximately 50% (Fuentes, Carmona, Agis, & Catena, 1994).[2]

Whereas facilitation is commonly found for SOAs less than 200 ms, inhibition—the traditional index of strategic processing—is small to non-existent at such short SOAs (Neely, 1991). Finally, at short SOAs, semantic priming occurs between a category name prime and exemplars of that category (e.g., *body-leg*), even when subjects are told to expect members of a different category (e.g., parts of buildings) to follow the prime (Burke, White, & Diaz, 1987; Favreau & Segalowitz, 1983; Neely, 1977; but see Balota, Black, & Cheney, 1992). Findings such as these are difficult to reconcile with a purely strategic account of priming.

Semantic priming, however, is not purely automatic. Two strategic processes have been identified and studied, *expectancy* and *semantic matching*. Expectancy refers to the active generation of candidates for the upcoming target, or at least the belief on the part of subjects that primes will be followed by semantically related targets (e.g., Becker, 1980). Semantic matching refers to the search for a relation from the target back to the prime (e.g., de Groot, 1983; Forster, 1981; Neely, 1976, 1977; Stanovich & West, 1983). The presence of a relation seems to bias a "word" response, whereas the absence of a relation seems to bias a "nonword" response. Each of these processes has the potential to produce facilitative or inhibitory effects in semantic priming. In the case of expectancy, responses may be facilitated if an expected target appears and may be inhibited if an expected target does not appear; in the case of semantic matching, success in finding a relation may produce facilitation for "word" responses, whereas failure to find a relation may produce inhibition for "word" responses and facilitation for "nonword" responses.

Several variables seem to influence the extent to which expectancy and semantic matching processes are employed. SOA may be the most important one. A traditional index of strategic processing in semantic priming tasks is inhibition (e.g., Neely, 1976). The reasoning is this: An expectancy process will yield an incongruent outcome on unrelated trials because the target is unrelated to the prime. Responses should therefore be slow in the unrelated condition relative to a condition in which expectancies are not generated. A neutral prime condition may provide such a baseline because neutral primes are effectively meaningless in the context of the experiment. Similarly, semantic matching will produce a bias to respond "nonword" in the unrelated prime condition. To the extent that semantic matching is not used in the neutral prime condition (perhaps because the neutral prime is recognized as having no potential for a match), responses will be slower in the unrelated condition than in the neutral condition. It is well documented that inhibition is small or nonexistent for SOAs shorter than 300 ms (e.g., de Groot, 1984; den Heyer, Briand, & Smith, 1985; Neely, 1977).[3]

In a direct examination of strategic processing, Neely (1977) instructed subjects to generate members of a specified category when given a different category name as the prime; for example, subjects were told to generate parts of the body in response to the prime *building*. On trials in which an expected target appeared (S-Ex-U; e.g., *building-leg*), significant facilitation did not appear until an SOA of 700 ms. On trials in which an unexpected target appeared (S-Ux-U; e.g., *building-canary*), significant inhibition appeared at an SOA of 400 ms (see Figure 9.1). Neely's results therefore suggest that expectancy requires somewhere between 400 and 700 ms to affect performance in lexical decision. To my knowledge, no one has tried to manipulate semantic matching strategies using instructions.

In Neely's (1977) experiment, the facilitation observed in the S-Ex-U condition had to be produced by expectancy because the primes and the targets were unrelated. It is noteworthy that this facilitation occurred much later in time than the facilitation observed for semantically related primes and targets and—according to Neely's results—even later in time than inhibition. The temporal ordering of these effects provides strong evidence for a distinction between automatic and strategic mechanisms in semantic priming.

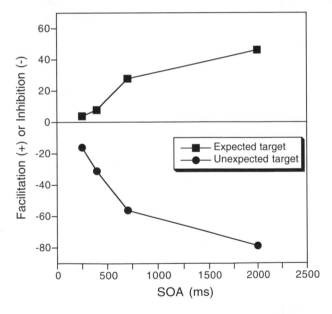

FIGURE 9.1. Facilitation for expected targets and inhibition for unexpected targets in Neely's (1977) experiment. Data are from the S-Ex-U and S-Ux-U conditions. Data for 2000 ms SOA are collapsed across the four conditions in Table 2 of Neely (1977).

It is easy to appreciate why expectancy would depend on the SOA between the prime and the target. The cognitive processes involved in using the prime to generate expected targets must be relatively complex and require time to develop. It is not as clear why semantic matching would depend on the SOA, as this process is triggered (presumably) when the target appears. Perhaps semantic matching is also a relatively high-level cognitive process that depends on attention being allocated to the prime and to the target for some critical amount of time. When the SOA is sufficiently brief, attention is not focused on the prime long enough to support semantic matching. Alternatively, semantic matching may be triggered by presentation of the context defined by the prime and may be interrupted when the target occurs too soon after the prime. Experimental results indicate that semantic matching is limited by the SOA, but to my knowledge, a satisfactory explanation of why it is so limited has not been proposed (for additional discussion, see Neely, 1991).

The relatedness proportion (RP) is a second factor that seems to influence strategic processing. The RP is defined as the proportion of related trials out of all word prime-word target trials (e.g., Neely, Keefe, & Ross, 1989). At long SOAs, facilitation and inhibition both increase in absolute magnitude as the proportion of related trials increases (e.g., de Groot, 1984; den Heyer, Briand, & Dannenbring, 1983; Tweedy, Lapinski, & Schvaneveldt, 1977). For example, in the 1040-ms SOA condition of de Groot's (1984) experiment, facilitation increased from +39 to +83 ms (113%) and inhibition increased from −20 to −40 ms (100%) as the RP increased from 0.25 to 0.75. The same experiments have also shown that the effect of RP is reduced or eliminated at short SOAs. For instance, in the 240-ms SOA condition of de Groot's experiment, facilitation increased from 44 to 60 ms (36%) and inhibition was constant at −14 ms as RP increased from 0.25 to 0.75. Priming in the naming task also increases with the RP (Keefe and Neely, 1990), suggesting that naming is also influenced by strategic processes.

The role that RP might have in expectancy is easy to appreciate. Higher RP corresponds to higher prime validity. The role of RP in semantic matching may not be as obvious. However, as Neely, Keefe, and Ross (1989) first observed, the RP is typically confounded with another variable that is plausibly related to semantic matching. In the standard lexical decision task, the presence of a semantic relation between the target and the prime is always informative about the lexical status of the target, as only word targets have related primes. However, the absence of a relation may or may not be informative, depending on the construction of the test list. One measure of the informativeness of the absence of a semantic relation is the nonword ratio (NR), which is the conditional probability that the correct response is "nonword" given that the word prime and the target are unrelated (Neely, Keefe, & Ross, 1989). As the nonword ratio deviates from 0.5, the absence of a semantic relation between the prime and the target becomes increasingly informative, signaling a nonword response when it is above 0.5, and a word response when it is below 0.5.[4]

The RP and the NR are naturally correlated because if the numbers of word and nonword targets are kept fixed, then as the RP increases, the number of unrelated word prime-word target trials necessarily decreases, which results in an increase in the NR. The only way to uncouple the RP and the NR is to change the ratio of word target to nonword target trials. Standard experimental procedures lead to NRs greater than 0.5, as investigators typically use equal numbers of word and nonword targets but use only word primes; hence, the number of word prime-nonword target trials exceeds the number of unrelated word prime-word target trials (assuming RP > 0).

Neely, Keefe, and Ross (1989) manipulated the RP and the NR in a lexical decision task in which primes were category names and targets were exemplars. Multiple linear regression analyses showed that the RP was correlated most strongly with priming for typical exemplars (e.g., *bird-robin*). The NR, however, was correlated with priming for both typical and atypical (e.g., *bird-penguin*) exemplars, and with nonword facilitation, which is defined as faster responses to nonwords primed by words than to nonwords primed by a neutral prime. Neely et al. argued that the effect of RP on priming for typical exemplars was a true expectancy effect, as subjects would be likely to generate typical but not atypical exemplars to category primes. According to Neely et al., the effect of NR was caused by semantic matching. The nonword facilitation effects are especially consistent with this interpretation, as when NR is high, nonword targets will benefit from a bias to respond "nonword" to targets unrelated to their word primes.

A fourth factor that may influence strategic processing is the task required of subjects. Tasks such as lexical decision that require accumulation of information to make an explicit binary decision are probably more susceptible to semantic matching than are tasks, such as naming, that do not involve an explicit decision (e.g., Forster, 1981; Keefe & Neely, 1990; Lorch, Balota, & Stamm, 1986; Seidenberg, Waters, Sanders, & Langer, 1984). The use of semantic matching in lexical decision but not in naming may explain why category-exemplar priming occurs for both typical and atypical exemplars in lexical decision (e.g., *bird-robin* and *bird-penguin*) but only for typical exemplars in naming (e.g., Lorch, Balota, & Stamm, 1986). The relatively weak semantic relations between category name primes and atypical exemplars may limit priming from automatic mechanisms (e.g., spreading activation) but may still be detectable by a semantic matching process (Neely & Keefe, 1989). Expectancy does not seem to be as affected by the task, as robust expectancy effects have been observed in naming and in lexical decision (e.g., Balota, Black, & Cheney, 1992; Neely, 1977).

McNamara and Altarriba (1988; see also Shelton and Martin, 1992) have argued that semantic matching, as well as expectancy, can be minimized by using a task in which the relations between primes and targets are not apparent to subjects. One method of achieving this goal is to use a "sequential" or "single-presentation" lexical decision task. In this task, stimuli are displayed one at a time and participants respond to each item as it appears. Primes precede targets in the test list, but their pairings are not apparent to subjects. Shelton and Martin found that inhibition and backward priming (e.g., prime *hop*, target *bell*; discussed in Chapter 13), which is usually attributed to semantic matching, did not occur in sequential lexical decisions.

Finally, a fifth factor that may influence strategic processing is the type of semantic relation existing between the prime and the target. To the extent that different patterns of facilitation and inhibition are indicative of different types of strategic processing, there is evidence that strategic processes may differ for associates and category-exemplar pairs. Associatively related words appear as mutual associates in free association, and are typically semantically related (see discussion in Chapter 10). Category-exemplar pairs may or may not be associated (e.g., *vehicle-car* vs. *vehicle-tank*). A common finding in the lexical decision task is that for associates, facilitation is at least as large as inhibition regardless of SOA (facilitation is typically much larger than inhibition at long SOAs), whereas for category-exemplar pairs, facilitation is greater than inhibition at short SOAs but inhibition is greater than facilitation at long SOAs (e.g., Becker, 1980; de Groot, 1984; den Heyer, Briand, & Smith, 1985; Neely, 1976, 1977; Smith, Briand, Klein, & den Heyer, 1987).[5] Greater facilitation than inhibition has been referred to as "facilitation dominance," and the reverse has been referred to as "inhibition dominance" (Becker, 1980). Results are less clear for the naming task, primarily because the appropriate experiments have not been conducted, but limited evidence indicates that semantic priming in naming is facilitation dominant at long SOAs for both associates and category-exemplar pairs (e.g., Keefe & Neely, 1990; Lorch, Balota, & Stamm, 1986). Given that naming rarely (if ever) produces inhibition in conditions in which inhibition is minimal in lexical decision, one can predict with some confidence that semantic priming in naming is facilitation dominant for both types of materials at short SOAs. These ostensibly complex findings can therefore be summarized quite simply: semantic priming tends to be facilitation dominant except for category-exemplar pairs, at long SOAs, in the lexical decision task.

A compelling explanation of this pattern of findings is elusive because the materials have differed in many ways other than the semantic relations between primes and targets. Associates and category-exemplar pairs have not been matched on target word frequency or prime-target associative strength, two variables known to affect semantic priming (e.g., Becker, 1979; Canas, 1990), and category-exemplar pairs typically have weaker associative strengths from category to exemplar than from exemplar to category (e.g., *tree-elm* vs. *elm-tree*). These observations not withstanding, the patterns of priming for associates and category-exemplar pairs may differ because of differences in the use of semantic matching.

As noted previously, it is commonly assumed that lexical decision is more prone to semantic matching than is naming. Also there is good evidence that strategic processes, such as semantic matching, take time to develop, having greater effects at longer SOAs. To the extent that semantic matching has a greater role in producing inhibition than facilitation (as suggested by Neely & Keefe, 1989), the inhibition dominance for category-exemplar pairs at long SOAs in the lexical decision task can be explained, at least qualitatively. This account, however, would seem to predict inhibition dominance for associates as well. Two unique features of most category-exemplar pairs (e.g., *tree-elm*) are that the prime is highly predictable from the target and the target and the prime form a simple, easily expressed proposition (e.g., *elm is a tree, robin is a bird*). The violation of this predictable, salient relation in unrelated pairs may be the cause of inhibition. Other explanations of the difference between associates and category-exemplar pairs are discussed later in this chapter.

Do expectancy and semantic matching differ in their relative propensities to produce facilitation or inhibition? Lorch et al. (1986), for example, argued that all inhibitory effects in lexical decision were produced by processes, such as semantic matching, that operate after the target has been recognized. Neely and Keefe (1989) looked at the literature available at the time and concluded that there was weak evidence that expectancy might be more involved in producing facilitation than inhibition and that the opposite might be true of semantic matching. I am not aware of any evidence that would lead to a revision of this conclusion. I am afraid that we will not have an answer to this question until someone has the courage to conduct a mega-experiment in which SOA, RP, and NR are manipulated jointly in both lexical decision and naming tasks. It would probably be a good idea to include associates and category-exemplar pairs as materials, given that priming for these types of items differs under certain conditions.

In summary, two types of strategic processes have been identified: expectancy and semantic matching. The employment of these processes seems to be affected by the stimulus-onset-asynchrony between primes and targets, relatedness proportion, nonword ratio, task (in particular, lexical decision vs. naming), and the type of semantic relation (in particular, associates vs. category-exemplar pairs). An investigator interested in the automatic component of semantic priming would be well advised to use a short SOA (e.g., 200 ms or less), a low RP (e.g., < 0.20?), and an NR of 0.50. Under these conditions, the task and the type of semantic relation do not seem to matter much.

The typical strategy for explaining strategic priming effects is to add additional mechanisms to an automatic priming model. A good example is Neely and Keefe's (1989; see also Neely, 1991) hybrid three-process theory of semantic priming discussed in Chapter 7. This theory combines an automatic spreading activation process, along the lines of the Collins and Loftus (1975) model, with expectancy and semantic-matching processes. Presumably, compound-cue models could be embedded in a similar framework of strategic processes.

As discussed in Chapter 2, Anderson's (1983a) production-system model of the lexical decision task accounts for priming without and with expectancy and predicts only facilitation in the absence of expectancy and both facilitation and inhibition if expectancy is operating. When expectancy is operating, automatic and strategic priming effects should be cumulative. If one assumes that expectancy processes require time to develop, the model predicts facilitation but not inhibition at short SOAs and, as discussed previously, this pattern is commonly observed. The model also predicts that if expectancy is operating (e.g., longer SOAs), an unexpected target that is related to the prime should produce less inhibition than an unexpected target that is unrelated to the prime because of the offsetting, facilitative effects of spreading activation. This pattern was observed by Neely (1977) and by Favreau and Segalowitz (1983). The model also predicts more priming for a target that is expected and is related to the prime than for a target that is expected but is unrelated to the prime. This effect was observed by Favreau and Segalowitz but not by Neely, who obtained the opposite result, although the difference was only marginally reliable at its largest. At least in Neely's results, the greater level of inhibition for unexpected-unrelated targets than for unexpected-related targets indicates that spreading activation was still having an influence at SOAs of 700 ms and beyond, whereas the roughly equal levels of facilitation for expected-related targets and expected-unrelated targets indicates that spreading activation was having no influence over the same time frame.

It may be possible to reconcile these findings in ACT* by assuming that subjects attended less consistently to the prime in the expected-related condition than in the other conditions (e.g., Neely, 1977, pp. 239–240). In Neely's experiments, subjects did not have to shift attention to another category when they saw the prime in the expected-related condition (Nonshift-Expected-Related), whereas they were required by the instructions to shift their attention to another category when they saw the prime word in the other conditions (Shift-Expected-Unrelated, Shift-Unexpected-Related, Shift-Unexpected-Unrelated). The shift instructions must have required more attentional focus than the nonshift instructions (one can imagine subjects repeating to themselves, "OK, when the prime is *body*, think of building parts; when the prime is *body*, think of building parts . . ."). As discussed in Chapter 2, activation will spread from the prime only if it is the focus of attention, and any disruption in this process will have the potential to reduce the spread of activation.

Anderson's model may be able to account for patterns of facilitation and inhibition in lexical decision and naming tasks for associates and category-exemplar pairs. One dimension on which associates and category-exemplar pairs may differ is the size of the expected set of targets (e.g., Becker, 1980). The set of targets expected to follow the prime may be smaller, on the average, for associates than for category-exemplar pairs. For example, if the test list contained a large number of antonym pairs, the set of expected targets for a prime such as *hot* would probably include only one word, *cold*. In contrast, if the test list contained a large number of category-exemplar pairs, and a given category name could be followed by any of several exemplars, the set of expected targets for a prime such as *bird* might include several possible exemplars, such as *robin, sparrow, eagle,* and so forth. In ACT*, an expectation requires that an assertion of the form "X is anticipated" be kept active in working memory. Capacity limitations of working memory place an upper bound on the number of assertions that can be kept active; in addition, activation from the stimulus must be divided among more elements in working memory as the number of expectations increases. These resource limitations cause ACT* to predict less facilitation and more inhibition as the size of the expectancy set increases (Anderson, 1983a, pp. 103–104). If one assumes that the effects of expectancy-based priming increase with SOA, the model may be able to account for the increase in inhibition for category-exemplar pairs in the lexical decision task at long SOAs. Anderson did not analyze the naming task in detail but suggests that it could be implemented with little more than the production that identifies a similar word (Anderson, 1983a, p. 105). This implementation would accurately predict facilitation dominance in the naming task, regardless of SOA and materials, but it could not account for expectancy effects (e.g., Balota, Black, and Cheney, 1992).

Anderson (1983a) acknowledges that SOA will control expectancy but does not discuss RP. The model also does not include a semantic matching process. However, allowing expectancy to be modulated by RP and adding a semantic matching process are entirely consistent with the architecture of the model. It is easy to see in this model, for example, why semantic matching might produce inhibition but not facilitation for "word" responses. The production that implements semantic matching may test for the absence of a semantic relation between the target and the prime and bias a "nonword" response if the condition is satisfied. Such a production would not be activated when the target was related to its prime.

Becker's model is often characterized as a strategic model of priming. As discussed in Chapter 3, my reading of the model is that generation of the semantic set is more automatic than strategic (see esp. Becker & Killion, 1977, p. 395; Becker, 1979, pp. 253–254). It is clear, however, from Becker's writings that he viewed generation of the semantic set to be under cognitive control at least some of the time (e.g., Becker, 1980; Eisenberg & Becker, 1982). If one assumes that generation of the semantic set can occur automatically and be under cognitive control, then Becker's model may be able to account for many of the complex patterns of facilitation and inhibition observed in semantic priming.

Because many commentators have assumed that generation of the semantic set is a strategic expectancy process, there is widespread belief that Becker's model cannot explain priming at short SOAs. If one assumes, however, that generation of the semantic set is an automatic consequence of recognizing the prime, then the model can explain priming at short SOAs without any difficulty. Semantic priming occurs in Becker's model because verification of a member of the semantic set allows feature analysis processes to be bypassed. Semantic sets are not generated for neutral primes. Targets preceded by neutral primes can be recognized only after successful verification of a member of the sensory set. Any delay between processing of the prime and processing of the target will allow some progress to be made in generation of the semantic set for a word prime, setting the stage for facilitation. Inhibition is the "cost" of facilitation. Targets preceded by unrelated primes are recognized only after an exhaustive and unsuccessful search of the semantic set. The longer those processes take, the greater the magnitude of inhibition.

Consider, for example, Neely's (1977) "Shift-Unexpected-Related" condition in which subjects were expecting an exemplar from category B to appear after the category A prime but an exemplar from category A appeared instead. For example, subjects might have expected the name of a building part (e.g., *window*) to follow the prime *body* but were presented with the target *heart* instead. Facilitation of +20 ms occurred at the SOA of 250 ms, but inhibition of –55 ms occurred at the SOA of 2000 ms (averaged across all 4 conditions). According to Becker's model, the early facilitation occurs because the related target is in the semantic set generated automatically to the prime, and the late inhibition occurs because the related target is not in the semantic set generated strategically for the other category.

Becker's model predicts that the magnitudes of facilitation and inhibition should depend on the size of the semantic set (Becker, 1980). As the semantic set gets larger, facilitation should decrease, because more and more items must be considered, on the average, before the correct item is found. Indeed, inhibition is predicted to occur in the semantically related condition for sufficiently large semantic sets (Neely, 1991). The magnitude of inhibition, however, increases with the size of the semantic set. Becker (1980) tested these predictions using antonyms and category-exemplar pairs. Becker assumed that small semantic sets would be generated for the primes in antonym pairs and larger semantic sets would be generated for category name primes. He obtained facilitation but little inhibition for antonyms and the opposite pattern for category-exemplar pairs.[6]

Becker (1980) used a relatively long SOA of 1050 ms. As discussed previously, subsequent studies have shown that priming is facilitation dominant for category-exemplar pairs at short SOAs. This finding can be explained in Becker's model by assuming that generation of the semantic set takes time and that SOA can be a limiting influence on set size (den Heyer, Briand, & Smith, 1985). The magnitude of facilitation for category-exemplar pairs does not seem to be influenced by SOA (Neely, 1991, Table 4—but see footnote 5). This fact implies that the increase in facilitation that should be produced by a reduction in semantic set size must be offset by a decrease in the probability of finding the exemplar target in the semantic set created for the category prime.

Becker did not apply his model to naming, but if one assumes that semantic priming in lexical decision and in naming are caused by the same processes, then Becker's model predicts the same pattern of facilitation and inhibition for both tasks (e.g., Lorch, Balota, & Stamm, 1986). As discussed previously, this prediction is largely supported by extant findings (at least qualitatively), with the exception of semantic priming for category-exemplar pairs at long SOAs; in these conditions, priming is inhibition dominant in lexical decision but facilitation dominant in naming. Lorch et al. (1986) suggested that Becker's model might be able to account for different patterns of inhibition in lexical decision and in naming if search of the semantic set and search of the sensory set occurred in parallel and inhibition was caused by a bias to respond "nonword" in the lexical decision task when the target was not in the semantic set. A generic bias of this kind, however, predicts the same pattern of inhibition for category-exemplar pairs and associates. Alternatively, the model could be augmented with a semantic matching process that (a) is more likely to be used in lexical decision than in naming, (b) has increasing effects as SOA increases, (c) tends to produce greater levels of inhibition than facilitation, and (d) is more sensitive to the superset-subset relations instantiated in category-exemplar pairs than to other types of semantic/associative relations.

Although data on the effects of RP were available at the time Becker was developing his model (e.g., Tweedy, Lapinski, & Schvaneveldt, 1977), I have not been able to find any discussion in Becker's articles of how RP effects might be explained in the verification model. As discussed previously, RP and SOA interact: at short SOAs, there is little influence of RP on facilitation or inhibition, whereas at long SOAs, facilitation and inhibition increase with RP. Becker's model may be able to account for this interaction if one assumes that priming at short SOAs is determined primarily by automatic generation and verification processes, whereas priming at long SOAs is also influenced by strategic modulation of those processes. As noted earlier, short SOAs may place limits on the sizes of semantic sets, producing a facilitation-dominant pattern, and also prevent strategic expectancy. At long SOAs, strategic expectancy processes may be more likely to be invoked.

Plaut's model (Plaut, 1995, 1997; Plaut & Booth, 2000; Plaut, McClelland, Seidenberg, & Patterson, 1996) is the only distributed network model of semantic priming that has been designed to account for associative and categorical priming and for patterns of facilitation and inhibition as a function of SOA. The model has not been applied to both sets of phenomena simultaneously but it probably has the mechanisms needed to account for different patterns of facilitation and inhibition for associates and categorically related items as a function of SOA (Plaut & Booth, 2000, p. 814). A unique feature of this model is that it explains patterns of facilitation and inhibition without invoking strategic priming mechanisms.

Associative priming occurs in the model because the network learns to make efficient transitions from the semantic representation of the prime to the semantic representation of the target if the prime precedes the target frequently during training. Associative priming increases in magnitude as the duration of the prime increases because the resulting pattern of activation is more similar to the pattern associated with that of the target. Most words have few strong associates and, therefore, the network learns to ignore most nonoverlapping patterns that precede a particular pattern during training. As a result, there is little inhibition from unrelated primes, and associative priming is facilitation dominant regardless of SOA.

Categorical priming occurs because the network gets a head start in processing the target if it is preceded by a semantically related prime. Categorical priming peaks at relatively short prime durations and then decreases with additional processing of the prime. The decrease in priming occurs because of hysteresis in the network. During training, the network learns to make particular patterns of activity stable, such that minor deviations from these patterns are corrected to the nearest attractor pattern. When a target follows a prime during testing, the network must make the transition to the target pattern from the prime pattern. As the network settles on a pattern of activation, it evinces greater degrees of inertia in moving to a nonassociated pattern of activation. Hence, for short prime durations, the network can move to the target pattern relatively efficiently, whereas for long prime durations, the network needs more time to make the transition to the target pattern. The overall result is that categorical priming is relatively weak and facilitation dominant at short SOAs but stronger and inhibition dominant at long SOAs.

One potential problem for the model is that it predicts that facilitation for categorically related items will decrease with SOA; in fact, facilitation for such materials is not influenced by SOA (see Chapter 10 and Neely, 1991, Table 4—but see footnote 5). Another possible problem is that the model predicts that associative priming will be larger than categorical priming, even at short SOAs. This relation holds for category members that do not share associative relations (see Chapter 10) but not for category-exemplar pairs, which tend to be moderately associated. Finally, the model would seem to predict similar patterns of facilitation and inhibition for lexical decision and naming, as both tasks require mapping written words onto their meanings, but, in fact, different patterns occur for category-exemplar pairs. An important fact to keep in mind, though, when evaluating the model's account of associative and categorical priming is that categorically related pairs in Plaut's simulations were members of a common category (e.g., *robin-sparrow*), not category-exemplar pairs.

Plaut's model does not yet have mechanisms corresponding to semantic matching, but it may be able to account for the effects of RP (D. C. Plaut, Personal Communication, 26 August 2003; see also, Plaut & Booth, 2000). The details have not been worked out formally, but the fundamental ideas are the following. Instead of accounting for response time with network settling time, response time is determined by a response system external to the lexical system (e.g., Usher & McClelland, 2001). For lexical decision, this response system could be implemented as a fourth layer consisting of two units, a *yes* unit whose input is the level of semantic stress for the current target and a *no* unit whose input is the average level of stress across all targets (see Figure 9.2). The *yes* and the *no* units compete on the basis of the relative strengths of their inputs. The network responds when the activation of one of the units exceeds a response criterion. In such a response system, the competition between the *yes* and the *no* units requires more time to resolve when the two units have inputs of similar magnitudes. Hence, *ceteris paribus,* a word that produces a high stress value will be responded to more quickly than a word that produces a stress value closer to the average, and a nonword that produces a very low stress value will be responded to more quickly than a nonword that produces a stress value closer to the average.

Semantic stress values are higher, on the average, for targets preceded by related primes than for targets preceded by unrelated primes. Because the stress levels for word targets preceded by unrelated primes and for nonword targets are not affected by the proportion of related trials, the average stress across all target stimuli will be higher in high RP lists than in low RP lists. Hence, the input to the *no* unit will be stronger in high RP than in low RP lists. Stronger input to the *no* unit forces a higher response criterion, which has the effect of increasing the difference in response time between targets in the related and the unrelated prime conditions (see Figure 9.3). This model of the effects of RP predicts that responses should be faster in low than in high RP lists because the response criterion is more aggressive in low than in high RP lists. A perusal of the relevant literature indicates this prediction is sometimes confirmed and sometimes falsified (e.g., de Groot, 1984; den Heyer, Briand, & Dannenbring, 1983; Neely, Keefe, & Ross, 1989; Perea & Rosa, 2002; Seidenberg,

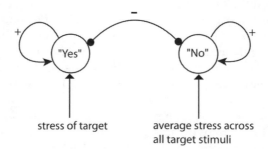

FIGURE 9.2. Depiction of a competitive response system for Plaut's model of semantic priming. Input to *yes* unit is semantic stress of current target; input to *no* unit is the average semantic stress across all target stimuli, including words and nonwords. Each unit sends activation to itself and inhibition to the other unit. Adapted from Plaut and Booth (2000, Fig. 16A).

Waters, Sanders, & Langer, 1984; Tweedy, Lapinski, & Schvaneveldt, 1977). A major limitation of those studies, for the purposes of evaluating the model's prediction, is that RP was manipulated between subjects. Between-subject comparisons of response times are notoriously unreliable. To my knowledge, only one published study has manipulated RP within subjects (Bushell, 1996), and it confirmed the predictions of Plaut's model, although the difference in response latencies was small: mean latencies in the unrelated prime condition were 676 ms and 689 ms for RP = 0.2 and 0.8, respectively (results for normal controls).

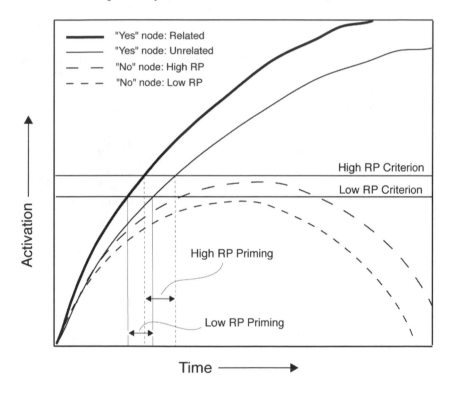

FIGURE 9.3. Response unit activation in a competitive response system as a function of time and input strength. Targets preceded by related primes produce stronger inputs to the *yes* unit than do targets preceded by unrelated primes. Hence, activation of the *yes* unit reaches criterion sooner in the related than in the unrelated condition. This difference in time to reach criterion is the semantic priming effect. The magnitude of the input to the *no* unit increases with RP. A higher response criterion is therefore needed to distinguish words from nonwords. Semantic priming increases in magnitude as a consequence. Adapted from Plaut and Booth (2000, Fig. 16B).

Proponents of multistage activation models eschew the traditional distinction between automatic and strategic priming (e.g., Stolz & Besner, 1999). Activation pathways can be placed under attentional control at any time, and in this sense, priming is never automatic. This conception of attentional control does not, however, imply conscious control. Stolz and Neely (1995) examined the role of RP in modulating feedback in a logogen-based model, and this explanation generalizes to the IA model (e.g., Smith & Besner, 2001, and Chapter 17). To my knowledge, however, the joint effects of SOA, RP, NR, task, and type of prime-target relation have not been examined in the context of a multistage activation model.

I want to end this chapter by unpacking the cautionary comment that I made in the beginning. The traditional two-process theory of automatic and strategic processes stipulates that these processes are independent (Posner and Snyder, 1975a). The influence of automatic processes should decrease across SOA, the influence of strategic processes should increase across SOAs, and there should be no evidence of an interaction between automatic processes, strategic processes, and SOA. There is evidence, however, that strategic processes may influence automatic processes, and the effect may depend on SOA.

In a conceptual replication of a subset of Neely's (1977) experimental conditions, Balota, Black, and Cheney (1992) orthogonally manipulated prime-target relatedness, expectancy, and SOA in the naming task. The authors assumed, as have previous investigators, that the relatedness effect indexed automatic processes and the expectancy effect indexed strategic processes. They found that the relatedness effect decreased across SOA in the expected condition, but there was little effect of relatedness, and little change across SOA, in the unexpected condition. The expectancy effect increased with SOA but primarily in the unrelated condition. This three-way interaction between relatedness, expectancy, and SOA is not consistent with the independent two-process model. Balota and colleagues also showed that a similar pattern was evident in the results of other experiments (Burke, White, & Diaz, 1987; Favreau & Segalowitz, 1983; Neely, 1977) when priming effects were defined with respect to an unrelated/unexpected word baseline rather than with respect to a neutral prime. Balota et al.'s results do not warrant abandoning the distinction between automatic and strategic processes, but they indicate that relations between these processes are more complex than is typically assumed. For instance, Balota et al. speculate that the allocation of attention is more efficient for familiar than for unfamiliar configurations in memory (e.g., *fruit-apple* vs. *fruit-robin*), thereby producing smaller effects of expectancy across SOA for related than for unrelated items.

As we shall see in Chapters 15, 16, and 17, similar conclusions have been reached in other lines of research on semantic priming. There is even evidence now that RP—long taken to be the independent variable most strongly associated with the strategic process of expectancy—affects subliminal semantic priming (see Chapter 14)! Bodner and Masson (2003; see also Bodner & Masson, 2004) found that semantic priming from briefly presented primes (45 ms, masked by the target) was 24 ms when RP was 0.80 and 13 ms when RP was 0.20 (data collapsed across Exps. 1 and 2). A similar effect occurred even when both groups received the same proportion of semantically related trials (0.20) but the high RP group received repetition primes on an additional 60% of the trials. Postexperimental interviews and direct assessment of prime perceptibility indicated that the results could not easily be attributed to conscious awareness of the primes. Bodner and Masson concluded that these results are particularly damaging to spreading activation theories of priming. In fact, their results are problematical for traditional interpretations of RP effects and really do not bear at all on the fundamental mechanism of priming. With the possible exception of Plaut's model, none of the models of priming explains effects of RP intrinsically.

Bodner and Masson's (2003) findings are intriguing but they should be interpreted cautiously. Cheesman and Merikle (1986) manipulated the proportion of congruent trials in a Stroop priming task—which is analogous to manipulating RP in a semantic priming task—and found that this variable did not affect the magnitude of priming when primes were presented at the subjective threshold (discussed in Chapter 14); indeed, they argued that manipulations of the proportion of congruent trials should affect the magnitude of priming only if subjects were aware of primes. Moreover, Perea and Rosa (2002) used procedures very similar to Bodner and Masson's but found no evidence of an effect of RP (0.82 vs. 0.18) on semantic priming at an SOA of 66 ms. Bodner and Masson speculated that subjects in Perea and Rosa's experiment might have been able to consciously perceive many of the primes and that conscious perception could have interfered, in some way, with the unconscious influences of RP. As discussed in Chapter 14, there is evidence that conscious perception of briefly presented primes can interfere with semantic priming, although this evidence does not provide any insight on why or how such an effect would produce equivalent levels of priming for both RP levels. Finally, it should be pointed out that Bodner and Masson's experiments confounded RP with NR. Hence, we really do not know which variable is moderating semantic priming. Although there may be some reluctance to think that NR may be affecting unconscious semantic priming, this reluctance stems from the same preconceptions that cause us to be surprised upon seeing an effect of RP on unconscious semantic priming!

CHAPTER

Associative Versus "Pure" Semantic Priming

As discussed in Chapter 1, the term "semantic priming" is an expository convenience used to refer to priming caused by many different kinds of interrelations, including both associative relations and true relations of meaning. Associative relatedness is defined in terms of free-association norms (e.g., Nelson, McEvoy, & Schreiber, 1991; Postman & Keppel, 1970). Words produced in response to each other in free association tasks are defined as being associatively related (e.g., *dog-cat;* as discussed in Chapter 13, associations can be asymmetrical).

Definitions of semantic relatedness have evolved over the years. In several early investigations (e.g., Hines, Czerwinski, Sawyer, & Dwyer, 1986; Lupker, 1984), semantically related words had to be members of a common semantic category, such as those appearing in Battig and Montague's (1969) norms (e.g., body parts, furniture, clothing). All other types of relations, including object-part relations (e.g., *camel-hump*) and functional relations (e.g., *car-drive*), were classified as nonsemantic. More recent investigations (e.g., McRae & Boisvert, 1998; Moss, Ostrin, Tyler, & Marslen-Wilson, 1995) have broadened the definition of semantic relatedness to include any relation that might appear in a good-faith attempt to define a word (e.g., *apples are red, a broom is used to sweep*). As defined here, "pure" semantically related words share such relations but are not associatively related (e.g., *goose-turkey, tent-cabin*).

It is well documented that associatively related words prime each other in lexical decision, naming, and similar tasks. The controversial issue has been whether priming occurs in the absence of association. Fischler (1977b) first investigated priming in the absence of association and reported a reliable pure semantic priming effect. However, several subsequent studies (e.g., Lupker, 1984; Moss, Ostrin, Tyler, & Marslen-Wilson, 1995; Shelton & Martin, 1992) failed to find pure semantic priming under various conditions; indeed, Shelton and Martin (1992) concluded that automatic priming was associative, not semantic. McRae and Boisvert (1998), on the other hand, have presented evidence that previous failures to find pure semantic priming can be attributed to the use of prime-target pairs that were weakly semantically related.

A recent meta-analysis may bring order to this apparent chaos. Lucas (2000) examined the results of 26 studies in which purely semantically related prime-target pairs were used as stimuli in lexical decision or naming (including Stroop) tasks. Most of those studies also included associatively related primes and targets. The average effect size (Cohen, 1977), weighted by the number of subjects in each sample, was 0.25 for pure semantic priming and 0.49 for associative priming. There was clear evidence therefore that pure semantic priming was present in the studies reviewed, and that associative priming was substantially larger than semantic priming. Because associatively related primes and targets also were related semantically, the larger effect size is best interpreted as an associative "boost" to priming. Further analyses indicated that the effect size for pure semantic priming was not influenced by the particular type of lexical decision task used, relatedness proportion, or stimulus onset asynchrony, suggesting that pure semantic priming was not strategically mediated.

Lucas (2000) also examined whether pure semantic priming varied with type of semantic relation. Category coordinates (e.g., *bronze-gold*), synonyms, antonyms, and script relations (e.g., *theater-play*) had similar average effect sizes, ranging from 0.20 to 0.27. In contrast, functional relationships (e.g., *broom-sweep*) had an average effect size of 0.55. This result supports the hypothesis that functional relations are central to word meaning (e.g., Tyler & Moss, 1997). Perceptually related prime-target pairs, in which primes and targets share referent shape (e.g., *pizza-coin*; Pecher, Zeelenberg, & Raaijmakers, 1998), had a very low effect size of 0.05. This estimate must be treated with caution, however, because only two studies in the corpus examined perceptual priming of this kind.

In summary, although the evidence on pure semantic priming has been mixed, with some studies finding evidence of such priming and others not, Lucas's (2000) meta-analysis indicates that pure semantic priming is a genuine phenomenon. This conclusion is important theoretically because distributed network models strongly predict pure semantic priming. Lucas's analysis also indicates that associative relations nearly double the magnitude of semantic priming relative to semantic relations alone. Finally, there is preliminary evidence that pure semantic priming varies in magnitude with the type of semantic relation, with the most priming occurring for functional relations.

Pure semantic priming and the associative boost to priming can be explained in at least three ways. According to one explanation, pure semantic priming is caused by overlapping semantic relations and the associative boost is caused by nonsemantic, associative relations that exist between words that co-occur frequently in experience (e.g., McKoon & Ratcliff, 1992). In principle, this explanation could probably be implemented in all of the models of priming, but only Plaut's model (e.g., Plaut, 1995) explicitly depends on such mechanisms. To the extent that associative relations can develop independently of semantic relations, one should be able to find evidence of associative priming in the absence of semantic relatedness. In fact, evidence of this kind is difficult to find (for reviews, see Hutchison, 2003; Lucas, 2000). For example, Pecher and Raaijmakers (1999) were able to find small priming effects as a function of experimentally learned associations, but these effects were context dependent: Lexical decision or perceptual identification was used in the study phase (along with other tasks), and both of these tasks were used in the test phase. Priming for newly learned associations was larger when the study and the test task matched than when they mismatched (priming was positive in mismatching tasks, but it was never statistically reliable). This pattern of results indicates that the observed priming effects were governed by the principle of transfer-appropriate processing (e.g., Franks, Bilbrey, Lien, & McNamara, 2000; Morris, Bransford, & Franks, 1977) and strongly implicates the role of episodic memory.

A second explanation of pure semantic priming and the associative boost assumes that words differ in their numbers of associates, and these differences are manifested in free association and in semantic priming. This explanation is fleshed out in some detail in Chapter 13. The fundamental idea is that the effectiveness of a word as a cue in free association and as a prime in a semantic priming task may depend on the number of associates of the word. Words with fewer associates may be better cues and primes than words with more associates. Associatively related primes and targets may be those semantically related pairs of words that have relatively few associations with other words, whereas purely semantically related primes and targets may be those semantically related pairs of words that have relatively large numbers of associations with other words. Presumably this conjecture could be tested by analyzing large corpora of free-association data.

A third explanation is that associatively related words simply share more or stronger semantic relations than do unassociated words (Lucas, 2000). Having devoted a fair amount of time perusing free-association norms, I challenge anyone to find two highly associated words that are not semantically related in some plausible way. Under this view, the distinction between purely semantically related words and associatively (and semantically) related words is an artificial categorization of an underlying continuum. This explanation of pure semantic priming and the associative boost could be implemented in all of the models of priming.

Mediated Versus Direct Priming

Mediated priming involves using primes and targets that are not directly associated or semantically related but instead are related via other words. For example, based on free-association norms (e.g., McNamara, 1992b), *mane* and *tiger* are not associates of each other, but each is an associate of *lion*. The associative relation between a prime and a target can be characterized in terms of the number of associative steps that separate them: one step, or directly related (e.g., *tiger-stripes*); two steps (e.g., *lion-stripes*); three steps (e.g., *mane-stripes*); and so on. Models of priming can be differentiated on the basis of whether or not they predict priming through mediated relations.

Early investigations suggested that two-step mediated priming occurred in naming but not in lexical decision (e.g., Balota & Lorch, 1986; de Groot, 1983). Subsequent studies showed that two-step, and even three-step, priming could be obtained in lexical decision if the task parameters were selected so as to minimize strategic processes, in particular, semantic matching (e.g., McNamara, 1992b; McNamara and Altarriba, 1988; Shelton & Martin, 1992). For example, McNamara and Altarriba (1988) obtained two-step mediated priming in a sequential lexical decision task in which items were presented one at a time on the computer screen and subjects responded to each as it appeared. Pace of presentation was rapid (80–100 ms response-stimulus interval). In this task, primes and targets are not distinguishable from the subject's point of view, and nonwords often immediately precede words. A semantic matching strategy is not effective because nearly all word targets are preceded by unrelated contexts (assuming that the RP is low). Another advantage of this task is that both primes and targets are processed sufficiently deeply to make a lexical decision. This feature of the task may be important when one is looking for relatively small priming effects. A disadvantage of using this task is that one cannot control precisely the interval of time between presentation of the prime and the target.

Mediated priming is strongly predicted by spreading activation models. For example, using the network in Figure 2.1, ACT* predicts an activation level of 1.45 for *stripes* in the unrelated-prime condition and an activation level of 1.61 when it is primed by *mane*.

Most of the remaining models are challenged to some degree by mediated priming. Becker's verification model cannot explain mediated priming because the semantic set is constructed on the basis of semantic and associative relations directly shared with the prime. Certain versions of compound-cue models can account for two-step priming but none predicts three-step priming (McNamara, 1992b). Two-step priming occurs in SAM because the compound cue gets a boost in familiarity when the prime and the target share an associate, even if they are not directly associated. Most distributed network models cannot explain mediated priming because priming in these models is produced by semantic features shared by the prime and the target. Plaut's model (1995; Plaut & Booth, 2000) may be able to account for mediated priming by taking advantage of the associative priming mechanism but, to my knowledge, this conjecture has not been tested. Logogen-based multistage activation models can account for mediated priming if the spread of activation in the semantic system continues for multiple associative or semantic steps (as in traditional spreading activation models). The IA model, however, does not have mechanisms for activation to spread within the semantic system. Only semantic representations that have direct connections to the prime's lexical representation will be partially activated in the semantic system.

A serious problem exists, however, in interpreting the mediated priming results. If the primes and the targets are directly related in some fashion, then all models predict priming between them. This issue has not gone unrecognized. For example, McNamara (1992b) collected free associations to all of the words in the three-step associative chains (e.g., *mane-lion-tiger-stripes*). At least 81 subjects provided associates to the primes, and at least 35 subjects provided associates to the other words. The average successive association (e.g., *mane-lion, lion-tiger*) was 0.39 and the average nonsuccessive association (e.g., *mane-tiger, mane-stripes*) was 0.004. These free-association data were used to identify the set of materials for which all nonsuccessive associations were exactly 0 and no extra-chain mediating word was ever listed for the primes and the targets (i.e., the three-step primes and targets were not two-step primes and targets in disguise). The average priming effect for these items was 10 ms, exactly the same as the average effect for all remaining items. The materials also were divided into a category of items that might plausibly be related semantically (e.g., *cheetah-turtle*) and a category of items that did not seem to share any semantic relations (e.g., *lifeguard-box*). The mean priming effects were 8 and 10 ms, respectively. Despite these valiant efforts, there is the nagging possibility that residual associations or semantic relations existed between the primes and the targets.

The best way to address this issue is in the context of a specific model. For example, McNamara (1992b) showed, using the memory model SAM (Gillund & Shiffrin, 1984), that if direct associations between three-step primes and targets were high enough to produce priming of the magnitude observed, then these primes and targets would have appeared as mutual associates in a free-association task at a much higher frequency than was observed. This analysis does not prove that the primes and targets were not directly related, and the conclusion is limited to one model of priming (viz., the compound-cue model conjoined with SAM). The contribution exists in demonstrating that a particular model would have difficulty accounting for both the mediated priming and the free-association results.

As another example of this approach, Livesay and Burgess (1998) used HAL, a high-dimensional model of semantic memory (e.g., Burgess and Lund, 2000), to compute semantic distances between the two-step mediated primes and targets developed by Balota and Lorch (1986), and subsequently used by McNamara and Altarriba (1988). Average semantic distance was *higher* between mediated primes and targets than between unrelated primes and targets. In addition, they found no relation between the magnitude of mediated priming and lexical co-occurrence frequency, contradicting predictions of McKoon and Ratcliff (1992).

In a similar application, Chwilla and Kolk (2002) developed a set of three-step primes and targets in Dutch. Free association was used to show that the primes and the targets were associated only via two mediating words. Reliable three-step priming was obtained in several experiments. Chwilla and Kolk then computed the semantic distances between the English translations of the primes and the targets using LSA (Landauer, 1998; Landauer & Dumais, 1997). They found that the semantic distances were smaller for the three-step primes and targets than for appropriate unrelated pairs. Hence, all models of priming would predict priming for these materials.

In summary, the status of mediated priming is somewhat ambiguous. Given the ready availability of tools such as HAL and LSA, a natural next step would be to try to construct mediated primes and targets that are not associatively related and are no more semantically related than control pairs using metrics provided by HAL and LSA. Finding priming for such materials would be a strong endorsement of some kind of spreading activation mechanism in priming. Alternatively, if one could show that multistep priming seems to occur only for semantically related primes and targets, as measured by HAL or LSA, then "mediated priming" could be eliminated as a test bed for models of priming.

Effects of Lag

Lag refers to the number of items that intervene between the prime and the target. The standard priming paradigm uses a lag of zero; the target immediately follows the prime. In lag-1 priming, the prime and the target are separated by one unrelated word (e.g., *lion, table, tiger*). Many studies have examined priming at lags of one, two, and even greater. The early literature on lag effects was ambiguous (for reviews, see Joordens and Besner, 1992; Masson, 1995; Neely, 1991). More recent investigations have shown that priming occurs over lags of at least one. Balota and Paul (1996), Joordens and Besner (1992), and McNamara (1992b) obtained priming at a lag of one in lexical decision, naming, or both. Averaged across those experiments, semantic priming at lag 1 was exactly half the magnitude of semantic priming at lag 0 in lexical decision (13 vs. 26 ms) and in naming (5 vs. 10 ms, but see Masson, 1995, for a demonstration of an absence of lag-1 priming in naming). McNamara (1992b) did not obtain priming at a lag of two in the lexical decision task.

There are at least two ways for a spreading activation model to explain lag-1 priming. One explanation is that activation decays at such a rate that it is still above baseline at a lag of one but not at a lag of two. Lag, of course, is defined in terms of the number of intervening items, not in terms of time. This explanation therefore depends on the existence of fortuitous correlations between lag and decay rate across the various experiments that have investigated lag effects. I am not aware of any experiments in which these variables have been manipulated independently. However, this explanation is not appealing in the face of Ratcliff and McKoon's (1988) results showing that activation apparently decays rapidly. Another explanation, and one that is consistent with ACT*, is that the prime is still a source of activation when the target appears. According to this explanation, the magnitude of priming as a function of lag is an index of the probability that the prime is still a source of activation.

In compound-cue models, lag effects are an index of the size of compound cues. Lag-1 priming implies that cues contain three items with some probability (prime, unrelated item, target); the absence of lag-2 priming implies that they rarely contain four items.

Proximity models can explain priming across intervening items by asserting that the semantic pattern of the prime is not completely replaced by semantic patterns of intervening items. Masson (1995) and Plaut (1995) were able to account for Joordens and Besner's (1992) finding of lag-1 priming in naming by incorporating this assumption into their models. In principle, similar mechanisms could be used in Becker's verification model and in multistage activation models. The idea is that one intervening item does not completely replace the semantic set of the prime or eliminate the prime's semantic representation.

Unfortunately for the models, experiments published by Becker, Joordens and their colleagues indicate that semantic priming may occur over lags much greater than one intervening item. Becker and Joordens (Becker, Moscovitch, Behrmann, & Joordens, 1997; Joordens & Becker, 1997) hypothesized, on the basis of theoretical considerations (see the discussion of distributed network learning models in Chapter 5), that semantic priming could be obtained at long lags if the primes and the targets were strongly semantically related and the task engaged semantic processing to a high degree. They constructed prime-target pairs that were semantically similar (e.g., *pontoon-raft, tulip-rose*) and used several methods to increase the semantic processing of target words. Becker et al. (1997) used an animacy decision task in which participants were required to decide whether each word referred to a living or a nonliving entity. Joordens and Becker (1997) used a lexical decision task in which nonwords were very wordlike (e.g., *brane*) or were studied preexperimentally. Priming at very long lags was obtained in several of these experiments (see Table 12.1).

Priming at long lags is predicted by distributed-network learning models but is a serious problem for all other models of priming. In principle, spreading activation models could explain such priming by making the decay of activation very slow, but this assumption would be inconsistent with other findings suggesting that activation decays quickly. Moreover, slow decay would probably leave so much residual

TABLE 12.1. Semantic priming (ms) as a function of lag in experiments designed to investigate long-term priming effects.

Study/Exp	Lag						
	0	1	2	4	8	10[a]	21.5[a]
Becker/1						43	
2							35
3	92			42	71		
Mean	92			42	71	43	35
Joordens/1					8		
2h	45	38	31	34	41		
2p	27	17	-10	11	12		
3	36			43	4		
4					63		
Mean[b]	41	38	31	38	29		

[a]Average lag.
[b]Means do not include Joordens/2p.
Notes: Citations are Becker, Moscovitch, Behrmann, & Joordens (1997) and Joordens & Becker (1997). Becker et al. used animacy decision: five primes per target in Exp. 1; one prime per target in Exps. 2 and 3. Joordens and Becker used lexical decision: nonwords were pseudohomophones (e.g., *brane*) in 1, 2h, and 3; only pronounceable in 2p (e.g., *brene*); and studied preexperimentally in 4.

activation in memory that basic semantic priming effects could no longer be predicted. In ACT*, priming at long lags implies that items can be sources of activation for very long periods of time (on the order of tens of seconds) without being rehearsed. This period of time, Δt, is a parameter of ACT*. It would be challenging to develop a principled explanation of why this parameter can range from 400 ms to tens of seconds in ostensibly very similar paradigms. Compound-cue models would need cues of between 23 and 24 items to explain priming at a lag of 21.5 (prime + intervening items + target). Cues of this size strain credibility. The mechanisms used by proximity models, multistage activation models, and Becker's model also will not work. Too many semantic representations get activated and too many semantic sets get created between the prime and the target.

There are at least two reasons to question these long-term semantic priming effects, however. First, the results seem to be unstable. Joordens and Becker (1997) obtained lag-8 priming in two experiments but did not obtain it in another two experiments. Second, and more important, the priming observed in these studies has peculiar properties. For example, in their second experiment, Joordens and Becker varied lag over the values 0, 1, 2, 4, and 8. One condition was designed to produce long-term semantic priming and used a lexical decision task with difficult nonwords (e.g., *brane*). There was little evidence of decay of priming across lags (Table 12.1, Joordens/2h). Another condition was designed not to produce long-term semantic priming and used a lexical decision task with easier nonwords (e.g., *brene*). Priming was significant at lag 0 but not at lags 1–8 (Table 12.1, Joordens/2p). These results suggest that semantic priming may have a long-term learning component and a short-term associative component (Joordens & Becker, 1997). Priming in the easy nonword condition would be attributed to the associative component alone, whereas priming in the difficult nonword condition would be attributed to the combined effects of both components. Even this two-process model, however, is not consistent with Joordens and Becker's findings, as it still predicts some decline in priming with lag, even in the difficult nonword condition. At lag 0, both associative and learning priming would occur, whereas at longer lags, only learning priming would occur. Perhaps experiments with greater power than those conducted by Joordens and Becker could detect these predicted differences.

I am not aware of any published replications of Joordens and Becker's findings. Zeelenberg and Pecher (2002) were unable to obtain long-term semantic priming in a lexical decision task, even when 12 primes were presented for each target and each prime appeared for 2 s (in one experiment subjects rated the primes on pleasantness). The nonwords in the lexical decision task were not pseudohomophones, as advocated by Joordens and Becker (1997), but they were pronounceable.

The long-term semantic priming effects discovered by Becker, Joordens, and their colleagues may be similar to the semantic transfer effects reported by Woltz (1990; Woltz, 1996) and by Hughes and Whittlesea (2003). In Woltz's experiments, subjects decided whether or not two words were synonyms (e.g., *moist-damp* vs. *moist-blue*). Responses to repeated comparisons (e.g., *moist-damp* followed by *moist-damp*) were faster than responses to first-time comparisons at lags greater than 400 trials. Hughes and Whittlesea obtained similar semantic transfer effects in a semantic categorization task. In the standard task, subjects saw a word flanked by two category labels (e.g., *animal-tiger-vitamin*) and had to choose the label matching the central word (e.g., *animal*). A primed trial was preceded by a trial containing a semantically related central word flanked by the same category labels (e.g., *animal-tiger-vitamin* preceded by *animal-lion-vitamin*). Priming in this task occurred at an average lag of 90 items.

These long-term semantic transfer effects have a strong episodic component, are specific to the decision made, and require extensive semantic processing in the prime and the test phases. Woltz (1990) found that priming in semantic comparisons decayed rapidly for synonyms (e.g., *soggy-wet* followed by *moist-damp*) and was virtually nonexistent at a lag of five. Woltz (1996) showed further that priming did not occur when the words in a semantic comparison (e.g., *moist-damp*) had been presented previously as members of lexically identical pairs (e.g., *moist-moist* and *damp-damp;* overlap in sensory-perceptual features was minimized by presenting the prime pairs and the target pairs in the auditory and the visual modalities, respectively). Similarly, Hughes and Whittlesea (2003) did not obtain priming effects between their semantic categorization task and a task that required subjects to select the flanker word representing a feature of the central word. For example, subjects might have seen *fruit-apple-bird* in the priming phase (*fruit* is the correct choice) and *peel-orange-hiss* in the test phase (*peel* is the correct choice). They also did not obtain priming between categorization and either naming or lexical decision.

Collectively, these findings indicate that long-term semantic transfer effects do not depend on the activation of abstract semantic representations but are produced instead by the reenactment of specific cognitive operations performed at an earlier point in time (e.g., Kolers, 1973, 1976). Hughes and Whittlesea (2003; see also, Whittlesea & Jacoby, 1990) speculate that this "processing account" of memory may explain all semantic priming effects. According to this account, processing the prime is a learning experience, which establishes a resource for performing similar mental activities on similar stimuli. The direction of causation in semantic priming is from the target back to the prime (as in semantic matching). Suffice to say that semantic priming phenomena would have received a very different interpretation if Hughes and Whittlesea had authored this book.

These comments aside, if priming at long lags holds up under additional experimental scrutiny, and if the paradoxical results obtained by Becker, Joordens, and their colleagues can be explained, long-term priming will provide compelling evidence in support of distributed-network learning models and virtually insurmountable evidence against other models of priming. The challenge for learning models will be to explain both long-term and short-term semantic priming.

Forward Versus Backward Priming

Associations between words can be asymmetrical. For example, *light* is frequently listed as an associate of *lamp*, whereas *lamp* rarely appears as an associate of *light* (Nelson, McEvoy, and Schreiber, 1991). Backward priming refers to the situation in which the association from prime to target is weak but the association from target to prime is strong (e.g., *light-lamp*). Koriat (1981) was the first to investigate backward priming, and he obtained equal amounts of priming in the forward (e.g., *lamp-light*) and the backward (e.g., *light-lamp*) directions. This result is surprising, because if priming depends on strength of association, it should be larger in the forward than in the backward direction.

Backward priming has now been examined in eight published articles (chronologically): Koriat (1981); Seidenberg, Waters, Sanders, and Langer (1984); Peterson and Simpson (1989); Shelton and Martin (1992); Chwilla, Hagoort, and Brown (1998); Thompson-Schill, Kurtz, and Gabrieli (1998); Kahan, Neely, and Forsythe (1999); and Hutchison (2002). A perusal of these articles reveals the following observations and findings (see Table 13.1).

One of the difficulties in comparing results across studies is that different materials have been used. Several studies have used asymmetrically associated, semantically related primes and targets (e.g., *lamp-light, eagle-bird*); other studies have used semantically unrelated compound words (e.g., *fruit-fly, sand-box*); and still others have used a mixture of these types of stimuli. Given the findings reviewed previously on pure semantic

TABLE 13.1. Forward and backward priming (ms) in lexical decision.

Study/Exp	Forward	Backward	SOA (ms)	Stimuli	RP	NR
Koriat/3	34	35	650	SR	.50	.67
Seidenberg/3	27	21	500	C	.50	.50
Peterson/2b		22	0[a]	C & SR	.50	.67
2b		26	200[a]	C & SR	.50	.67
1b	40	37	500	C & SR	.50	.67
Shelton/2s	3	-26	500[b]	C	.09[c]	na
2l	38	19	750	C	.24	.45
2h	32	25	750	C	.76	.72
Chwilla/1	48	35	0[a]	C & SR	.75	.80
1	30	22	500[a]	C & SR	.75	.80
Thompson-Schill/1	24	17	250	SR	.50	.67
2	25	17	250	SR	.36	.60
Kahan/1		26	150	C	.80	.875
1		30	150	SR	.80	.875
1		24	500	C	.80	.875
1		26	500	SR	.80	.875
Hutchison/1	36	-4	700[b]	SR	.50	.50

[a]Interstimulus interval for auditorially presented primes.
[b]Response-stimulus interval in sequential lexical decisions.
[c]Proportion of word target trials preceded by related primes.
Notes: Citations are Koriat (1981); Seidenberg, Waters, Sanders, & Langer (1984); Peterson & Simpson (1989); Shelton & Martin (1992); Chwilla, Hagoort, & Brown (1998); Thompson-Schill, Kurtz, & Gabrieli (1998); Kahan, Neely, & Forsythe (1999), and Hutchison (2002). In Shelton and Martin's second experiment, three tasks were used: sequential lexical decision (2s), paired presentation with low RP (2l), and paired presentation with high RP (2h). C = compounds, SR = semantically related noncompounds.

priming, one would expect to find some priming in the forward and in the backward directions for semantically related pairs, regardless of differences in associative strength. In contrast, one wonders why priming would occur at all for semantically unrelated compounds, unless it is strategically mediated. Of the 20 compounds introduced into the literature by Seidenberg et al. (1984) and subsequently used by Shelton and Martin (1992) and by Thompson-Schill et al. (1998), 18 prime words appear in the Nelson, McEvoy, and Schreiber (1991) free-association norms. The associative strength in the forward direction (e.g., *fruit-fly*) has a modal value of 0 and a mean of 0.02! Given that these items are neither semantically nor associatively related, automatic priming would not be expected for them.

There is good evidence that forward and backward priming for compounds is produced by strategic processes. Shelton and Martin (1992, Exp. 2; see Table 13.1) did not obtain priming in the forward or the backward directions for compound words in the sequential lexical decision task. Thompson-Schill et al. (1998, Exp. 3) examined priming for compounds in the naming task, under conditions at least marginally consistent with automatic processing (RP = 0.50, SOA = 200 ms). No priming was obtained in either the forward or the backward direction. Those studies reporting reliable priming for compounds (Chwilla, Hagoort, & Brown, 1998; Kahan, Neely, & Forsythe, 1999; Seidenberg, Waters, Sanders, & Langer, 1984; Shelton & Martin, 1992, Exp. 2, "paired" conditions) employed task parameters consistent with strategic processing: high RP, high NR, or long SOA. I include in this mix experiments using the naming task, as there is evidence that naming is not immune to strategic processing (e.g., Keefe and Neely, 1990).

It seems likely that expectancy and semantic matching play a role in priming for compounds. Especially with high RP, subjects may expect primes and targets to be related in some manner. They may then check for a relation, from prime to target or from target to prime, before responding. Although naming is usually assumed to be immune from semantic matching strategies, I can imagine that even this task could be influenced by these strategies if the conditions were appropriate. Strategic processes in naming are implicated by comparing Kahan et al.'s (1999) naming conditions to those of Thompson-Schill et al. (1998, Exp. 3). SOAs were approximately the same (150 vs. 200 ms), and similar materials were used, but whereas RP = 0.80 and NR = 0.875 in Kahan's experiments, RP = 0.50 in Thompson-Schill's (NR was not defined because nonwords were not included in the lists). Backward priming for compounds was 13 ms in Kahan's experiment and –2 ms in Thompson-Schill's (see Table 13.2).

Asymmetrically associated, semantically related pairs (e.g., *lamp-light*) seem to prime each other in both directions, and there is weak evidence that priming is greater in the forward than in the backward directions. Only four published studies have examined priming in both directions for semantically related pairs: Koriat (1981), Chwilla et al. (1998), Thompson-Schill et al. (1998), and Hutchison (2002). Relevant data can be found in Table 13.1, with the following two additions: Chwilla et al. reported 61 ms of forward priming and 27 ms of backward priming for semantically related items, collapsing across ISI, when those items were analyzed separately from the compounds. In a naming task, Thompson-Schill et al. obtained 11 ms of forward priming and 13 ms of backward priming for semantically related items (RP = .50, SOA = 200 ms). Ignoring what may be important procedural and task differences, priming has averaged 32 ms in the forward direction and 18 ms in the backward direction for

TABLE 13.2. Backward priming (ms) in naming.

Study	SOA (ms)				Stimuli	RP	NR
	0	150	200	500			
Seidenberg				-7	C	.50	
Peterson	22[a]		7[a]	-6	C & SR	.50	
Thompson-Schill			-2		C	.50	
			13		SR	.50	
Kahan		13		5	C	.80	.875
		13		4	SR	.80	.875
Mean	22	13	6	-1			

[a]Primes presented auditorially; value of SOA is ISI between prime and target.
Notes: Citations are Seidenberg, Waters, Sanders, & Langer (1984); Peterson & Simpson (1989); Thompson-Schill, Kurtz, & Gabrieli (1998); and Kahan, Neely, & Forsythe (1999). C = compounds, SR = semantically related noncompounds. An empty cell for NR means that nonwords were not included in the test list.

asymmetrically associated, semantically related items. This pattern of results is exactly what is expected if both associative and semantic relations contribute to priming.

An important fact to keep in mind when comparing the magnitudes of forward and backward priming is that direction of priming is confounded with target word frequency. Backward targets are usually of lower word frequency than are forward targets (e.g., *wood-termite* vs. *termite-wood*). This confound may produce a bias in favor of backward priming because priming is greater for low- than for high-frequency words (see Chapter 17).

Backward priming in the naming task may depend on SOA. As shown in Table 13.2, backward priming in naming seems to decrease in magnitude with SOA/ISI. This effect does not seem to be modulated by the type of relation between the prime and the target. A notable feature of past experiments is that all have used RPs of 0.50 or greater, which suggests that strategic processes may be contributing to the apparent dependence of backward priming on SOA. It is not clear why backward priming would appear at short but not at long SOAs in naming, but then not much is known about strategy use in naming. More research is clearly needed to unravel these unusual findings on backward priming in naming.

Although the data on backward priming may seem to be bewildering, a clear pattern emerges: Automatic priming should not occur for compounds because they lack associative and semantic relations, and, in fact, semantic priming is not obtained in lexical decision or in naming when task parameters are in the automatic regime. Automatic priming should occur for asymmetrically associated, semantically related pairs and, indeed, priming occurs in the forward and in the backward directions for these items; there is weak evidence that the magnitude of priming tracks associative strength.

ACT* can account for asymmetrical priming in at least two ways. One possible explanation is that the asymmetry is caused by differences in node strength. All else equal, stronger nodes will be better primes than weaker nodes because they have more activation to send. This explanation, however, is not consistent with the direction of the asymmetry in free association or in semantic priming. In asymmetrically associated pairs, the prime is usually of lower word frequency—and, presumably, of lower node strength—than the target in the forward direction (e.g., *stork-baby, termite-wood*). A more promising explanation assumes that the primes and the targets in asymmetrically associated pairs differ in numbers of associates. In ACT*, the strength of the association from node A to node B is defined as the strength of B divided by the sum of the strengths of all nodes linked to A. This definition guarantees that activation emanating from A is partitioned across all of the nodes directly linked to A according to their relative strengths. If A and B are directly linked, but A is linked to fewer nodes than is B, then A will be a better prime for B than B is for A. Consider, for example, *mane* and *lion* in Figure 2.1, and assume that all nodes are of equal strength. The activation of *lion* is 3.4 when *mane* and *lion* are sources of activation and is 1.9 when *lion* alone is a source, producing a "forward" priming effect of 1.5. By way of contrast, the activation of *mane* is 1.5 when *lion* and *mane* are sources and is 1.2 when *mane* alone is a source, producing a "backward" priming effect of 0.3. The asymmetry is produced because all of *mane*'s activation is sent to *lion* when *mane* is a prime, but only one fifth of *lion*'s activation is sent to *mane* when *lion* is a prime. The direction of this asymmetry parallels those found in free association and in semantic priming.

Becker's model should be able to account for associative and semantic priming by including the appropriate features in the conceptual representations. However, it is difficult to envision how this model could account for asymmetrical priming effects.

The predictions of compound-cue models depend on which model of memory serves as the base. The two models that have figured most prominently in investigations of priming are SAM (Gillund and Shiffrin, 1984) and TODAM (Murdock, 1982). SAM predicts backward priming and, with appropriate parameter values, greater priming in the forward than in the backward directions. Suppose the strength of association in Figure 4.1 between D and E' is reduced from 0.7 to 0.2. Now D is no more associated with E than it is with any other unrelated item (e.g., F–L) but E is strongly associated with D. The familiarity of the cue {D E} is 3.77 and the familiarity of the cue {E D} is 3.59. These are the related conditions. The familiarities are reversed from what one might expect because the familiarity of E is greater than the familiarity of D (because of the reduced associative strength from D to E). Unrelated primes must be chosen so that their familiarities match the familiarities of the related primes. For example, the unrelated prime for E must have the same overall familiarity as D. To accomplish this using the matrix in Figure 4.1, another associative strength must be changed. Suppose S(H,I') is also reduced to 0.2. Item H can now be used as a prime for E because its familiarity is the same as that of D (3.7). The familiarity of a cue containing {H E} is 3.59, producing a backward priming effect of 3.77–3.59 = 0.18. K, like E, is associated with two items and therefore has the same familiarity as E. The familiarity of {K D} is 3.40, producing a forward priming effect of 3.59–3.40 = 0.19. Different parameter values yield larger differences between backward and forward priming. For example, if the strength of association from each cue to itself (e.g., A-A') in Figure 4.1 is increased from 1 to 10, the predicted backward and forward priming effects are 0.63 and 1.32.

TODAM also predicts backward priming, but, because associations are modeled by a commutative operation, it has difficulty explaining asymmetrical priming. To account for priming in TODAM, the compound cue must contain, at the bare minimum, the target and the prime-target association (e.g., Dosher & Rosedale, 1989; McNamara, 1992a, 1992b; McNamara & Diwadkar, 1996). For example, given prime B and target A, the cue must contain $\{\mathbf{A} + \mathbf{A}^*\mathbf{B}\}$, where $\mathbf{A}$ and $\mathbf{B}$ are vectors representing items A and B, and $\mathbf{A}^*\mathbf{B}$ is the convolution of the vectors (e.g., Bracewell, 1978). The familiarity of the cue is higher when the prime-target association is present in memory than when it is not, but because convolution is commutative ($\mathbf{A}^*\mathbf{B} = \mathbf{B}^*\mathbf{A}$), familiarity is not affected by the order of the prime and the target.

Forward and backward priming are defined in terms of asymmetries in free association, which can be viewed as a form of cued recall. TODAM can predict asymmetrical cued recall if the members of associated pairs have different numbers of associates (e.g., Kahana, 2002). The mechanism is similar to the one discussed previously for ACT*. In particular, if B has fewer associates in memory than does A (e.g., *stork* and *baby*, respectively), then B will be a better retrieval cue for A than A is for B (e.g., producing *"baby"* in response to *"stork"* is more likely than producing *"stork"* in response to *"baby"*).

Unlike cued recall, item recognition (and, by generalization, lexical decision) in TODAM depends only on the familiarity of cues. The expected value of the familiarity of a cue is not affected by other items or by associative information in memory. Hence, the familiarity of a forward-priming cue (B primes A; cue = {**A** + **A*****B**}) would be the same, on the average, as the familiarity of a backward-priming cue (A primes B; cue = {**B** + **B*****A**}), even if B has fewer associates than does A. The variance of the distribution of familiarity is affected by item and associative information in memory, but these effects are probably too small to explain asymmetrical priming. As the number of associates of an item increases, the variability of the distribution of familiarity for that item also increases. Variability increases because partial matches (e.g., A vs. A*C) introduce more variance than complete mismatches (e.g., B vs. A*C; see Weber, 1988, Table 2). The increase in variance is of order $\frac{1}{N}$ for each partial match, where N is the number of features needed to represent an item. N is a parameter of the model and typically ranges from 200 to 500 in fits to episodic recall and recognition data (Weber, 1988). The increases in variance are therefore very small and are unlikely to be useful in modeling asymmetrical semantic priming. In summary, in its basic form, TODAM cannot readily explain asymmetrical priming.

All of the distributed network models predict priming for semantically related primes and targets, but only Plaut and Booth's (2000) model has an associative mechanism that would allow it to predict greater priming in the forward than in the backward associative direction.

Multistage activation models may be able to explain asymmetrical priming effects, depending on details of the implementations. In logogen-based models, the semantic system would have to allow for asymmetrical associative strengths between semantic representations. In the IA model, the key would be for feedforward connections from the lexical level to the semantic level to differ in strength from prime to target and from target to prime.

In summary, forward vs. backward semantic priming may be an important arena for testing models of semantic priming. For example, several of the models of priming would be challenged by a convincing demonstration of asymmetrical priming for asymmetrically associated, semantically related primes and targets under automatic priming conditions (i.e., short SOA, low RP, neutral NR).

14
CHAPTER

Conscious Versus Unconscious Priming

There is probably no more controversial issue in the semantic priming literature than "subliminal" or "unconscious" priming. The question is, can semantic priming occur even when the prime is presented under conditions in which it cannot be identified or its presence cannot be detected? This question is a species of the genus "Can perception occur without awareness?" That question may not be as old as the hills, but it is certainly as old as the science of psychology, some of the earliest experiments having been published in the 19th century (cited in Adams, 1957). Although a negative answer to the perception question would probably entail a negative answer to the priming question, the inverse is not true. For instance, accessing the meaning of a word may not require awareness but semantic priming may. For this reason and because this book is about semantic priming, not about perception and consciousness, I will focus my attention on the narrower question of whether or not semantic priming requires awareness of the prime.

Backward masking of the prime has emerged as the method of choice for investigating subliminal semantic priming (Holender, 1986). The prime is presented for a brief period of time (on the order of tens of ms) and followed by a pattern mask. The target is then displayed and subjects name or make a lexical decision to the target. The goal is to find an SOA between the prime and the mask such that subjects are not aware of the prime, yet semantic priming still occurs. The thorny conceptual and methodological issues involve defining and measuring awareness of the prime.

The concept of a sensory or perceptual threshold is not well defined in contemporary psychophysical theory (e.g., Macmillan, 1986). However, one can empirically define the maximum level of stimulus duration or energy that produces a desired level of perceptual awareness. It has been known since at least the 19th century that people can respond above chance, yet claim they are only guessing (Adams, 1957). Cheesman and Merikle (1984) considered two definitions of awareness and distinguished between two associated awareness thresholds. According to one definition, subjects were unaware of the prime if they said they could not perceive it. The subjective threshold was defined as the maximum level of stimulus presentation at which subjects reported no phenomenal awareness of the prime. According to the other definition, subjects were said to be unaware of the prime if they could not reliably make a forced-choice decision (e.g., present-absent, word-nonword) on the prime. The objective threshold was the maximum level of stimulus presentation to produce chance performance in a task requiring a forced-choice decision on the prime.

Many investigators are reluctant to use objective thresholds to define awareness because such thresholds do not account for phenomenal experience (e.g., Fowler, 1986; Kunimoto, Miller, & Pashler, 2001; Paap, 1986). A fundamental problem with defining awareness in terms of subjective thresholds is that the criteria for making awareness judgments are unknowable, and reports may be influenced by response biases (e.g., Eriksen, 1960). For example, when subjective thresholds are assessed after blocks of trials using retrospective evaluations, they are substantially higher than objective thresholds (e.g., Cheesman & Merikle, 1984; Kunimoto, Miller, & Pashler, 2001). However, when subjective and objective thresholds are estimated by applying signal-detection analyses to trial-by-trial measures of confidence and accuracy, they differ trivially (Kunimoto, Miller, & Pashler, 2001). In Kunimoto et al.'s experiments, for example, the stimulus-mask SOAs for subjective and objective thresholds differed by 3.2 ms, on average. In other words, perception preceded awareness by about 3 ms. These results indicate that people underestimate their ability to make sensory discrimination judgments (e.g., Bjorkman, Juslin, & Winman, 1993) and may report that they are guessing or cannot identify a stimulus even though they are aware of having obtained partial information about the stimulus. Another problem is that for complex stimuli, such as words and pictures, the subjective threshold marks the endpoint of a continuum of partial awareness based on fragments of information extracted from the stimulus (e.g., Holender &

Duscherer, 2004; Lupker, 1986). Unconscious semantic processing may appear to have occurred if people are able to use partial awareness to reconstruct or guess the "subliminally" presented stimulus (Kouider & Dupoux, 2004).

Awareness of the prime, however it is defined, must be measured at some point. The most common strategy is to establish the awareness threshold for each subject individually in the first phase of the experiment and then to use these thresholds in the second semantic priming phase. A potential problem with this method is that thresholds may decrease during the course of the experiment because of learning, adaptation, and so forth (Holender, 1986). Primes thought to be presented below threshold would then be above threshold. To address this problem, some investigators have retested the threshold after the priming phase of the experiment. Ideally one would like to know for each trial whether or not the subject was aware of the prime, and a few studies have required subjects to identify or to make a decision on the prime in each trial of the semantic priming phase of the experiment.

The first investigations of subliminal semantic priming using backward masking appeared in the early 1980s. Those studies indicated that semantic priming occurred even when the prime was presented under conditions in which it could not be identified or its presence could not be detected (e.g., Balota, 1983; Carr, McCauley, Sperber, & Parmelee, 1982; Fischler & Goodman, 1978; Fowler, Wolford, Slade, & Tassinary, 1981; Marcel, 1983; McCauley, Parmelee, Sperber, & Carr, 1980). After conducting a comprehensive review of this literature, Holender (1986) concluded that the effects were unreliable and that the stimuli had probably been consciously identified. Holender's conclusion was vindicated by failures to find unconscious semantic priming when more sensitive measures of prime awareness were employed (e.g., Cheesman & Merikle, 1984).

A second generation of investigations of unconscious priming used improved methods for defining and assessing awareness of the prime. Dagenbach, Carr, and Wilhelmsen (1989) established prime awareness thresholds using four tasks: detection, in which subjects were required to decide whether any word or a blank field had been presented before the mask; constrained detection, in which subjects were required to decide whether a specific word or a blank field preceded the mask; word-word discrimination, in which subjects decided which of two alternative words preceded the mask; and semantic similarity, in which subjects decided which of two words was semantically associated with the stimulus that appeared before the mask (a given subject participated in at most two of these tasks). One of these thresholds was assessed before and again after the semantic priming phase of the experiment (in Exps. 1–3, the detection threshold; in Exp. 4, either the detection or the semantic similarity threshold). The crucial analyses of semantic priming data were based on those subjects whose thresholds did not decrease in the retest. (Hines, Czerwinski, Sawyer, and Dwyer, 1986, used a similar approach.) As an additional check that subjects were not consciously aware of the primes, at the conclusion of the first threshold-setting session, subjects were shown a series of words presented at the just-estimated threshold (or the longer of two thresholds in Exp. 1) and asked to guess the identities of the words. None of these words could be identified. To monitor subjects' awareness of the primes during the semantic priming phase, Dagenbach et al. required subjects to guess the identity of the prime after they had responded to the target on approximately one fifth of the trials. Identification rates were higher in the related than in the unrelated condition (levels of performance were not reported). The authors attributed these successes to guesses generated by free associating to the targets (more on this subsequently).

There were two major findings from these experiments. First, statistically reliable semantic priming was obtained in the condition in which primes were presented at the detection threshold. For example, in Experiment 1, semantic priming was 32 ms at detection threshold for subjects who participated in detection and constrained detection tasks, and in Experiment 4, semantic priming was 27 ms at detection threshold for subjects in the detection task condition. Importantly, these results were obtained for subjects who were at or near chance in both threshold setting sessions. Second, the threshold-setting task influenced the pattern of priming results in the semantic priming phase. Although these patterns were not consistent in their details across experiments, the trend was for semantic priming to decrease with increasing SOA when the detection tasks were used to estimate the threshold and for semantic priming to be less robust, and even negative (i.e., inhibition was observed), when the semantic similarity task was used to estimate the threshold.

Despite the extraordinary steps Dagenbach et al. (1989) took to ensure that primes were presented at an objective threshold and that subjects were phenomenally unaware of the primes, their experiments suffer from a severe limitation. The sequences of stimuli presented during the threshold-setting phases and the semantic priming phase were not the same; in particular, primes were not presented in the context of related targets during threshold setting. Several studies have shown that briefly presented primes are better identified, classified lexically (word vs. nonword), and recognized when followed by semantically related targets than when followed by semantically unrelated targets (e.g., Bernstein, Bissonnette, Vyas, & Barclay, 1989; Briand, den Heyer, & Dannenbring, 1988; Dark, 1988; Dark & Benson, 1991). Moreover, those studies have also shown that semantic priming can be positively correlated with prime identification (Briand, den Heyer, & Dannenbring, 1988, Exp. 2; Dark, 1988; Dark & Benson, 1991; but see Carr, McCauley, Sperber, & Parmelee, 1982; Fischler & Goodman, 1978; McCauley, Parmelee, Sperber, & Carr, 1980). These results raise the possibility that primes followed by related targets in the semantic priming phase were above threshold because of processing facilitation created by the targets. Awareness thresholds estimated in the context of related targets almost certainly would be lower than those estimated in the context of unrelated targets, and they might be sufficiently low to eliminate semantic priming itself.

Hirshman and Durante (1992) tried to address this problem by interleaving prime identification and target lexical decision trials. Each trial began with a cue that indicated to the subject whether the prime should be identified or a lexical decision should be made to the target. This procedure has several advantages over standard threshold-setting procedures. With the exception of the cue, the experimental conditions and stimuli are identical on prime identification and target lexical decision trials. In addition, prime identification and semantic priming are measured at the same time (albeit from responses collected on different trials). An advantage of this procedure over the concurrent responding procedure used by Briand et al. (1988), Dagenbach et al. (1989), Dark (1988), and Dark and Benson (1991, Exp. 1 but not Exps. 2 and 3) is that identification of the prime cannot interfere with lexical decisions to the target, and vice versa.

Hirshman and Durante (1992) obtained several important results. First, semantic priming was obtained even when prime identification was very low. In Experiment 2, with a prime presentation duration of 33 ms, semantic priming averaged 43 ms and prime identification averaged 6%. Second, subjects were able to identify primes more often when the primes were followed by related targets than when they were followed by unrelated targets (e.g., in Exp. 2, 7% vs. 4%, respectively). Third, there was no evidence that prime identification was based on free association, as suggested by Dagenbach et al. (1989). A free-association strategy predicts that at least some of the errors in prime identification will be semantic associates of the target. In fact, none of the errors at the prime duration of 33 ms was semantically associated with the target or the prime.

Given that prime identification was greater than zero, semantic priming might have been caused by the small subset of trials in which primes were identified. The authors examined several predictions of such an explanation and did not find support for any of them. In particular, there was no correlation across subjects between the magnitude of semantic priming and prime identification rate. Another alternative explanation is that the semantic priming effect is really a prime identification effect. The idea is that prime identification itself may reduce lexical decision latencies on targets. This explanation predicts that the semantic priming effect and the prime identification effect will be positively correlated. In fact, the correlation was negative and approached statistical significance. This result suggests that prime identification might have interfered with target lexical decision (e.g., Fischler & Goodman, 1978). In subsequent work using the pre-cueing paradigm, Durante and Hirshman (1994) presented evidence that the magnitude of masked semantic priming decreased as the prime identification rate increased.[1]

A third generation of investigations of subliminal priming has been characterized by additional methodological innovations. The most significant may be Greenwald, Klinger, and Schuh's (1995) use of linear regression to assess subliminal priming. The ostensibly subliminal effects of primes on responses to targets are predicted with an independent measure of prime perceptibility. For example, semantic priming with briefly presented primes could be predicted with a measure of the perceptibility of those primes under the same presentation and display conditions. Subliminal priming is indicated by a statistically significant y intercept: priming (y) is nonzero when prime perceptibility (x) is at zero sensitivity. The principal advantage of this approach is that the search for subliminal priming effects is transformed from one that requires establishing chance performance for all subjects on a measure of prime awareness to one that capitalizes on the between-subject variability in the measure of prime awareness to examine the functional relation between that measure and the measure of semantic priming.

This regression method has been criticized by several authors (e.g., Dosher, 1998; Merikle & Reingold, 1998; Miller, 2000). A common criticism is that the method requires strong assumptions, including linearity of the relationship, rational zero points on the measures of semantic priming and of prime perceptibility, and absence of measurement error in the measure of prime perceptibility (x). Concerns have also been expressed about whether the measures of semantic priming and prime perceptibility were comparable, in the sense that they used similar stimuli, procedures, and response metrics (e.g., Reingold & Merikle, 1988). In response, Greenwald and colleagues have considered alternative functional relations between the criterion and the predictor variables and used regression methods that make weaker assumptions about the data (see Greenwald & Draine, 1998; Klauer & Greenwald, 2000). Although opinions are likely to differ, my reading of these critiques and responses is that the linear regression method cannot be dismissed solely for technical reasons.

Greenwald and his colleagues (e.g., Draine & Greenwald, 1998; Greenwald, Draine, & Abrams, 1996) have claimed that large, robust subliminal priming effects can be obtained under the proper experimental conditions. These experiments have several atypical if not unique features:

1. The experiments use a response-window procedure. Participants are required to respond within a very narrow time frame (e.g., 133 ms) following the target. Because accuracy is well below ceiling using this method, a measure such as d' can be used to assess priming. This method was used because of concerns that speed-accuracy tradeoffs might obscure subliminal priming effects (e.g., Wickelgren, 1977). The hope is that the requirement to respond within a narrow time frame will force priming effects onto a single dimension of performance (error rate) instead of allowing them to be distributed across two dimensions (response latency and error rate). An appealing by-product of using d' to measure priming is that the measures of prime perceptibility and semantic priming are on the same scale and therefore are directly comparable (e.g., Eriksen, 1960; Reingold and Merikle, 1988).
2. Rather than using standard semantic priming tasks (e.g., lexical decision or naming), Greenwald and his colleagues have used evaluative or gender judgments. For example, in the evaluative judgment task, participants judge whether words have positive or negative meanings (e.g., *happy* vs. *vomit*). Priming is assessed by comparing trials in which the prime and the target are from the same category (e.g., *happy-love*) to trials in which the prime and the target are from different categories (e.g., *vomit-love*).
3. Primes are preceded and followed by a pattern mask ("sandwich masking"), and brief prime-target SOAs (e.g., 100 ms) are typically used.
4. Linear regression, as described previously, is used to assess subliminal priming.

Using these methods, Greenwald and his colleagues have obtained evidence of subliminal priming. For example, in Experiment 1, Draine and Greenwald (1998) used evaluative judgments as the priming task and a subsequent discrimination task (words vs. strings of Xs and Gs) as the measure of prime perceptibility. The stimuli and procedures used in these tasks were similar; in particular, target words were also presented in the prime perceptibility task. At prime durations of 33 and 50 ms, reliable priming was obtained ($d' = 0.24$ and 0.21). Intercepts in the regression analyses were positive and statistically significant. In terms of Cohen's (1977) **d**, the intercept effects were substantial (0.79 at 33 ms, 0.54

at 50 ms). These findings indicate that when participants' direct perception of the prime approached zero sensitivity to whether the prime was a word or an XG string, the prime nevertheless increased the probability of responding in a manner consistent with the prime's category membership.

Klinger, Burton, and Pitts (2000) replicated these findings but also showed that they can best be explained as a response congruency effect (see also De Houwer, Hermans, Rothermund, & Wentura, 2002). In addition, the results of their experiments indicated that semantic priming of the lion-tiger variety does not occur in this paradigm. In Klinger et al.'s third experiment, lexical decision was used as the priming task and as the measure of prime perceptibility. On each trial of the priming task, a word or a nonword was presented as the masked prime, and a word or a nonword was presented as the target. Participants judged whether the target was a word or a nonword. Half of the word prime-word target pairs were semantically related and half were unrelated. Exactly the same materials and display parameters were used to measure prime perceptibility, except that participants were required to judge whether the brief, masked flash (i.e., the prime) was a word.

The results showed that word and nonword responses were influenced by the lexical status of the prime, even when word-nonword discrimination of the prime approached zero sensitivity. Concretely, participants were more likely to respond "word" to words primed by words than to words primed by nonwords, even though the primes were not perceptible. Using the regression analysis, the intercepts were 0.44 and 0.54 for word and nonword target trials respectively. These findings replicate those of Greenwald and his colleagues.

A subset of these data, namely, the word prime-word target trials, was then used to evaluate semantic priming. In the regression analysis, semantic priming d' was predicted with performance in masked word-nonword discrimination of the primes. The intercept did not differ significantly from zero. There was no evidence of semantic priming in the absence of conscious awareness of the primes.

A subsequent experiment showed that if primes and targets varied orthogonally on two meaning dimensions (positive vs. negative and living vs. nonliving), only the dimension of meaning relevant to the target decision was activated unconsciously. The evaluative status of the prime influenced evaluative judgments but not animacy judgments on targets, whereas the animacy status of the prime influenced animacy judgments but not evaluative judgments on targets. These results provide convincing evidence that subliminal priming in this paradigm is a response congruency effect. Klinger et al. (2000) explain their finding by appealing to response competition mechanisms (e.g., Logan, 1980) similar to those used to explain the Stroop effect (1935).

Another wrinkle is that the subliminal categorical priming observed in this paradigm may be affected by whether or not primes previously appeared as targets. Abrams and Greenwald (2000) showed that practiced primes produced large subliminal priming effects, whereas unpracticed primes produced little or no priming (see also Abrams, Klinger, & Greenwald, 2002; Damian, 2001). Contrasting results were obtained by Naccache and Dehaene (2001). They found that practiced and unpracticed primes produced equivalent levels of categorical priming in a task similar to Greenwald's and, moreover, that semantic priming (of a sort) occurred. Subjects in these experiments decided whether a target digit or digit name (e.g., "one") was greater than or less than 5 (five never appeared as a target or prime). Only the numbers 1, 4, 6, and 9 were used as targets. The forward and backward masked prime was also a digit, a digit name, or the neutral symbol "$." All nine numbers between 1 and 9 could appear as primes. Hence, 2, 3, 7, and 8 appeared as briefly presented primes but never as targets. Target responses were faster when the prime and the target fell on the same side of 5 (congruent) than when they fell on opposite sides of 5 (incongruent). Relative to the neutral condition, this effect consisted of inhibition on incongruent trials, not facilitation in congruent trials. This categorical priming effect did not interact with prime familiarity. In addition, on congruent trials, responses were faster as the numerical distance between the prime and the target became smaller (e.g., 2–1 faster than 4–1). If one assumes that numerically closer digits are more highly associated, then this distance effect is analogous to a semantic priming effect.

Naccache, Blandin, and Dehaene (2002) also have presented evidence that masked priming in their digit classification paradigm depends on temporal attention. In the standard subliminal priming experiment, subjects know exactly when the target will appear (and if informed, when the "invisible" prime will appear) and can focus their attention on this temporal window. In one experiment, Naccache et al. manipulated the predictability of target occurrence and obtained masked priming only when targets were temporally predictable. In another experiment, a visual cue signaled the temporal onset of one third of the targets. Masked priming was observed for cued but not uncued targets. Lachter, Forster, and Ruthruff (2004) presented evidence that masked primes did not produce repetition priming unless they were attended.

Frankly, I am not sure what to make of the third generation of subliminal priming research. On the one hand, the studies of Greenwald and his colleagues set a new standard of theoretical and methodological sophistication in investigations of subliminal priming. On the other hand, the results of those studies, in particular, Klinger's, are not consistent with the results of other compelling studies of subliminal semantic priming, such as Dagenbach et al.'s (1989) and Hirshman and Durante's (1992). Moreover, Dehaene's experiments produce findings inconsistent with those of Greenwald and his colleagues. An obvious difference between these two lines of research is that Dehaene's experiments have used only one task and one small stimulus set, whereas Greenwald's experiments have used several tasks and a multitude of materials. This difference may be crucial, as Kouider and Dupoux (2004) presented evidence that when the stimulus set is small and participants have expectations about the identities of the stimuli, partially perceived primes can cause priming in a Stroop task; indeed, under partial awareness conditions, pseudo color words (e.g., *gener*) were as effective as real color words (e.g., *green*) in producing a congruency priming effect. Clearly what is needed is a systematic examination of the interactions among tasks, stimulus materials, and the various types of priming observed using this categorization paradigm.

Finally, it should be noted that subliminal priming effects have been observed in various psychophysiological and neurophysiological measures (see also Chapter 18). Dehaene et al. (1998) showed that the congruency priming effect observed in their digit-classification task also could be observed in ERPs and in brain activation as measured by fMRI. Unfortunately, these results are not as compelling as other demonstrations of subliminal priming for several reasons. Prime awareness was apparently only assessed in separate experiments using different samples of subjects and, moreover, as measured by d', prime awareness was greater than 0 for the prime duration used in the experiments (see Dehaene et al., 1998, Table 1). Although the mean d's (0.3 for a detection task; 0.2 for a discrimination task) were not statistically different from zero, my estimates of the power to detect differences of these magnitudes are under 0.3 (Agresti, 1990).

So where do we stand on subliminal semantic priming? For reasons discussed previously, the categorization paradigm introduced by Greenwald and his colleagues does not yet provide compelling evidence for subliminal semantic priming of the nurse-doctor variety. The best one can say at this point is that the method is promising and deserves to be explored further. Although one can certainly find fault with aspects of the methods used by Dagenbach et al. (1989) and by Hirshman and Durante (1992), their findings are difficult to dismiss. At the bare minimum, their experiments show that semantic priming can still be obtained when primes are presented so briefly that subjects claim that they cannot see anything and have difficulty detecting, classifying, and identifying the primes.

For better or worse, models of priming are mute on subliminal priming. Collins and Loftus (1975) do not mention consciousness in their discussion of spreading activation processes. The claim that only one concept can be processed at a time because of the "serial nature of the human central process" (p. 411) might be interpreted to imply that conscious processing of the prime is necessary to produce priming; however, such an interpretation does not find much support elsewhere in the text. Anderson (1983a, p. 309) explicitly disavows equating activation with consciousness. The language used to describe compound-cue models (e.g., "combining cues" and "searching memory") might give the impression that conscious awareness of the prime is necessary for priming to occur in the compound-cue model. However, features of the prime could be extracted and combined with features of the target even if the prime were not consciously perceived. Although Becker's model is commonly believed to depend on conscious control processes to explain priming, this belief is, in my opinion, mistaken. Distributed network models are also noncommittal on whether semantic priming requires conscious awareness of the prime, as long as the networks can converge on appropriate patterns of activation in the absence of awareness. Finally, proponents of multistage activation models reject any connection between attentional control and consciousness (e.g., Stolz & Besner, 1999).

In closing, I suggest to anyone who is interested in investigating subliminal priming, or more generally, perception without awareness, that he or she begin by reading the following articles: Eriksen (1960), Holender (1986), Macmillan (1986), Reingold and Merikle (1988), and Greenwald, Klinger, and Schuh (1995). These articles provide essential theoretical and methodological background on subliminal priming, and in my opinion, are required reading on the topic.

Prime-Task Effect

Given that semantic priming occurs even when primes are presented so briefly that subjects claim to see nothing, one might predict that semantic priming would occur regardless of the task performed on the prime. In fact, this is not true. Henik, Friedrich, and Kellogg (1983) and Smith, Theodor, and Franklin (1983) discovered that semantic priming in lexical decision was greatly reduced if subjects searched the prime for a given letter. Semantic priming is also reduced in magnitude when the prime is searched for a repeated letter (e.g., Smith, Meiran, & Besner, 2000) or when the area surrounding the prime is searched for a visual probe (e.g., Smith, Theodor, & Franklin, 1983).[1] These findings are surprising when one considers that semantic priming is consistently found when the prime word requires no response (e.g., Neely, 1977), is named (e.g., Henik, Friedrich, & Kellogg, 1983), is classified as a word or a nonword (e.g., Tweedy, Lapinski, & Schvaneveldt, 1977), or is the object of a semantic decision of some kind (e.g., living vs. nonliving; Smith, Theodor, & Franklin, 1983). Similar prime-task effects also occur for Stroop interference (e.g., Parkin, 1979).

Five conclusions seem to be emerging from research on the prime-task effect (see also, Maxfield, 1997):

1. The prime-task effect does not occur just because the prime word is processed at a relatively shallow level. Chiappe, Smith, and Besner (1996) showed that identifying the color of the prime

word did not reduce the magnitude of semantic priming in lexical decision.

2. Evidence indicates that letter search and similar tasks interfere with the initial activation of the prime's semantic representation or its semantic associates. The underlying mechanism does not seem to involve decay or active suppression of fully activated representations. For example, the prime-task effect occurs even when SOAs of 200–240 ms are used between the prime and the target (Henik, Friedrich, Tzelgov, & Tramer, 1994; Smith, Bentin, & Spalek, 2001). In addition, visual or auditory preview of the prime restores semantic priming in lexical decision (Friedrich, Henik, & Tzelgov, 1991; Stolz & Besner, 1996). For example, Friedrich et al. (1991) had the experimenter read the prime word aloud just prior to visual presentation of the probe letter and the prime. Under these conditions, semantic priming was just as large after letter search as after naming the prime. Stolz and Besner (1996) obtained similar results by presenting visual primes 200 ms prior to probe letters. These prime-preview results show that letter search does not interfere with already activated semantic representations.

3. There is evidence that lexical access occurs for the prime word. Put another way, the prime-task effect does not seem to be caused because only letter-level information about the prime is accessed or activated. Repetition priming (e.g., prime *table*, target *TABLE*) and, more generally, morphological priming (e.g., prime *mark*, target *MARKED*) are not reduced by letter search on the prime (Friedrich, Henik, & Tzelgov, 1991; Stolz & Besner, 1998). There is ample evidence in the word recognition literature that these types of priming are not produced because of overlap of individual letters (e.g., Feldman & Moskovljevic, 1987). Moreover, semantic priming from words to pictures shows the same pattern of results; namely, a letter-level task on the prime greatly reduces semantic priming (e.g., prime is the word *table*, target is a picture of a chair) but does not reduce repetition priming (e.g., prime is the word *table*, target is a picture of a table; Smith, Meiran, & Besner, 2000).

4. The prime-task effect is not caused by competition between semantic analysis and generic search processes. Brown, Roberts, and Besner (2001, Exp. 3) used prime displays that contained an irrelevant word in the middle, flanked above and below by a string of unique digits and a probe digit (repeated to match the

length of the digit string, as in the standard letter search task). The prime task was digit search. The digit search task did not reduce semantic priming between the ignored word and the target. Similarly, MacNevin and Besner (2002) showed that searching the prime for a letter of a particular color did not interfere with morphological priming or semantic priming. These results (see also point #1 above) indicate that the competition for attentional resources is specific to a domain of processing (Chiappe, Smith, & Besner, 1996; Brown, Roberts, & Besner, 2001). The idea is that perceptual and cognitive tasks can be grouped into domains based on the mental representations and processes involved. Tasks within a domain compete for resources (e.g., letter search and word recognition), whereas tasks in different domains do not (e.g., color or digit perception and word recognition).[2]

5. The reduction of semantic priming following letter search on the prime depends on context. Henik, Friedrich, Tzelgov, and Tramer (1994) showed that semantic priming in lexical decision was restored when the proportion of related pairs (RP) was very high.[3] Collapsing across experiments, semantic priming in lexical decision after letter search on the prime averaged 4 ms for low to moderate RP levels (0.2–0.5) and 44 ms for high RP levels (0.8). By comparison, the same figures for naming of the prime were 29 ms and 117 ms, respectively. Similarly, Stolz and Besner (1996) showed that when standard search trials and prime-preview trials (discussed previously) were randomly intermixed, semantic priming occurred in both conditions. They did not include a control condition in which primes were read silently or named, but the magnitudes of priming (~30 ms) were comparable to those obtained in other studies in which primes were read or named.

Collectively, these findings suggest that attention is needed to retrieve or to activate the meanings of words (e.g., Lachter, Forster, & Ruthruff, 2004; Stolz & Besner, 1999). Activation of semantic representations is an optional, not an unavoidable, consequence of reading a word. The precise nature of this attentional control—where and how in the information-processing stream it has its effects—is the focal point of current research.

Stolz and Besner (Stolz & Besner, 1996, 1998, 1999; Stolz & Neely, 1995) have explained these findings in the context of multistage activation models. They assume that explicit letter identification processes involved in searching the prime for a particular letter are more resource demanding at the letter level than are the implicit letter identification processes involved in reading or naming the prime. Attention is involved in redirecting activation away from levels of representation in which it is not needed to levels in which it is needed. They argue that in the case of letter search and similar tasks, the flow of activation from the lexical level to the semantic level (pathway B in Figure 6.2) is blocked, allowing more activation to be available at the lexical level, and because of feedback (pathway D in Figure 6.2), at the letter level as well (for a similar argument, see Friedrich, Henik, & Tzelgov, 1991). Efficiency of letter search is improved at the expense of activation of semantic representations. The extent to which resources are reallocated seems to depend on demand, as the strength of the prime-task effect scales with the difficulty of the letter-level task (Smith, Bentin, & Spalek, 2001). The attentional mechanisms implied by this explanation are qualitatively different from those implied by the traditional distinction between automatic and strategic priming (as discussed in Chapter 9); in particular, they need not be conscious.

Brown et al. (2001) concluded that the entire pathway from the lexical level to the semantic level is blocked based on the results of experiments that have examined priming from unattended, task-irrelevant words in the prime display. In Experiments 1 and 2, they used prime displays in which the prime and the probe letter were displayed in red and an irrelevant word was displayed in white. The three letter strings were stacked one above the other (in Exp. 1, the probe was in the middle; in Exp. 2, the ignored word was in the middle). Subjects were told to attend to the red items and ignore the white one. Semantic relatedness was varied between the prime and the target and between the ignored word and the target. When subjects read the prime word silently, semantic priming occurred between the prime and the target and between the ignored word and the target (e.g., Fuentes, Carmona, Agis, & Catena, 1994; Fuentes & Tudela, 1992). However, letter search on the prime eliminated semantic priming from the prime and from the ignored word. Brown et al. (2001) concluded from these findings that the entire pathway B in Figure 6.2 was blocked, not just the pathway or connection specific to the prime word. This conclusion is weakened, however, by the results of similar experiments reported by Marí-Beffa, Fuentes, Catena, and Houghton (2000). They obtained semantic priming between the task-irrelevant, unattended words and the targets regardless of the task performed on the prime.

A strong prediction of Stolz and Besner's analysis of prime-task effects is that semantic context should not affect a letter search task. Results on this prediction are mixed. In one of the first investigations of prime-task effects, Smith (1979) found that letter search was facilitated by the prior presentation of a semantically related prime. Similar findings were reported by Schvaneveldt and McDonald (1981). However, Blum and Johnson (1993) and Smith and Besner (2001) failed to find an effect of semantic context on letter search. Smith and Besner did not discuss the inconsistencies between their findings and those of Smith (1979) and of Schvaneveldt and McDonald (1981).

In summary, Stolz and Besner's interpretations of multistage activation models provide useful frameworks for understanding prime-task effects, even though a few key predictions are not well supported by extant data. Prime-task effects create difficulties for all of the remaining models of priming. The fundamental problems are that the models do not cast the proper roles for attention or they do not distinguish between levels of representation in a manner that would allow, for instance, attention to be directed to one level (e.g., lexical) but not to another (e.g., semantic), or both. These problems are not insurmountable, but they are not trivial to solve, either.

A limitation of this entire line of research is that it is predicated on the assumption that an absence of semantic priming necessarily implies that the prime's semantic representation was not activated (Marí-Beffa, Houghton, Estévez, & Fuentes, 2000). This assumption may be false (e.g., Luck, Vogel, & Shapiro, 1996). Marí-Beffa, Houghton, et al. (2000) have proposed that letter search on the prime inhibits semantic activation caused by the prime word. The automatic activation and attentional inhibition offset or partially offset each other, producing a net reduction in semantic priming for the target. To test this hypothesis, Marí-Beffa, Houghton, et al. constructed a new version of the prime-task paradigm in which the prime display contained a word and a string of symbols containing a single letter (e.g., ###S#). The subject's task was to search either the word or the symbol string for a previously supplied letter. After the subject responded, the target word for lexical decision appeared. When subjects searched for the letter in the word, semantic priming was not significant (although it averaged +23 ms across two experiments), but when subjects searched the symbol string, negative priming occurred between the prime word and the target (mean = –50 ms). These results do not show that the meaning of the prime was activated when it was searched, but they do indicate that the meaning of the prime was activated when another object next to it was searched.

A major problem for the model advanced by Marí-Beffa, Houghton, et al. is that the prime-task effect occurs even when the SOA between the prime and the target is as short as 200 ms (Henik, Friedrich, Tzelgov, & Tramer, 1994; Smith, Bentin, & Spalek, 2001). However, negative priming from ignored primes does not seem to occur at SOAs this short. Ortells, Abad, Noguera, and Lupiáñez (2001) examined the time-course of negative priming created by ignored prime words, using SOAs of 200,

300, 600 and 1000 ms. Positive priming from ignored words occurred at the SOA of 200 ms, and reliable negative priming did not occur until the SOA of 600 ms. Although Marí-Beffa, Houghton, et al.'s explanation of the prime-task effect does not seem to be viable, their observation that all other explanations depend on the assumption that an absence of semantic priming implies an absence of semantic access is valid.

In closing, I briefly summarize two alternative explanations of the prime-task effect. One is inspired by the ROUSE model (see Chapter 7). Perhaps the prime-task effect is caused by discounting of prime features (e.g., Huber, Shiffrin, Lyle, & Ruys, 2001; see also Ratcliff & McKoon, 2001). Semantic information identified with the prime may be discounted during processing of the target, thereby reducing semantic priming. Discounting may result from the attempt to distinguish events that occur closely in time but have incompatible processing goals. In ROUSE, discounting is greater when more conscious attention is directed to the prime; so, too, the magnitude of the prime-task effect increases—that is, semantic priming decreases—as the difficulty of the letter-level task on the prime increases (Smith, Bentin, & Spalek, 2001). Clearly, this highly speculative proposal would need to be developed in much greater detail to account for the rich array of data on the prime-task effect.

A better developed interpretation of the prime-task has been advanced by Neely and Kahan (2001). They proposed that prime-task effects may be caused, at least in part, by effects of spatial attention on visual feature integration. The hypothesis is that when attention is directed to individual components of prime words, such as letters, the visual features of unattended letters may not be properly integrated and, hence, the primes may not be perceptually encoded as words. Semantic activation of the primes would not be expected under such circumstances. Neely and Kahan's explanation is intriguing, but it cannot readily account for why semantic priming is preserved when subjects search the prime for a letter of a particular color, why letter search on the prime does not eliminate repetition or morphological priming, or why the prime-task effect is context dependent.

16
CHAPTER

List Context Effects

It has been known for a long time that the context created by the types of semantic relations present in a test list could influence patterns of semantic priming. To my knowledge, Becker (1980) published the first demonstration of such a finding. He showed that priming for category-exemplar pairs became more facilitation dominant when a list containing such items followed a list containing antonyms or when category-exemplar pairs were intermixed with antonyms and semantic associates in a single list. Since the publication of Becker's article, several analogous phenomena have been discovered.

One series of studies has shown that list context may even modulate whether semantic priming occurs at all. For example, McKoon and Ratcliff (1995) placed a small number of prime-target pairs related in a particular way (e.g., opposites, *close-far*) in a list in which more than half of all prime-target pairs were related in a different manner (e.g., synonyms, *mountain-hill*). Semantic priming in lexical decision and in naming was virtually eliminated for the "mismatching" items. The high RP in these experiments almost certainly plays a role in producing the list context effect (cf. Fischler, 1977a). Hess, Foss, and Carroll (1995) obtained similar results by varying the global context established by short vignettes preceding target words.

Similar results also have been shown for procedural variables. Smith, Besner, and Miyoshi (1994) presented primes for short durations (84 ms prime + 14 ms mask + 400 ms ISI) or long durations (280 ms prime + 14 ms mask + 400 ms ISI) in pure blocks or in intermixed blocks. Semantic priming for short-duration primes averaged 25 ms in the blocked condition but only 6 ms in the intermixed condition. Repetition priming was unaffected by the blocking manipulation. Stolz and Besner (1997) presented evidence that this effect interacted with RP: semantic priming for short-duration primes in intermixed conditions was present when RP was 0.25 but not when RP was 0.50 (the level of RP in Smith et al.'s experiments).

Additional examples of list context effects were reviewed in Chapter 15. Henik et al. (1994) showed that the prime-task effect was mitigated—that is, semantic priming was present following letter search on the prime—when the RP was very high, and Stolz and Besner (1996) showed that when standard letter search trials and prime-preview trials were randomly intermixed, semantic priming occurred in both conditions.

Explanations of these list and procedural context effects have invariably emphasized the role of top-down cognitive influences on semantic priming. Becker (1980) proposed that subjects can engage in two processing modes, which he referred to as the "prediction strategy" and the "expectancy strategy." The prediction strategy is characterized by the generation of a small number of semantic features most appropriate to the prime and its immediate context. This process tends to produce small semantic sets and, hence, facilitation-dominant patterns of priming. The expectancy strategy is characterized by the generation of a larger number of semantic features appropriate to many meanings of the prime. This process tends to produce large semantic sets and, hence, inhibition-dominant patterns of priming. The relative balance of these processing modes depends on the context created by the list. In Becker's experiments, the effect of list context was asymmetric. The context created by antonyms had a substantial effect on the relative magnitudes of facilitation and inhibition for category-exemplar pairs, whereas the context created by category-exemplar pairs had relatively little effect on patterns of priming for antonyms. Becker did not advance an explanation of why the list context effect appeared to be asymmetric.

McKoon and Ratcliff (1995) considered several possible explanations of their findings, framed in terms of spreading-activation and compound-cue models of priming, and concluded that none was satisfactory. Hess et al. (1995) concluded that all semantic priming effects were determined by global context. This conclusion is not defensible. There is just too much evidence that semantic priming occurs in the most infelicitous of conditions (see Chapter 9).

Smith et al. (1994) proposed a signal-detection explanation of their finding that priming for short-duration primes was negligible when such trials were intermixed with long-duration primes. The idea was that the relatively small amounts of activation created by short-duration primes in the lexical system were blocked from spreading to the semantic system if the variability in activation levels in the lexical system was sufficiently high. Assuming that long-duration primes produce more activation in the lexical system, then variability would be higher in the intermixed condition.

Stolz and Besner (1997) proposed an alternative explanation based on a "center-surround" attentional mechanism (e.g., Dagenbach, Carr, & Wilhelmsen, 1989). According to this explanation, when meaning is relevant to a task and subjects are having difficulty processing items, they employ an attentional process that enhances processing of the focal item (center) and suppresses related items (surround). In Smith et al.'s (1994) experiments, the relatively high RP of .50 made semantics salient. When short and long duration primes were intermixed, the short duration primes were relatively hard to perceive. Participants therefore used the center-surround mechanism to enhance processing of the short-duration primes in the intermixed condition. According to Stolz and Besner, when this mechanism was successful, it would produce priming, presumably because activation of the successfully retrieved semantic representation of the prime would overcome inhibition of the semantically related target, but when this mechanism was unsuccessful, only inhibition would occur. An appropriate mixture of these two outcomes across trials could produce a net result of little or no semantic priming. Stolz and Besner's account depends on the assumption that short-duration primes were not difficult to perceive—or at least were not perceived by subjects to be difficult to perceive—in the pure blocks. Hence, their account, like Smith et al.'s, depends on some kind of criterion setting by subjects as a function of context (see also Lupker, Brown, & Colombo, 1997; Taylor & Lupker, 2001).

Stolz and Besner reasoned that the center-surround and signal-detection explanations could be tested by reducing the RP. According to the center-surround explanation, reducing RP should make semantics less salient and therefore reduce the likelihood that subjects would invoke the center-surround mechanism. Stolz and Besner assumed that reducing RP would not affect the variability of activation in the lexical system and, therefore, would not, according to the signal-detection explanation, have an effect on priming for short-duration primes in the intermixed conditions. As discussed previously, Stolz and Besner found that a reduction of RP from 0.50 to 0.25 restored priming for short-duration primes in the intermixed condition.

Finally, Henik et al. (1994) suggested that semantic priming was reduced by letter search on the prime because processing resources were directed away from the semantic level. Raising the RP to sufficiently high levels allowed some of these resources to remain at the semantic level. This explanation is consistent with the IA model. RP may influence the flow of activation from the lexical level to the semantic level (Pathway B in Figure 6.2). Stolz and Besner (1996) argued that the dependence of the prime-task effect on the presence or the absence of prime-preview trials was one more example of how semantic priming was not automatic, in the sense of being an unavoidable consequence of perceiving a word. Stolz and Besner framed their explanation in terms of the IA model and proposed that the experimental "set" adopted by subjects (e.g., Luchins, 1942) determined how activation flowed through the system.

These global context effects challenge models of priming for many of the same reasons that prime-task effects do. The fundamental problem is that most of the models do not have mechanisms to allow low-level recognition and retrieval processes to be influenced by high-level processes, such as goals, conceptions of the task, and experimental "set." ACT* and multistage activation models may be the only exceptions.

CHAPTER 17

Word Frequency, Stimulus Quality, and Stimulus Repetition

Some of the most important results in the semantic priming literature may exist in the joint effects of semantic context, word frequency, stimulus quality, and stimulus repetition. I begin this chapter by looking at the effects of the first three of these variables and end by examining stimulus repetition (see Table 17.1 for a summary).

The magnitude of semantic priming in lexical decision is larger for low-frequency words than for high-frequency words, even with associative strength equated (e.g., Becker, 1979; Stone & Van Orden, 1992). Semantic priming is also larger for degraded targets (e.g., masked or presented at low contrast) than for intact targets (e.g., Meyer, Schvaneveldt, & Ruddy, 1975). According to the additive factors logic proposed by Sternberg (1969), these interactions indicate that semantic context and word frequency affect the same stage of processing and that semantic context and stimulus quality affect the same stage of processing. However, stimulus quality and word frequency are additive: stimulus degradation influences high-frequency words as much as low-frequency words (e.g., Becker & Killion, 1977; Borowsky & Besner, 1993).[1] This pattern of results—context and word frequency interact, context and stimulus quality interact, but word frequency and stimulus quality are additive—is difficult to explain in most models of word recognition (e.g., Besner & Smith, 1992; Borowsky & Besner, 1993).

TABLE 17.1. Empirical relations among semantic context (Cx), word frequency (WF), stimulus quality (SQ), stimulus repetition (Rp), and short-term stimulus repetition (Rp_{ST}).

	WF	SQ	Rp	Rp_{ST}
Cx	⊗	⊗	+	?
WF		+	⊗	+
SQ			⊗	?

Notes: + = variables combine additively; ⊗ = variables interact; ? = unknown. Higher-order interactions among these variables have not been observed.

Stolz and Neely (1995) have shown further that RP moderates the interaction between context and stimulus quality.[2] They obtained interactions between context and stimulus quality when RP was 0.5 but not when RP was 0.25. Their results are summarized in Table 17.2. The semantic priming effects in Table 17.2 constitute the effect of context. As shown, when RP = 0.25, the effect of context is approximately the same for bright and for dim targets (31 vs. 35 ms), but when RP = 0.5, the effect of context is smaller for bright than for dim targets (43 vs. 63 ms). For the SOA of 200 ms, the interaction between context and stimulus quality seems to occur only for strong associates, whereas for the SOA of 800 ms, it occurs for both strong and weak associates.[3] Importantly, there is almost no evidence of an interaction between RP and context at an SOA of 200 ms: mean priming effects are +35 ms and +37 ms for RP = 0.25 and 0.5, respectively. The absence of an RP-context interaction indicates that the strategic process of expectancy was not operating at the SOA of 200 ms, a conclusion consistent with the results summarized in Chapter 9.

Compound-cue models and most spreading-activation models are too simple to explain the complex relations among semantic context, word frequency, stimulus quality, and RP. These models will need to be embedded in more complex information-processing architectures to explain such findings. Along these lines, Anderson (1983a, p. 103) discusses how ACT* could handle the interaction between semantic context and stimulus quality. The productions that perform the spelling check are sensitive to properties of the physical stimulus and to the spelling pattern in memory. Stimulus degradation lowers the level of activation from the physical stimulus, increasing processing time. The relative influence of activation of the spelling pattern (which is boosted by the appearance of the semantically related prime word) increases, thereby increasing the priming effect. ACT* is sufficiently powerful that it can almost certainly be programmed to account for the complex interactions among semantic context, word frequency, stimulus quality, and RP, although the model has not been applied to these phenomena, to my knowledge.

TABLE 17.2. Summary of results of Stolz and Neely's (1995) experiments.

	RP = .25		RP = .50	
SOA = 200	Bright	Dim	Bright	Dim
Strong	+34	+46	+31	+52
Weak	+31	+29	+30	+34
SOA = 800				
Strong	+45	+48	+88	+120
Weak	+15	+18	+22	+47

Notes: Values in the table are semantic priming effects (unrelated-related). Strong and weak refer to the strength of the associative relation between primes and targets. SOA was manipulated between experiments.

Becker's verification model can explain some of the empirical relations between word frequency, stimulus quality, and semantic context (Becker, 1979; Becker & Killion, 1977). The key assumptions are that stimulus quality affects the rate of feature extraction in the feature analyzer and that the verification process is unaffected by stimulus quality.

The interaction between stimulus quality and context occurs because stimulus quality influences a process that is essential for recognizing words in an unrelated context but is bypassed for words in a related context (Becker & Killion, 1977). Targets preceded by unrelated primes are recognized as a result of successful verification of a member of the sensory set (after first exhaustively searching the semantic set constructed for the unrelated prime word). Stimulus degradation decreases the rate of feature extraction, creating a delay in the construction of the sensory set and, therefore, a delay in recognition. The delay in recognition will occur only if the time needed to construct the sensory set exceeds the time needed for an exhaustive and unsuccessful search of the semantic set (Neely, 1991). Targets preceded by related primes are (usually) recognized by verification of a member of the semantic set, which is created independently of sensory features. Construction of the semantic set and the verification process are not influenced by a change in the rate of feature extraction. Becker's explanation of the stimulus quality by context interaction assumes that stimulus degradation has relatively little effect on construction of the representation of the stimulus in visual sensory memory and on comparisons between that representation and representations generated from candidates in the sensory or semantic sets.

The explanation of the interaction between word frequency and context is formally similar. Word-frequency effects are explained by assuming that sampling from the sensory set is determined by word frequency: high-frequency words are selected before low-frequency words and, therefore, on the average, will be recognized faster (e.g., Rubenstein,

Garfield, & Millikan, 1970).[4] Members of the semantic set, however, are ordered according to associative strength (Becker, 1979). Targets preceded by unrelated primes are recognized by verification of a member of the sensory set and, therefore, will show a word frequency effect. Targets preceded by related primes are recognized by verification of a member of the semantic set and, therefore, will not show a word frequency effect. In fact, the usually observed pattern is that word frequency effects are larger for words out of context than for words in context (e.g., Becker, 1979). The small effect of word frequency on recognition of words in context can be explained by assuming that verification on the semantic set fails for a proportion of such words.

Finally, the additive relation between word frequency and stimulus quality occurs because common and rare words are equally affected by stimulus quality but verification is unaffected by stimulus quality (Becker & Killion, 1977). Stimulus degradation slows the rate of feature extraction for all words, regardless of frequency, creating a delay in the construction of the sensory set. Once the sensory set has been constructed, verification is blind to processes that created it.

The presence of an interaction between stimulus quality and semantic context for both short and long SOAs is not a problem for Becker's model, contrary to the claims of some authors (e.g., Borowsky & Besner, 1993; Stolz & Neely, 1995). As explained in Chapter 3, generation of the semantic set and verification could be fast-acting processes. Becker's model has difficulty, however, explaining the effects of RP on this interaction. The interaction is produced because performance is harmed by the delay in the construction of the sensory set when the prime is unrelated to the target but is relatively unaffected by this delay when the prime is related to the target. It is not clear why this delay would be affected by RP.[5] Moreover, if generation and verification of the semantic set can be fast-acting processes, as I have claimed, then an interaction between semantic context and stimulus quality should occur if there is an effect of semantic context. Stolz and Neely's results clearly violate this prediction.

Plaut's model (Plaut, 1995; Plaut & Booth, 2000) can account for several of the effects examined in this chapter. As explained in Chapter 5, this network learns to map written words onto their meanings. The written form of each word is represented by a pattern of activation over a set of orthographic units, and its meaning is represented by another pattern of activation over its semantic units. Semantic relatedness among words is determined by the extent of overlap of semantic features, and associative relatedness is determined by the frequency with which one word follows another during training. The crucial assumption that allows the model to explain interactive and additive effects between context, word frequency, and stimulus quality is that the mapping from inputs to activation levels is S-shaped (e.g., logistic). This nonlinear mapping has the property that equal differences in input can be mapped onto equal or unequal differences in output, depending on the magnitude of the input.

The mechanism is illustrated in Figure 17.1. A, B, and C correspond to the total input for three types of stimuli, such that the overall magnitude of input is greater for C than for B, and greater for B than for A. The arrowheads correspond to weaker (W) and stronger (S) inputs within each type. The difference between the weaker and the stronger input is identical for each type, but depending on the overall magnitude of the input, these differences get mapped onto equal differences in activation levels (e.g., A vs. B) or unequal differences in activation levels (e.g., B vs. C). To be concrete, A might correspond to the inputs for low-frequency

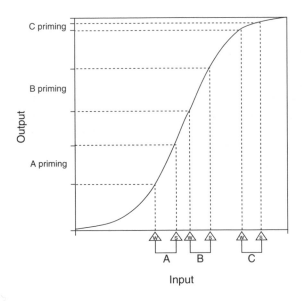

FIGURE 17.1. Illustration of the relative magnitudes of priming effects using a sigmoidal mapping from input to activation levels. A, B, and C correspond to the total input for three types of stimuli (e.g., increasing stimulus quality). W and S correspond to weaker and stronger inputs within each type (e.g., targets preceded by unrelated versus related primes). The difference between the weaker and the stronger input is identical for each type, but depending on the overall magnitude of the input, these differences get mapped onto equal differences in activation levels (e.g., A vs. B) or unequal differences in activation levels (e.g., B versus C). Adapted from Plaut and Booth (2000, Fig. 1).

words and C might correspond to the inputs for high-frequency words. Within each condition, W and S might correspond to unrelated and to related priming conditions, respectively.

In Plaut's network, context, word frequency, and stimulus quality can be implemented so that they affect input strength. Although the mechanisms for associative and semantic priming differ, the two are similar in that semantic units receive stronger inputs in a related priming condition than in an unrelated priming condition. High-frequency words are presented more frequently during training than are low-frequency words. Because they are trained more often, high-frequency words have greater impact on the weights learned by the network and, hence, produce stronger input to the semantic units than do low-frequency words. Finally, levels of stimulus quality can be implemented by varying the strength of inputs to the orthographic layer, which affect inputs to the semantic layer.

Whether two variables are additive or interactive depends on the logistic function of their inputs. For example, if A in Figure 17.1 corresponds to low frequency words, C corresponds to high-frequency words, and W and S correspond to unrelated and related priming conditions, then the model will produce greater priming for low- than for high-frequency words. However, if A corresponds to poor stimulus quality, B corresponds to high stimulus quality, and W and S correspond to low- and to high-frequency words, then an additive relation between stimulus quality and word frequency is produced. Plaut (1995) showed that the model could be implemented in such a way that context interacted with word frequency and with stimulus quality.[6]

An intriguing property of this model is that the nature of the relationship between two variables is not necessarily fixed by the architecture of the model but may depend on their total impact on how quickly the network settles into a stable state. For example, the pattern of the interaction between context and word frequency will change if input levels are altered appropriately. Suppose B corresponds to high-frequency words, and the level of input from low frequency words A, is reduced even further; eventually, the priming effect for A will be less than the priming effect for B.

Plaut and Booth (2000) have demonstrated effects of this kind. They found that subjects with low perceptual ability, as assessed by the Symbol Search Test of the WISC-III (Wechsler, 1991), did not show an interaction between word frequency and semantic context. The assumption is that the overall strength of input is less for low- and than for high-ability readers. In terms of Figure 17.1, A and B might correspond to low and to high-frequency words for low-ability participants, whereas B and C might correspond to low and to high-frequency words for high-ability participants. There was even evidence that the interaction between context and word frequency reversed direction (i.e., more priming for high than for low-frequency words) for low-ability participants under certain conditions (e.g., Exp. 3).

It is unclear whether Plaut's model can explain the interaction between context, stimulus quality, and RP. The context by stimulus quality interaction occurs in the lexical system. As discussed in Chapter 9, Plaut and Booth (2000) propose that effects of RP may reside in a general decision-making system, outside the lexical system. Given that the decision-making system has not been formally implemented in Plaut's model, it is probably premature to speculate on how these two systems may interact.

One final comment on Plaut's model: the logistic function of inputs does most of the heavy lifting in explaining the interactive and additive relations among context, word frequency, stimulus quality, and other variables. In principle, similar input-output nonlinearities could be incorporated into other models. This undertaking is not trivial, however, as the function would need to be integrated into the model in a way that preserves the model's internal consistency and integrity.

To my knowledge, distributed network learning models have not been applied to these findings. However, given that the architecture of those models is similar to that of proximity models, and they are governed by similar principles, it should be possible to postulate mechanisms in those models that would allow them to account for at least some of the empirical relations among context, word frequency, stimulus quality, and RP.

Borowsky and Besner (1993) and Stolz and Neely (1995) explained the relations among context, word frequency, stimulus quality, and RP in a logogen-based multistage activation model. Given that Stolz and Besner, in particular, have in recent years adopted the IA model as a foundation for explaining word recognition, I shall do the same here, although my interpretation may differ from one that they might propose.

According to the model, stimulus quality would affect the letter level by slowing the rate of accumulation of evidence for letters in the word. To account for the additive relation between stimulus quality and word frequency, representations in the letter level probably need to be thresholded (Besner and Roberts, 2003; Reynolds and Besner, 2002, 2004), as in logogens. Activation is accumulated until a criterion level is reached, at which point activation is forwarded to the next level. Using such a mechanism, low stimulus quality will add a fixed delay in the output of the letter level to the lexical level, which appears to be necessary to account for the additive relation between stimulus quality and word frequency. Incorporating this process into the IA model transforms the model into a hybrid of continuous and discrete processing stages (cf. McClelland, 1987).

Semantic context has effects at the semantic level and, because of feedback, at lower levels (see Figure 6.3). Recognition of a word partially activates, in the semantic level, the semantic representations of semantically similar words. This residual activation feeds back to the lexical level, partially activating the lexical representations of those semantically related words, and activation at the lexical level feeds back to the letter level, partially activating letter representations of those semantically related words (e.g., Hino & Lupker, 1996; Pexman, Lupker, & Hino, 2002). Because of bottom-up support and within-level competition, the letter, lexical, and semantic representations of the word actually presented will usually be the most active.

Semantic context has its effects by lowering the criterion needed for recognition. For a given rate of accumulation of evidence, a lower criterion will be exceeded sooner than a higher criterion. This difference constitutes the semantic priming effect. If the rate of accumulation of evidence is slowed, the magnitude of the difference between the time needed to exceed the lower criterion and the time needed to exceed the higher criterion will increase. Hence, any variable that slows the rate of accumulation of evidence in a particular stage of processing will produce a corresponding increase in the magnitude of the priming effect in that stage of processing (*ceteris paribus*). These ideas are illustrated in Figure 17.2. This relation explains why semantic context interacts with stimulus quality. Semantic context lowers the criterion for recognition in the letter level, and poor stimulus quality slows the rate of evidence accumulation in the letter level.

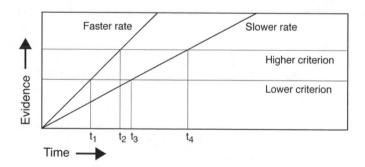

FIGURE 17.2.   Time to reach criterion (t_i) as a function of the rate of accumulation of evidence over time and the criterion level. $(t_4 - t_3) > (t_2 - t_1)$. Faster vs. slower rates might correspond to intact vs. degraded stimuli or to high- vs. low-frequency words. Higher vs. lower criteria might correspond to targets preceded by unrelated vs. related primes. Adapted from Borowsky and Besner (1993, Fig. 2).

Word frequency influences processing in the pathways that carry activation from the lexical level to the semantic level (pathway B in Figure 6.3). The efficiency of these pathways increases as word frequency increases. This results in faster rates of accumulation of evidence in the semantic level for high- than for low-frequency words. Context and word frequency interact in the semantic level for the same reason that context and stimulus quality interact in the letter level. Because stimulus quality and word frequency affect different levels, and because representations in the letter level are thresholded, stimulus quality and word frequency do not interact. Poor stimulus quality causes a delay in when information reaches the semantic level, affecting high- and low-frequency words equally.

Stolz and Neely's (1995) finding that RP modulates the context-stimulus quality interaction indicates that RP influences the pathway from the semantic level to the lexical level (pathway C in Figure 6.3). According to the model, the source of the interaction between semantic context and stimulus quality is feedback from the semantic level to the letter level by way of the lexical level. A reduction in this feedback will reduce the size of the context-stimulus quality interaction. This kind of modulation of activation is consistent with explanations of the prime-task effect discussed in Chapter 15. But why should feedback from the semantic level to the lexical level depend on RP? One of the functions of feedback must be to reduce the amount of bottom-up information needed for activation of appropriate representations in the lexical level. It is plausible to assume that the gain on feedback is sensitive to the likelihood that the feedback will be helpful. When RP is low, relatively few primes are followed by semantically related targets and, hence, feedback based on semantics will not usually contribute to activating the target representation, whereas when RP is high, relatively many primes are followed by semantically related targets and, hence, feedback based on semantics will tend to be more useful (Stolz & Neely, 1995).

Stolz and Neely (1995) proposed that RP modulates feedback from the semantic level to the lexical level regardless of SOA. This feature is needed to explain the effect of RP on the context-stimulus quality interaction for SOAs of 200 and 800 ms. Presumably, at very brief SOAs, activation in the semantic level would be minimal, limiting potential feedback to lower levels. Stolz and Neely also suggested that at long SOAs, RP modulates the strategic process of expectancy. Although Stolz and Neely did not discuss the effects of RP and NR on semantic matching, their proposal is consistent with a more general one, which is that at long SOAs, RP and NR modulate expectancy and semantic matching. It seems that the IA model must be augmented in this manner to account for the findings reviewed in Chapter 9.

To explain the finding that the context-stimulus quality interaction occurred only for strong associates at an SOA of 200 ms, Stolz and Neely (1995) hypothesized that the rate of feedback from the semantic level to the lexical level increased with associative strength between the prime and the target. At a short SOA, only targets that were strongly related to their primes would have their representations in the lexical level activated. At longer SOAs, sufficient time would pass for feedback to produce activation of representations in the lexical level even for targets weakly related to their primes. This mechanism does not have any natural implementation in the IA model. Parameters of the feedback connections from the semantic representation of a target word to its lexical representation would need to be modifiable by the strengths of the feedforward connections between the lexical representations of all possible prime words and the target word's semantic representation. Given that this result is a relatively minor one, it probably should be replicated before theorists expend a great of energy trying to explain it.

An interesting prediction of this model is that word frequency effects should not occur in lexical decision if pathway B of Figure 6.3 is blocked. The reason is that word frequency effects occur in the semantic level and pathways to it. Blocking these pathways should eliminate effects of word frequency. Stolz and Besner (1996) have argued that letter search on the prime blocks pathway B (see Chapter 15). Hence, the model predicts that letter search on the prime word should eliminate word frequency effects in lexical decisions to target words. To my knowledge, this prediction has not been tested.

To close this discussion of the IA model, I want to comment on the model's use of criterion changes to explain semantic priming. There is ample evidence that semantic priming is revealed in measures of sensitivity and bias (see Chapter 8). The use of criterion changes in the IA model to account for effects of semantic context might lead one to wonder whether the model can predict sensitivity effects in semantic priming. Norris (1995) presented evidence from model simulations that pure criterion-bias models, such as the logogen model (e.g., Morton, 1969) and the context-checking model (e.g., Norris, 1986), are able to predict increases in sensitivity due to related primes. However, Pastore, Crawley, Skelly, and Berens (2003) used an ideal observer analysis to show that Norris's (1995) model, at least as implemented, could not predict effects of related primes on sensitivity; related primes only influenced bias.

The status of the IA model is unclear. The operation of criterion changes in the IA model is quite different from their operation in Norris's (1995) model. In the IA model, semantic context lowers criteria for recognition at multiple levels of the system, and these changes interact with bottom-up information from lower levels and within-level inhibitory competition. The hypothesized net result is an increase in the efficiency of word recognition. Semantic context therefore has the potential to influence the statistical separation of evidence for words and nonwords and thereby increase sensitivity (e.g., Pastore, Crawley, Skelly, and Berens, 2003). Unfortunately, this conjecture cannot be tested because the IA model does not yet generate quantitative predictions and has little to say about how nonword decisions are made.

As if the just-reviewed findings were not sufficiently complex by themselves, they omit the effects of a variable that is known to influence the speed and the accuracy of word recognition, namely, stimulus repetition. Lexical decision and naming are faster on the second presentation of a word than on the first (e.g., Forbach, Stanners, and Hochhaus, 1974; Kirsner & Smith, 1974; Scarborough, Cortese, and Scarborough, 1977).[7] Stimulus repetition and semantic priming combine additively (den Heyer, Goring, & Dannenbring, 1985; Durgunoglu, 1988; Wilding, 1986), but stimulus repetition interacts with word frequency, such that the word frequency effect is larger on the first than on the second presentation (den Heyer, Goring, & Dannenbring, 1985; Norris, 1984; Wilding, 1986), and with stimulus quality, such that the difference between intact and degraded stimuli is larger on the first than on the second presentation (Besner & Swan, 1982; Norris, 1984). It is not clear that any of the models can account for this constellation of findings. Consider, for example, the IA model: The interaction between stimulus repetition and stimulus quality indicates that repetition affects the letter level, and the interaction between stimulus repetition and word frequency indicates that repetition affects the semantic level. Repetition should therefore interact with semantic context—as semantic context also affects each of these levels—but it does not.

A possible saving grace for the models is that repetition priming for words seems to have at least two components produced by different mechanisms: a short-term effect that lasts a few seconds (perhaps fewer than 10 s) and is produced by lexical processes and a long-term effect that can last hours or even days and is produced by episodic memory processes (e.g., Feustel, Shiffrin, & Salasoo, 1983; Forster & Davis, 1984; McKone, 1995; Ratcliff, Hockley, & McKoon, 1985; Versace & Nevers, 2003). There is strong evidence that word frequency interacts with the long-term but not the short-term repetition effect (Forster & Davis, 1984; McKone, 1995; Versace & Nevers, 2003). Much less is known about how semantic context and stimulus quality combine with the short-term effect. With one exception, previous investigations of the effects of repetition, semantic context, and stimulus quality have used repetition lags of approximately 9 s and greater and therefore would seem to be sensitive to the long-term effect. The exception is an experiment published by den Heyer and Benson (1988, Exp. 2). They manipulated semantic context, stimulus quality, and target repetition and varied the lag between repetitions (0, 1, 3, or 7 items; 2.5 to 20+ s). They obtained an interaction between semantic context and repetition—unlike previous studies—and an interaction between stimulus quality and repetition—like previous studies. Neither interaction varied significantly with lag. Den Heyer and Benson concluded that repetition effects have sensory, lexical, and episodic components. Only the lexical component interacts with semantic context, whereas only the episodic component interacts with stimulus quality. These conclusions are quite fragile, however, as they depended on the nonsignificance of several interactions, including the absence of an interaction between semantic context and stimulus quality. Moreover, the experiment may be limited by its design: RP and NR were both 1.0 (only related prime and neutral prime conditions were included) and the SOA was 750 ms. The patterns of results might therefore have been affected by strategic processes.

These findings may provide some breathing room for the models. In the IA model, for example, the additive relation between word frequency and short-term repetition can be explained by placing short-term repetition effects in the letter or the lexical levels. If semantic context and stimulus quality both interact with the short-term effect, then short-term repetition effects could be isolated to the letter level. Other patterns, of course, would lead to different conclusions.

18
CHAPTER

Cognitive Neuroscience of Semantic Priming

In this chapter, I take a look at the findings from three areas of research aimed at uncovering the brain bases of semantic priming: hemispheric asymmetries, event-related potentials, and functional neuroimaging.

☐ Hemispheric Asymmetries in Semantic Priming

The specialization of the left cerebral hemisphere for many language functions (e.g., Whitney, 1998) suggests that semantic priming, at least for linguistic materials, may evince hemispheric asymmetries. Such asymmetries exist and are potentially revealing about semantic priming processes.

The anatomy of the visual system is such that all stimuli presented to the left of fixation (left visual field) are initially transmitted to the right visual cortex, and all stimuli presented to the right of fixation (right visual field) are initially transmitted to the left visual cortex. Although the cerebral hemispheres share information through the corpus callosum, qualitatively different patterns of behavior may be produced when processing is initiated in the right vs. the left hemisphere (Hellige, 1993).

Hemispheric asymmetries in semantic priming can be investigated by presenting primes or targets to the left or the right visual field. Asymmetries seem to be greater when both stimuli are presented laterally (either to the same visual field or to different visual fields) than when the prime is presented centrally and the target is presented laterally (e.g., Chiarello, Burgess, Richards, & Pollock, 1990).

Baselines. Shears and Chiarello (2003) examined the effects of using unrelated word baselines and neutral baselines (*blank* and *ready*) in a standard lexical decision task and in a go/no-go lexical decision task (described subsequently). Their results indicated that neutral and word primes may differ in processing load and that these differences may affect each hemisphere differently and interact with the processing demands of the task. For example, they found that in the go/no-go task, neutral primes slowed left-hemisphere processing of target words relative to unrelated word primes. Shears and Chiarello's results indicate that the effects of using neutral primes in experiments that use lateralized presentation of primes or targets may be quite different from those effects in experiments that use central presentation.

Automatic Versus Strategic Priming. Many experiments have obtained bilateral semantic priming under experimental conditions that limit the contributions of strategic processes (for reviews, see Chiarello, 1998, 2003). For example, Chiarello, Liu, Shears, Quan, and Kacinik (2003) examined the time course of semantic priming in lexical decision for associatively and semantically related primes and targets (e.g., *cat-dog*) using RP = 0.25 and NR = 0.57. SOAs ranged from 150 ms to 800 ms. Semantic priming occurred at all SOAs and did not interact with visual field at any SOA. There was some evidence of delayed onset of priming in the right relative to the left hemisphere (e.g., at the SOA of 150 ms, priming was 9 ms in the right hemisphere and 20 ms in the left hemisphere). A second experiment used the same materials in a go/no-go lexical decision task with an SOA of 300 ms. In this task, subjects respond to words and make no response to nonwords. Researchers have speculated that the go/no-go lexical decision task may be less prone to semantic matching than is the standard lexical decision task (e.g., Neely, 1991; VanVoorhis and Dark, 1995). Robust semantic priming was obtained in both hemispheres.

Several studies have attempted to determine the relative contributions of each cerebral hemisphere to strategic priming by examining facilitation and inhibition as a function of SOA or by manipulating RP or NR (e.g., Beeman, Friedman, Grafman, Perez, Diamond, & Lindsay, 1994; Burgess & Simpson, 1988; Chiarello, 1985; Chiarello, Burgess, Richards, & Pollock, 1990; Chiarello, Richards, & Pollock, 1992; Collins, 1999; Koivisto, 1999; Koivisto & Laine, 2000; Nakagawa, 1991; Shears & Chiarello, 2003). Two theoretical perspectives have emerged from this research. According to one view, automatic priming occurs in both hemispheres but semantic processing tends to be more rapid and precise in the left than in the right hemisphere, whereas strategic priming occurs primarily in the left hemisphere (e.g., Beeman, Friedman, Grafman, Perez, Diamond, & Lindsay, 1994; Burgess & Simpson, 1988; Chiarello, 1998, 2003; Collins, 1999; Nakagawa, 1991). According to the other view, automatic priming is limited to the left hemisphere (at least for unassociated category coordinates) but strategic priming occurs in both hemispheres, with the left hemisphere primarily responsible for expectancy and the right hemisphere primarily responsible for semantic matching (e.g., Koivisto, 1998, 1999; Koivisto & Laine, 2000). Although these theoretical perspectives would seem to make quite different predictions about patterns of facilitation and inhibition as a function of SOA and about effects of RP and NR, extant results do not clearly distinguish between them.

A potential limitation of visual half-field investigations of strategic priming is that expectancy has not been manipulated experimentally (e.g., Neely, 1977) nor have facilitation and inhibition been assessed in a single experiment in which RP and SOA were manipulated parametrically and factorially (e.g., de Groot, 1984). It is therefore difficult to interpret the results of visual half-field experiments in light of the wealth of results available in the canonical behavioral literature. To confound matters further, there are reasons to suspect that strategic processing may be quite different when primes or targets are presented laterally from when both are presented centrally (e.g., Shears & Chiarello, 2003).

Associative Versus "Pure" Semantic Priming. Priming for associatively and semantically related primes and targets (e.g., *cat-dog*) seems to occur in both hemispheres under a wide range of conditions (e.g., Chiarello, Liu, Shears, Quan, & Kacinik, 2003). Priming for purely semantically related primes and targets (e.g., *goat-dog*) seems to be limited to the left hemisphere when the experimental conditions limit strategic processing (e.g., Collins, 1999; Koivisto, 1997, 1998; Koivisto & Hämäläinen, 2002). Greater pure semantic priming has been obtained in the right than in the left hemisphere at long SOAs (500 ms) even when RP is low and NR is neutral (e.g., Chiarello, 1985; Chiarello, Burgess, Richards, & Pollock, 1990; Chiarello & Richards, 1992; Koivisto, 1997), although this finding may depend on the task used (e.g., Koivisto, 1998; Koivisto & Hämäläinen, 2002).

If one assumes that the major difference between these types of materials is that associatively and semantically related primes and targets share more or stronger semantic relations than do purely semantically related primes and targets (as suggested in Chapter 10), then priming for purely semantically related items may initially be greater in the left than in the right hemisphere because semantic processing is more efficient in the left hemisphere and therefore is better able to capitalize on relatively weak semantic relations (e.g., Chiarello, Liu, Shears, Quan, & Kacinik, 2003).

Visual half-field experiments have also investigated priming for "purely" associated words (e.g., *cradle-baby, miner-coal*). According to contemporary standards, these materials would be considered semantically related (e.g., *babies sleep in cradles, miners mine coal*), with moderately asymmetrical prime-target associations (see Chapters 10 and 13). To my knowledge, priming for such items has not been investigated under conditions of low RP and brief SOA. Chiarello et al. (1990) did not obtain priming in lexical decision or in naming using RP of 0.25 and SOAs of 575 ms and 600 ms (NR = 0.57 in lexical decision). Abernethy and Coney (1993) investigated priming for such items in go/no-go lexical decision using an SOA of 250 ms but the RP and the NR were 1.0 (only related and neutral prime conditions were included). Under those conditions, priming was obtained in the left but not the right hemisphere. For an SOA of 450 ms, priming was obtained in both hemispheres. The findings are therefore not entirely clear for this category of materials.

Finally, several studies have investigated hemispheric asymmetries in semantic priming for dominant and subordinate meanings of homographs (e.g., *bank-money* vs. *bank-river*). Results are not entirely consistent across studies, but the following patterns seem to hold (for a review, see Chiarello, Liu, Shears, Quan, and Kacinik, 2003). Priming for the dominant meaning is bilateral across a wide range of SOAs. Priming for the subordinate meaning seems to be stronger in the left than in the right hemisphere at brief SOAs (< 100 ms), bilateral at somewhat longer SOAs (100–200 ms), and stronger in the right than in the left hemisphere at long SOAs (750 ms). All of the relevant studies have used relatively high RP (0.50) and central presentation of the prime word.

Mediated Versus Direct Priming. Mediated priming is robust in both hemispheres for a wide range of SOAs (Livesay & Burgess, 2003; Richards & Chiarello, 1995).

Effects of Lag. Faust and Chiarello (1998) manipulated the lag (1 vs. 6) between primes and targets in sentences or scrambled versions of the sentences. The latter condition is of most interest because it corresponds most closely to other investigations of lag effects. Subjects read lists of three (lag 1) or eight (lag 6) words and then received a target stimulus for lexical decision. Semantic priming was not significant in the lag-6 condition (–8 ms and 5 ms for right and left hemisphere, respectively) but was reliable in the lag-1 condition (31 ms for each hemisphere). These results are consistent with findings reviewed in Chapter 12.

Forward Versus Backward Priming. The data on backward priming are limited, but they indicate that backward priming occurs in the right hemisphere and is caused by semantic matching. Koivisto (1999, Experiment 2) manipulated RP and NR jointly (0.25/0.50 vs. 0.75/0.75) in lexical decision using backward associated primes and targets (e.g., *tail-beaver*) and an SOA of 750 ms. The only significant priming effect was in error rates, and it was limited to the right hemisphere in the high RP/NR condition. Koivisto's third experiment included forward and backward related pairs, high RP and NR (0.75/0.75), and an SOA of 750 ms. Forward priming occurred in both hemispheres, although it was larger in the left than in the right hemisphere (103 ms vs. 44 ms), but backward priming occurred only in the right hemisphere (-8 ms vs. 114 ms). These forward priming effects were probably also caused by strategic processes. When similar materials were presented in the forward direction in a go/no-go lexical decision task using an SOA of 750 ms (Exp. 1), semantic priming did not occur for high or for low RP (0.75 vs. 0.25; NR was constant at 0.50). The only condition yielding semantic priming was one in which RP was high (0.75) and subjects were told that the prime and target would often be related and that they should use the prime to predict the target. Priming in this condition was limited to the left hemisphere. Koivisto concluded from these and other findings that the left hemisphere was primarily responsible for the strategic process of expectancy and the right hemisphere was primarily responsible for the strategic process of semantic matching.

Summary. Investigations of hemispheric asymmetries in semantic priming suggest that the cerebral hemispheres both support automatic priming but differ in their contributions to strategic priming, although the nature of those differences is a matter of debate. Several types of priming are bilateral, including priming between associatively and semantically related items, priming for dominant meanings of homographs, mediated priming, and priming that spans an unrelated intervening item. Other types of priming reveal strong hemispheric asymmetries: pure semantic priming is stronger in the left than in the right hemisphere, at least when strategic processing is minimized; priming for subordinate meanings of homographs changes lateralization patterns depending on SOA; and backward priming is limited to the right hemisphere. A crucial issue that needs to be addressed in this line of research is whether the empirical findings and models generated from experiments using central presentation generalize to experiments using lateral presentation, especially with regard to the difference between automatic and strategic processing.

☐ Semantic Priming and N400

Active neurons produce voltage fields. Voltage fluctuations produced by large populations of neurons can be measured with electrodes on the scalp. The trace of voltage across time is referred to as the electroencephalogram (EEG). When the EEG is time-locked to an event, such as the presentation of a stimulus, it is referred to as the event-related potential (ERP). The ERP consists of phases of positive and negative potentials of varying latency. These waves of positive and negative activity are identified by their valence and latency from stimulus onset.

The N400 is a negative going shift in potential, peaking approximately 400 ms after stimulus onset. Since the discovery of the N400 by Kutas and Hillyard (1980), there has been an enormous amount of research aimed at determining the cognitive processes signaled by the N400 (e.g., Kutas & Van Petten, 1994). The N400 is especially sensitive to semantic processing. For example, a large N400 component is produced by the comprehension of a word when it is preceded by a semantically unrelated word, whereas the N400 component is greatly reduced or even absent when a word is preceded by a semantically related word (Bentin, McCarthy, & Wood, 1985; Rugg, 1985). This effect is often referred to as the "N400 priming effect." The balance of evidence indicates that the N400 priming effect is produced by various processes involved in integrating semantic information with context. The easier it is for new information to be incorporated into immediate context, the smaller is the amplitude of the N400 component (e.g., Chwilla, Kolk, & Mulder, 2000; Osterhout & Holcomb, 1995). Effects of several of the independent variables examined in previous chapters have also been explored in the N400. These effects are reviewed in the following sections.

Baselines. Brown, Hagoort, and Chwilla (2000) examined ERPs to related, unrelated, and neutral primes ("blanco" in Dutch, or "blank") in the lexical decision task and in a silent reading task (e.g., McNamara & Healy, 1988). ERPs to related and unrelated primes did not differ, which would be expected given that these primes were very similar (although different words were used). However, the neutral prime produced a large positive deflection that began to appear at approximately 300 ms and continued for the remainder of recording (up to 700 ms). This effect did not interact with relatedness proportion. Brown et al. suggested two explanations of this effect. The positive deflection might be a repetition effect, as neutral primes but not related and unrelated primes were repeated (e.g., Rugg, 1985). Another possible explanation is that the effect is an "oddball" effect. If subjects implicitly classified the primes as "words" vs. "blank," then the neutral prime "blank" would be a low probability event. The positive deflection might therefore be a version of P300 (e.g., Donchin, 1981). Regardless of the cause of this positive deflection, its existence shows that a neutral priming condition defined by the repeated presentation of a particular word may be fundamentally different from priming conditions in which primes are not repeated. As discussed in Chapter 8, the same conclusion has been reached on the basis of results from behavioral experiments.

Relatedness Proportion and SOA. Several studies have examined the effects of relatedness proportion on N400 priming effects. For the most part, N400 priming effects mirror behavioral priming effects: For long prime-target SOAs, N400 priming and semantic priming are larger for high than for low RP (Holcomb, 1988, SOA = 1150 ms; Brown, Hagoort, & Chwilla, 2000, SOA = 700 ms), whereas for short SOAs, N400 and semantic priming are unaffected by RP (Silva-Pereyra, Harmony, Villanueva, Fernández, Rodríguez, Galán, Díaz-Comas, Bernal, Fernández-Bouzas, Marosi, & Reyes, 1999, SOA = 300 ms). One possibly important difference in results for the two measures was reported by Brown et al. (2000). Lexical decision response time revealed a pattern of facilitation and inhibition in the high RP condition but only a pattern of facilitation in the low RP condition. The amplitude of N400, however, was the same for unrelated and neutral primes for both levels of RP; that is, there was no pattern in N400 comparable to inhibition in response time. The meaning of this apparent dissociation is not clear.

Associative Versus "Pure" Semantic Priming. Hagoort, Brown, and Swaab (1996) were the first to compare N400 priming effects for associatively and semantically related word pairs. The primary goal of this experiment was to investigate lexical-semantic impairments in aphasic patients. ERPs were recorded while participants listened passively to auditorially presented word pairs. Associatively related pairs (e.g., *bread-butter*) were chosen from word association norms; the target was the dominant associate of the prime for most pairs. Semantically related pairs (e.g., *church-villa*) were selected from common semantic categories and were not associatively related according to word association norms. N400 priming effects were obtained for both types of prime-target relation and were of similar magnitude. The only indication of an effect of type of relation on N400 priming occurred for patients with right-hemisphere lesions. They showed a normal N400 priming effect for associatively related pairs but a diminished priming effect for semantically related pairs.

Koivisto and Revonsuo (2001) compared priming for semantically unrelated compound words (e.g., *wind-mill*) to semantically related words that were "not strongly lexically associated but . . . belonged to the same semantic category and shared semantic features" (the procedures used to create these materials were not described and the stimuli were not provided). Behavioral priming effects were present for both types of stimuli and had comparable magnitudes. N400 priming was present for the compounds in two time windows (250–375 ms and 375–500 ms) but present for the semantically related pairs only in the earlier time window. Priming for the compounds was probably produced by strategic processes, as the RP and NR were 0.67 and the SOA was 715 ms (see Chapter 13). These results are also difficult to evaluate because the associative relations between primes and targets were not verified by free association (10 subjects rated the prime-target pairs on "associative strength and semantic feature overlap").

The third project investigated priming between words that have perceptually similar referents, such as *button-coin* (Kellenbach, Wijers, & Mulder, 2000). There was no evidence of semantic priming in lexical decision response times or error rates, but statistically reliable N400 priming was observed.

Mediated Versus Direct Priming. Several studies have examined mediated priming using ERPs (Chwilla, Kolk, & Mulder, 2000; Hill, Strube, Roesch-Ely, & Weisbrod, 2002; Kiefer, Weisbrod, Kern, Maier, & Spitzer, 1998; Silva-Pereyra, Harmony, Villanueva, Fernández, Rodríguez, Galán, Díaz-Comas, Bernal, Fernández-Bouzas, Marosi, & Reyes, 1999; Weisbrod, Kiefer, Winkler, Maier, Hill, Roesch-Ely, & Spitzer, 1999). Generally, these studies indicate that the N400 priming effect is produced by integrative processes. Perhaps most telling are Chwilla et al.'s experiments. N400 priming effects were observed for mediated pairs only when they appeared in lists that did not contain directly related pairs and under conditions that made the semantic relations between such items more salient (e.g., in the second block of testing or in a task in which primes and targets were presented simultaneously and subjects decided whether or not both were words). Chwilla et al. concluded that the N400 priming effects in their experiments were produced by language comprehension processes that search for meaningful connections between linguistic events (e.g., words) and general context (e.g., previously presented words, the experimental task and setting).

Effects of Lag. I was able to find only one experiment that examined N400 priming effects when the prime and target were separated by unrelated intervening items. Deacon, Hewitt, and Tamny (1998) used a task in which three words were presented in succession and then a probe word was presented. The task was to decide whether the probe was one of the three words previously displayed. The first and third words or the second and third words or none of the words were semantically related. Each word was presented for 185 ms and the SOA was 250 ms (no description is provided of what was on the screen for the remaining 65 ms). N400 amplitudes were consistently smaller in the lag-1 priming condition (first and third words related) than in the unrelated condition (all three words unrelated), but the N400 priming effect was only marginally significant.[1]

Forward Versus Backward Priming. To my knowledge, only one study has examined backward priming using the N400 priming effect. Chwilla, Hagoort, and Brown (1998) included bidirectionally related pairs (e.g., *spider-web*), bidirectionally unrelated word pairs (e.g., *bird-soap*), unidirectionally forward-related pairs (e.g., *mouse-cheese*), and unidirectionally backward-related pairs (e.g., *stick-lip*) in a cross-modal lexical decision task. Primes were presented auditorially; targets were presented visually. Approximately 60% of the unidirectionally related pairs were compounds (e.g., *lip-stick*). The RP was 0.75 and the NR was 0.80, conditions appropriate for strategic processing. In lexical decision response times, priming effects were largest for bidirectionally related pairs and intermediate for forward-related and backward-related pairs (60 ms, 39 ms, and 29 ms, respectively, collapsed across the two prime-target ISIs of 0 and 500 ms). Within the sets of unidirectionally related pairs, priming for compounds was 25 ms and 29 ms in the forward and the backward directions, whereas priming for noncompounds was 61 ms and 27 ms in the forward and the backward directions. N400 priming effects also were largest for bidirectionally related pairs and intermediate for forward-related and backward related pairs; comparisons of N400 priming effects for compounds and noncompounds were not made.

These behavioral results are consistent with the conclusions reached in Chapter 13; namely, priming for compounds is produced by strategic processes, whereas priming for noncompounds is produced by automatic and strategic processes. Note in particular that priming in the forward direction for noncompounds is of the same magnitude as priming for bidirectionally related pairs. Processing of both of these types of items has the potential to benefit from automatic processes and strategic processes. In contrast, priming is of smaller magnitude for backward-related noncompounds and for compounds. These items benefit less or not at all from automatic priming mechanisms. Chwilla et al. (1998) concluded that the ERP results were consistent with their assumption that N400 was sensitive to semantic integration processes; in particular, N400 priming effects for forward and backward related pairs were of the same magnitude. They assumed that semantic integration processes were not sensitive to direction of association but that expectancy and spread of activation would be so sensitive. However, on the basis of their data alone, one cannot rule out the possibility that the N400 priming effects also were produced by memory-retrieval processes, such as spreading activation. One way to get at this question would be to examine N400 priming effects for compounds and noncompounds separately as a function of direction of association. Unfortunately, Chwilla et al. (1998) did not report such an analysis.

Conscious Versus Unconscious Priming. To the extent that the N400 reflects semantic integration processes, which are strategic in the classical sense (see Chapter 9), one would expect N400 priming effects to be reduced or eliminated if primes were presented outside conscious awareness. Brown and Hagoort (1993) tested this hypothesis using forward and backward masking of primes in a lexical decision task. The N400 priming effect was completely eliminated in the masked condition. They concluded that presenting primes outside conscious awareness prevented semantic integration processes and, hence, eliminated N400 priming. More recent experiments indicate that N400 priming effects are reduced, but not eliminated, by masking (e.g., Deacon, Hewitt, Yang, & Nagata, 2000; Kiefer, 2002; Stenberg, Lindgren, Johansson, Olsson, & Rosen, 2000). These findings suggest that the N400 priming effect is not produced solely by semantic integration processes. It is possible, however, that semantic integration processes operate even when primes (i.e., context) are presented outside conscious awareness. This conjecture may not be so far fetched given recent demonstrations of effects of RP on unconscious semantic priming (e.g., Bodner & Masson, 2003). Kintsch (1988) proposed a model of text comprehension that includes automatic integration processes of this kind (see also Norris, 1986).

Stimulus Quality. In two experiments, Holcomb (1993) showed that whereas semantic priming in lexical decision response time was larger for degraded than for intact targets, the magnitude of the N400 priming effect was not affected by stimulus quality. The only apparent effect of poor stimulus quality on the N400 was to delay it by approximately 40 ms. According to the explanation favored by Holcomb, semantic context and stimulus quality affected relatively early word recognition processes, whereas the N400 was produced by semantic integration processes occurring relatively late in processing. This view is quite consistent with contemporary models of word recognition (as discussed in Chapter 17).

Summary. Research on the effects of semantic context on the N400 seems to have converged on the conclusion that the N400 is produced by processes involved in integrating semantic events with previous context. Although a fair amount of research has been conducted on N400 priming effects, a perusal of the literature shows that ERP methods have been vastly underutilized as a tool for investigating the effects of semantic context on word recognition and memory retrieval. A frustrating feature of many of the studies conducted to date is that the methods, especially stimulus preparation and stimulus counterbalancing across experimental conditions, have not met the high standards established in behavioral investigations of semantic priming (notable exceptions include studies by Bentin, Chwilla, Holcomb, Kutas, and Rugg). For example, it is fairly common for different stimuli to be used in the unrelated and the related priming conditions. Methodological problems such as these are relatively easy to solve, but until they are addressed, much of the N400 research will be viewed with some skepticism by behavioral researchers.

☐ Functional Neuroimaging of Semantic Priming

Remarkably little research has been conducted on semantic priming using functional neuroimaging methods. To my knowledge, the first such study was published by Mummery, Shallice, and Price (1999), who used positron emission tomography (PET) to investigate the neural correlates of semantic priming. Subjects were scanned while performing a lexical decision task. Related pairs were category coordinates that did not share associative relations (e.g., *pig-horse*). A word prime and either a word or a nonword target were presented on each trial; the SOA was 250 ms. RP was varied across scans from 0% to 100% (in 25% increments). In the control task, two consonant letter strings were presented on each trial, and the task was letter decision on the second letter string ("Is there a 'b' present?").

Several areas of the brain were differentially active for lexical decision and for letter decision, and these areas were predominantly left lateralized (especially those areas more active for lexical decision than for letter decision). Of primary interest were areas more active for lexical decision than for letter decision and also in which activity correlated with RP. Two such areas were identified: left anterior temporal lobe and anterior cingulate. In the left anterior temporal lobe, activity was relatively high for RPs of 0% and 100% and relatively low otherwise. In anterior cingulate, activity decreased monotonically with RP. Activity in two additional areas was related to RP: right superior parietal lobe and right premotor region. Neither of these regions was selectively activated by the lexical decision task.

Rossell and her colleagues (Rossell, Bullmore, Williams, & David, 2001; Rossell, Price, & Nobre, 2003) were the first to investigate semantic priming with functional magnetic resonance imaging (fMRI). Because the second of these two projects used superior methods, I will focus my attention on it. This study included parallel ERP and event-related fMRI (efMRI) experiments.[2] Semantically related pairs were category coordinates (assessment of associative relations was not discussed). SOAs of 200 and 900 ms were used; RP and NR were both .5.

Behavioral results for both ERP subjects and efMRI subjects revealed an interaction between semantic priming and SOA, such that priming was larger for the short than for the long SOA (44 ms vs. 31 ms). N400 priming was significant for both SOAs, but it had an earlier onset (300 ms vs. 360 ms) and greater amplitude for the long than for the short SOA. Strategic processes were probably minimal at the SOA of 200 ms; we can therefore assume that priming at this SOA was dominated by the contributions of automatic mechanisms. The N400 results indicate that semantic integration processes were more prevalent at the long SOA and presumably contributing more to the overall priming effect. The fact that the overall magnitude of priming decreased with SOA indicates that contributions of automatic processes decreased with SOA and at a faster rate than contributions of strategic processes increased.

Activity in several areas of the brain was reliably related to semantic priming. Left anterior medial temporal cortex was more active in the unrelated prime condition than in the related prime condition, whereas the left supramarginal gyrus of the inferior parietal lobe was less active in the unrelated prime condition than in the related prime condition. Anterior cingulate was more active for long than for short SOAs. Finally, activity in the posterior portion of the right superior temporal gyrus, at the junction with the supramarginal gyrus, was affected by the interaction between semantic priming and SOA. Activity was greater for unrelated pairs than for related pairs and more so for the long SOA than for the short SOA.

A second efMRI investigation of semantic priming was recently published by Rissman, Eliassen, and Blumstein (2003). Stimuli were word-word or word-nonword pairs presented auditorially; subjects made a lexical decision to the second member of each pair. The interstimulus interval (ISI) between the prime and the target was 50 ms, but because primes required 541 ms, on the average, to be spoken, this brief ISI is not comparable to an SOA of 50 ms under visual presentation conditions. Related prime-target pairs shared semantic and associative relations. The RP was 0.5 and the NR was 0.67. In the tone control task, subjects heard pairs of tones and alternately pressed the right or the left response key after hearing the second tone.

For present purposes, the most important comparisons involve the unrelated and the related prime conditions. Five areas of the brain were more active in the unrelated than in the related condition: left superior temporal gyrus, left precentral gyrus, middle frontal gyrus bilaterally, and right caudate. No areas were more active in the related than in the unrelated condition. Investigations of the time course of the BOLD response showed that it peaked at the same time or later, and decayed more slowly, in the unrelated condition than in the related condition. An unfortunate limitation of this experiment, relative to the previously discussed functional neuroimaging experiments, is that it did not parametrically manipulate any variable plausibly related to the magnitude of priming (e.g., RP, SOA).

Summary. Although very few functional neuroimaging investigations of semantic priming have been conducted, a few patterns seem to be emerging in the findings. Regions of left temporal cortex (anterior temporal, anterior medial temporal, and superior temporal gyrus) and anterior cingulate are often activated in semantic priming. Left anterior temporal cortex seems to be involved in aspects of semantic processing, whereas anterior cingulate seems to be involved in more attentional aspects (Rossell, Price, & Nobre, 2003). The precise roles that these and other areas of the brain may have in producing and modulating semantic priming remain to be discovered.

SECTION IV

Summary and Conclusions

CHAPTER

What Have We Learned About Semantic Priming and What Does the Future Hold?

My goal in this chapter is to survey the semantic priming scene from "30,000 feet," with any eye for general patterns or principles. I begin by offering bullet-point summaries of each of the preceding chapters:

- Chapters 2–7: Models. The most influential models of semantic priming have been spreading activation models, Becker's verification model, compound-cue models, distributed network models, and multistage activation models. Other notable models include Forster's models, Norris's context-checking model, Neely and Keefe's hybrid model, and ROUSE.
- Chapter 8: Methodological Issues. To ensure that semantic priming is not confounded with irrelevant differences between materials, primes and targets should be counterbalanced through experimental conditions (e.g., related vs. unrelated prime), such that each item occurs in each experimental condition across subjects but is not repeated within subjects. The ANOVA for such a design should include counterbalancing test list as a between-subjects factor; there is no need, however, to conduct separate analyses across subjects and items. If facilitation and inhibition need to be estimated independently, the best choice for the neutral prime condition may

be orthographically regular, pronounceable nonwords. Semantic priming is revealed in SDT measures of sensitivity and bias. These measures reflect the behavior of an entire memory or word recognition system and, hence, are not by themselves informative about the information-processing stage at which semantic context has its effects (e.g., perceptual vs. postperceptual).

- Chapter 9: Automatic Versus Strategic Priming. Semantic priming is produced by automatic processes and by strategic processes. Two types of strategic processes have been identified, expectancy and semantic matching. Strategic processes seem to have greater effects (a) as the SOA increases, (b) as the relatedness proportion increases (especially, expectancy), (c) as the nonword ratio increases (especially, semantic matching), (d) in lexical decision than in naming (especially, semantic matching), and (e) for category-exemplar pairs than for associates. Models of priming differ greatly in how they explain automatic and strategic priming. One approach is to overlay strategic processes on a base automatic priming model; at least one model attempts to explain effects attributed to strategic processes (e.g., inhibition) with automatic processes; and in another model, all priming is under attentional control.

- Chapter 10: Associative Versus "Pure" Semantic Priming. Semantic priming occurs for primes and targets that are only semantically related (e.g., *goat-dog*) and is even larger for primes and targets that are also associatively related (e.g., *cat-dog*). The magnitude of semantic priming seems to depend on the type of semantic relation, with the greatest priming occurring for functionally related primes and targets (e.g., *broom-sweep*). Although few models of priming specify associative or semantic representations in much detail, all of the models could be extended in relatively minor ways to account for pure semantic priming and the "boost" provided by associative relations.

- Chapter 11: Mediated Versus Direct Priming. Mediated priming has been obtained for primes and targets separated by up to three associative steps (e.g., *mane-stripes*). Only spreading activation models predict this result. However, the finding is not decisive because of the inherent difficulty in ruling out the possibility that the primes and the targets are directly related in some manner.

- Chapter 12: Effects of Lag. Under standard test conditions, semantic priming is reduced by 50% when one unrelated word intervenes between the prime and the target and is eliminated entirely when two words intervene. Recent evidence, however, suggests that semantic priming may occur over lags of nearly 100. Only distributed network learning models can account for priming over such long lags. It is unclear at this point whether long-term semantic priming is caused by lexical-semantic processes or by episodic memory processes.

- Chapter 13: Forward Versus Backward Priming. There is weak evidence that more priming occurs in the forward than in the backward associative direction for asymmetrically associated semantically related primes and targets (e.g., *lamp-light* vs. *light-lamp*). Forward priming and backward priming for compounds (e.g., *fruit-fly* vs. *fly-fruit*) are almost certainly produced by strategic processes. Becker's model, TODAM, and distributed network models other than Plaut's model may have difficulty explaining automatic asymmetrical priming.

- Chapter 14: Conscious Versus Unconscious Priming. Semantic priming seems to occur even when subjects claim that they cannot see the primes and have difficulty making forced-choice decisions about the primes (e.g., word vs. nonword). None of the models is challenged by these findings because none of them has anything to say about conscious vs. unconscious processing.

- Chapter 15: Prime-Task Effect. The magnitude of semantic priming is greatly reduced when people search the prime for a particular letter. Findings on the prime-task effect indicate that models of priming must distinguish between levels of lexical-semantic representation (e.g., features, letters, words, meanings) and that attentional processes—but not necessarily conscious attentional processes—are needed to activate or to retrieve the meanings of words. Multistage activation models are the only models of priming that have been applied to the prime-task effect.

- Chapter 16: List Context Effects. The magnitude of semantic priming can depend on the context established by the test list. For example, the magnitude of the prime-task effect depends on the relatedness proportion, and priming for antonyms seems to be eliminated if they are embedded in a list containing mostly synonyms. Most models of priming have difficulty accounting for these findings because they do not have processing architectures in which high-level cognitive processes, such as conceptions of the experimental "set," can affect low-level processes.

- Chapter 17: Word Frequency, Stimulus Quality, and Stimulus Repetition. Semantic priming is larger for low- than for high-frequency words and larger for perceptually degraded than for intact targets, but low- and high-frequency words are affected equally by stimulus degradation. The interaction between semantic context and stimulus quality is present for high but not for low values of relatedness proportion. Stimulus repetition seems to have a short-term lexical component and a long-term episodic memory component. Short-term repetition effects combine additively with word frequency, but their relations with semantic context and stimulus quality are largely unknown. Collectively, these results challenge all of the models of priming and imply that models need to distinguish between stages of processing (possibly corresponding to levels of lexical-semantic representation) and incorporate processes by which cognitive processes can influence more low-level recognition processes.

- Chapter 18: Cognitive Neuroscience of Semantic Priming. Studies of hemispheric asymmetries in semantic priming indicate that the cerebral hemispheres contribute equally to some kinds of priming (e.g., priming under automatic conditions, mediated priming) but differentially to other kinds of priming (e.g., priming under strategic conditions, pure semantic priming). An important but unresolved issue in this research is whether findings obtained from experiments using central presentation generalize to experiments using lateral presentation, as lateral presentation may alter semantic processing in fundamental ways. Investigations of semantic priming using event-related potentials have focused primarily on the N400 component. Research seems to be converging on the conclusion that the N400 is produced by processes involved in integrating semantic events with previous context. Functional neuroimaging studies are just beginning to uncover the brain networks involved in semantic priming. The limited evidence that is available indicates that left anterior temporal cortex and anterior cingulate are recruited in semantic priming tasks.

Given this complex pattern of findings, a natural question is whether we are looking at diverse manifestations of one phenomenon or a multifarious collection of phenomena (e.g., Hughes and Whittlesea, 2003). Perhaps no single model should be able to account for all of these findings. I think one would have a tough time making the case that, *ceteris paribus*, priming for associatively and semantically related words is different in kind from priming for purely semantically related words, or that mediated and direct priming are caused by different mechanisms, or that priming at a lag of 0 is caused by different processes from those producing priming at a lag of 1, or that separate models should be developed to explain the interactions between semantic context and word frequency and between semantic context and stimulus quality. However, natural clefts exist elsewhere.

The clearest theoretical division exists between automatic and strategic priming processes. The findings reviewed in Chapter 9 show that semantic priming can have very different properties, depending on subjects' explicit expectations, the SOA between prime and target, relatedness proportion (RP), nonword ratio (NR), task, and the type of semantic relation between the prime and the target. It is difficult for me to imagine how this complex array of findings could be explained without positing categories of theoretical mechanisms akin to automatic processes and strategic processes. There is mounting evidence, though, that aspects of the two-process theory of automatic and strategic processing will need to be revised. I will return to this issue later in this chapter.

A second theoretical cut point may exist between short-term and long-term semantic priming effects. As discussed in Chapter 12, the long-term semantic transfer effects investigated by Woltz and by Hughes and Whittlesea seem to be caused by very different processes from those responsible for semantic priming in standard paradigms. The status of the long-term priming effects discovered by Becker, Joordens, and their colleagues remains uncertain. If those effects turn out to be produced by episodic memory processes, then models of semantic priming may not need to accommodate long-term semantic priming. By contrast, if long-term semantic priming is a lexical-semantic effect, and distributed network learning models are unable to explain short-term and long-term priming with a common mechanism, then different processes may be needed to explain these two types of semantic priming.

Finally, a third theoretical division may exist between unconscious and conscious priming. This distinction is highly correlated with that between automatic and strategic processes. Investigators commonly assume that semantic priming from masked primes can be produced only by automatic processes. This assumption has high face validity: If subjects are not consciously aware of the prime, how can they use it to generate expected targets or determine whether it is related to the target? Semantic priming from visible primes, on the other hand, can be produced by automatic or strategic processes, depending on the procedure. To the extent that different component processes are used to account for automatic and strategic priming effects, so, too, different types of processes will probably be needed to explain unconscious priming and certain forms of conscious priming.

In summary, semantic priming phenomena almost certainly cannot be explained by a unitary process. Multiple mechanisms will be needed. There is compelling evidence that models will need to honor the distinction between automatic and strategic priming processes (although perhaps in modified form); there is at least some evidence that different mechanisms may underlie short-term and long-term priming effects; and to the extent that semantic priming produced by masked primes is purely automatic, then different processes may apply to unconscious and to conscious priming.

☐ Automatic and Strategic Processing

The two-process theory of automatic and strategic processing has formed the foundation of several models of semantic priming and the backdrop for much of the experimental work over the past 30 years. As noted in several chapters, this theory has now been challenged on many fronts.

At the level of theory, two models have been proposed in which the automatic-strategic distinction is questioned. Plaut and Booth (2000; see Chapters 5 and 17) showed that some inhibition effects can be explained in a distributed network model without invoking strategic processes such as expectancy or semantic matching. At the other extreme, Stolz and Besner (1996; Stolz and Besner, 1999, see Chapters 6, 15, and 17) have argued that activation of word meanings requires attention and, that in general, processing pathways in word recognition can be placed under attentional control at any time. These models represent important advancements in understanding semantic priming mechanisms, but they do not supplant the distinction between automatic and strategic priming processes. Plaut and Booth acknowledge that their model cannot account for all strategic effects and that models of word recognition must include top-down influences on processing. Similarly, Stolz and Besner's conception of attention is different from the standard conception in the semantic priming and word recognition literatures. Attention, according to Stolz and Besner, implies nothing about consciousness of processing or speed of processing or the relative mix of benefits and costs.

At an empirical level, the traditional conception of automatic versus strategic priming is challenged by several results, including interactions among relatedness, expectancy, and SOA (Chapter 9); effects of RP on masked priming (Chapter 9); dependence of response-congruity masked priming on temporal attention (Chapter 14); prime-task effects (Chapter 15); and list-context effects (Chapter 16). Although these findings will certainly complicate a model's job in accounting for semantic priming effects, they do not yet justify abandoning the theoretical distinction between automatic and strategic components of priming.

The finding with the clearest theoretical impact may be the interaction between relatedness, expectancy, and SOA. This interaction can be described in terms of expectancy, wherein expectancy effects increase more as a function of SOA for unrelated than for related primes and targets, or in terms of relatedness, wherein relatedness effects decrease more as a function of SOA for expected targets than for unexpected targets. This interaction has now been observed in four independent studies (see Chapter 9). Balota et al. (1992) sketch possible ways that the traditional two-process theory could be extended to account for this interaction. For instance, expectancy effects for unrelated primes and targets may depend heavily on SOA because time is needed to retrieve and use the recently learned relations between the words (e.g., "when the prime is *metal*, think of types of trees"), whereas expectancy effects for related primes and targets may be minimally influenced by SOA because preexisting relations are retrieved and processed efficiently (e.g., "when the prime is *flower*, think of types of flowers"). Regardless of how this interaction is eventually explained, the results indicate that automatic and strategic processes are not independent.

With respect to the other findings:

(a) As discussed in Chapter 9, there are reasons to be cautious about accepting the demonstration of RP effects in masked priming. Assuming these effects are genuine, they may be produced by modulation of feedback from semantic to lexical levels of representation (Bodner and Masson, 2003). Such a mechanism was used in multistage activation models to account for the effects of RP on the interaction between semantic context and stimulus quality (see Chapter 17). There is no reason to believe that processes of this type are incompatible with traditional strategic processes. Hence, RP may influence high-level cognitive processes, such as expectancy and semantic matching, and low-level processes, such as the flow of information between levels of lexical-semantic representation.

(b) As explained in Chapter 14, findings on response-congruity masked priming may not generalize to masked priming of the *lion-tiger* variety.

(c) Finally, prime-task and list-context effects are challenging to explain but they do not provide direct evidence against the two-process theory.

But in the interest of fostering minority influence, let us suppose that all of these findings can be accepted at face value. What do they imply about semantic priming mechanisms? Collectively they suggest (a) that high-level cognitive processes, such as expectations, goals, and interpretations of context, can influence and be influenced by low-level processes, such as the flow of activation through stages of word recognition, and (b) that attentional control need not be conscious.

Modifying the two-process theory so that automatic and strategic processes can interact seems to be necessary to account for several findings reviewed in this book. An important methodological implication of this view is that one cannot assume that the impact of top-down processes has been mitigated just because a short SOA or a particular task, such as naming, has been employed in an experiment. The experimental set established by high relatedness proportion, for example, may have effects on patterns of priming despite other features of the experimental design.

The second suggested modification to the two-process theory naturally invites questions about whether all cognitive processes are under attentional control or whether conscious and unconscious attentional processes differ in ways other than awareness. It is unknown, for example, whether unconscious attentional processes produce inhibition.

The two-process theory of automatic and strategic processes identified two categories of cognitive processes on the basis of features that were correlated behaviorally (e.g., fast onset and little inhibition). It has long been acknowledged that those features corresponded to values on dimensions of cognitive processing: onset time, extent of conscious awareness, susceptibility to attentional control, and propensity to produce benefits and costs. Experimental results summarized in this book indicate that values on at least two of those dimensions—conscious awareness and attentional control—may not be correlated in the population of cognitive processes.[1] The concepts "automatic" and "strategic" will have to be updated to accommodate this discovery, and the two-process theory will undergo substantial evolution. However, models of semantic priming, in particular, and of word recognition, in general, will nevertheless need to characterize cognitive processes in terms of onset time, extent of conscious awareness, susceptibility to attentional control, and propensity to produce benefits and costs. Those dimensions remain fundamental even if the space of cognitive processes turns out to be populated in ways that theorists never originally imagined.

☐ Status of Models of Semantic Priming

The body of evidence on semantic priming has become sufficiently complex that it can no longer be explained by a few simple processes, such as spreading activation, compound cuing, or even combinations of one of these mechanisms with expectancy and semantic matching. Comprehensive, explicitly specified models are needed. Which models offer the most hope for the future? An answer to this question may hinge on the nature of Becker and Joorden's long-term semantic priming effects.

If long-term semantic priming effects can be replicated successfully and consistently, and research indicates that they are produced by lexical-semantic processes, then distributed network learning models will stand alone in this arena. None of the other models of priming or word recognition has mechanisms that can account for such long-term priming effects. The challenge for proponents of learning models will be to develop a corresponding explanation of the complex findings on short-term priming reviewed in this book. However, if long-term semantic priming turns out be a species of the long-term semantic transfer effects documented by Woltz and by Hughes and Whittlesea, then the other models have a fighting chance.

The findings on prime-task effects, list-context effects, and the complex interactions among semantic context, stimulus quality, stimulus repetition, word frequency, and RP place powerful constraints on models of semantic priming and word recognition. First, these findings indicate that models must distinguish between levels of lexical-semantic representation, such as features, letters, words, and semantics. Second, the models must allow for the flow of information between levels to be guided by processing goals. Only multistage activation models have been applied to such effects so far. A major limitation of those applications is that they have been qualitative and descriptive. It remains to be seen whether multistage activation models can account for quantitative aspects of a wide range of semantic priming phenomena.

Two additional promising models are Plaut's distributed network model (e.g., Plaut & Booth, 2000) and ROUSE (e.g., Huber, Shiffrin, Lyle, & Ruys, 2001). Plaut's model is especially intriguing because it attempts to account for a wide range of semantic priming phenomena with a single underlying mechanism and without relying on strategic processes. This model has been implemented computationally and fared reasonably well in predicting qualitative patterns of semantic priming findings, but parameters of the model have not been estimated from data. Plaut's model also distinguishes between levels of representation in the manner that seems to be necessary. ROUSE's major strengths exist in its explicit mathematical form and its ability to account for the quantitative properties of an array of results that poses serious challenges to other models (e.g., preferences for prime-related words when the prime is processed shallowly but preferences against prime-related words when the prime is processed deeply in a primed perceptual-identification task). This model, at least in its newest incarnation, nROUSE (e.g., Huber & O'Reilly, 2003), also distinguishes between levels of lexical-semantic representation. ROUSE's major limitation is that it has not been applied to many of the significant issues and paradigms in the semantic priming field.

The scientific understanding of semantic priming has advanced enormously in the past 30 years. Although the findings are by no means simple and easy to apprehend, there has been closure on several crucial issues and consistent themes have emerged in explanations of semantic priming phenomena. It seems clear that future investigations of semantic priming will need to be framed in the broader contexts of models of word recognition, memory, or both. I look forward to seeing the fruits of these endeavors and remain optimistic about future scientific progress.

Appendix

This appendix collects several ideas for experiments that occurred to me while I was writing this book. Perhaps a thesis or two can be found among them.

- The nature of attentional control of cognitive processes responsible for semantic priming needs to be explored in more depth by manipulating prime-mask SOA (such that masked and visible primes are used), RP, prime-target SOA, and type of prime (related, unrelated, neutral). NR should either be held constant at 0.5 or manipulated as well. Key questions are whether or not inhibition occurs for masked primes and how patterns of facilitation and inhibition are affected by masking, RP, and SOA.
- Understanding of the relative propensities of expectancy and semantic matching to produce facilitation and inhibition would be advanced by the results of an experiment in which SOA, RP, and NR were manipulated jointly in both lexical decision and naming tasks. Given that patterns of facilitation and inhibition are affected by the type of prime-target relation, the experiment should use associates and category-exemplar pairs as materials.
- The role of semantic matching in lexical decision and in naming would be better understood if this strategic process were manipulated explicitly, as has been done with expectancy. One approach might be to have subjects judge whether the target stimulus is related to the prime and manipulate factors hypothesized to affect semantic matching, such as RP, NR, and SOA. It might be possible to encourage semantic matching in lexical decision or naming by mixing standard lexical decision or naming trials with trials that require an explicit judgment of target-prime relatedness.
- Plaut's model of the effects of RP on semantic priming predicts that overall response time should be faster in low than in high RP lists. This prediction should be tested within subjects. To my knowledge,

only one study has manipulated RP within subjects. That study provided evidence consistent with the prediction but was not designed to test it.

- Mediated priming would have strong theoretical implications if one could provide additional evidence that primes and targets did not share residual semantic or associative relations. One possible approach to this problem would be to collect existing data sets and then determine (a) whether a subset of items meets the criterion of being semantically unrelated according to HAL and LSA and (b) whether those items evince priming. Of course, another approach is to construct new mediated primes and targets that are not semantically related according to HAL or LSA and then determine whether such materials produce priming.
- Long-term semantic priming may have enormous theoretical impact. Hence, the long-term semantic priming effects discovered by Becker, Joordens, and their colleagues need to be replicated, and the relations between those effects and short-term semantic priming and long-term semantic transfer effects must be determined with greater precision. One line of attack would be to examine how long-term semantic priming combines with word frequency, stimulus quality, and stimulus repetition.
- Several models of priming would be challenged by a convincing demonstration of asymmetrical priming for asymmetrically associated, semantically related primes and targets (e.g., *lamp-light*) under conditions that limit strategic processing (e.g., brief SOA, low RP, neutral NR of 0.5).
- Results on backward priming in naming present a confusing array of findings in which priming occurs for short but not long SOAs and for some types of materials but not for others. This area of research would benefit from an experiment that manipulated SOA (from a minimum of 200 ms to at least 500 ms), RP, and type of prime-target relation (asymmetrically associated, semantically related items vs. compounds). To keep matters simple, I would not include nonwords initially, but because they may influence strategic processes, the NR also needs to be manipulated at some point.
- Results of experiments that have investigated the relations between the magnitudes of masked priming and retrospective priming (i.e., the effect of prime-target relatedness on prime identification) are contradictory, with some studies showing a positive correlation and others showing a negative correlation. A resolution of this paradox would help explain the role of attention in semantic priming and word recognition.

- The relations between visual and auditory word recognition should be explored by conducting a prime-task experiment in which the presentation modality of the prime is crossed with the presentation modality of the target (visual vs. auditory).
- Stolz and Besner's interpretation of the IA model predicts that letter search on the prime will eliminate word frequency effects in lexical decisions (and presumably naming as well). This prediction has never been tested.
- The RP modulates the interaction between semantic context and stimulus quality. Does it also modulate the interaction between semantic context and word frequency? Does the NR play a role in modulating these interactions?
- Stimulus repetition effects have two components, a short-term effect that lasts a few seconds and a long-term effect that can last days or weeks. Almost nothing is known about the relations among short-term repetition effects, semantic context, and stimulus quality.
- Event-related potentials and fMRI have been vastly underutilized as methods of investigating semantic priming. The N400, for example, could be used to test whether letter search on the prime blocks activation of the prime's semantic representation (e.g., Luck, Vogel, and Shapiro, 1996). The functional neuroimaging literature is so sparse that just about any investigation will be informative, although it would be heartening if future studies were motivated by empirical and theoretical controversies in the behavioral literature and used methods (especially stimulus counterbalancing) that met the high standards that have been established in behavioral experiments.

Notes

[Chapter 2]

1. Given that *lion* and *tiger* are strong mutual associates (e.g., Nelson, McEvoy, and Schreiber, 1991), one might wonder why they are not directly linked in Figure 2.1. It is important to distinguish associative networks empirically derived from free association (e.g., McNamara, 1992b) from semantic networks, which are hypothetical models of memory. The links in Figure 2.1 correspond to propositional relations between concepts (e.g., Anderson, 1983a). Additional propositional relations certainly exist (*lions are mammals, tigers are mammals, lions are similar to tigers* etc.). Presumably free association is sensitive to the strength and number of links between concepts. This issue also arises in Chapter 10.
2. Collins and Loftus (1975) were not very clear about the relation between processing and the duration of the release of activation. They stated in assumption #1 that "when a concept is processed . . . activation spreads out along the paths of the network" and in assumption #2 that "the longer a concept is continuously processed . . . the longer activation is released from the node of the concept at a fixed rate" (p. 411). My reading of these statements is that the release of activation starts when a concept is processed, and stops eventually, but can continue even when the concept is not actively processed. Other interpretations are also possible.
3. This is my interpretation of assumption #1, p. 411, of Collins and Loftus (1975).

[Chapter 5]

1. The input from other units is subjected to a logistic transformation to yield activation levels, as discussed in Chapter 17.

[Chapter 6]

1. Stolz and Besner (1996) identify only the semantic and the lexical levels as sites of facilitation. However, processing letter representations also should be facilitated because of feedback from the lexical to the letter level.

[Chapter 7]

1. According to Norris (1986), each member of the candidate set is "weighted according to its frequency." However, it is unclear how, or even whether, word frequency is used to establish the candidate set.

[Chapter 8]

1. If stimuli are treated as a fixed effect, the approach outlined by Pollatsek and Well—which is simpler than that advocated by Raaijmakers—will suffice, although it does not permit separate statistical tests of the main effect of materials and the within-subject component of the materials by treatment interaction (but see Pollatsek and Well, 1995, Appendix A and Table A2). I cannot imagine when such tests would be of interest. However, if stimuli are treated as a random effect, then the approach outlined by Raaijmakers may be necessary to obtain unbiased statistical tests of treatment effects.

2. René Zeelenberg and Diane Pecher discovered the differences in instructions by visiting each of our labs in March 1995 and participating in the experiments. One wonders how many other controversies in the sciences might be resolved by having investigators swap labs for a day! See Latham, Erez, and Locke (1988) and Mellers, Hertwig, and Kahneman (2001) for more formal and systematic approaches to resolving scientific disputes.

[Chapter 9]

1. Of course, benefits in one component of a task may produce costs in another, as in Stroop interference.

2. Subjects in Fuentes's experiments might very well have attended to parafoveal primes on at least a proportion of trials (Lachter, Forster, and Ruthruff, 2004). Even so, it seems unlikely that subjects used the primes strategically under such conditions.

3. Antos (1979) obtained significant inhibition at an SOA of 200 ms. In those experiments, a limited set of materials was repeated many times, and the target could be uniquely predicted from the prime on related trials because they consisted of category *exemplar-*category *name* pairs. Subjects could very well have learned the prime-target pairings over the course of the experiment. Antos's experiments are probably more informative about episodic learning and decision processes than about semantic priming.

4. I follow Neely et al.'s (1989) lead in defining RP and NR and exclude neutral prime trials. This practice is eminently reasonable when the neutral prime is not a word (e.g., XXXXX). I can see the merit of treating neutral prime trials as unrelated prime trials when the neutral prime is a word such as *blank* or *ready*. However, if such trials appear with sufficient frequency, subjects almost certainly categorize them differently from word prime trials. For this reason, and to avoid the necessity of computing RP and NR differently depending on what kind of neutral prime is used in an experiment, I consider unrelated word prime and neutral prime trials as different and exclude the latter in the computation of RP and NR.

5. For the record, I want to point out that priming effects for den Heyer et al. (1985) in Neely's (1991) Table 6 are incorrect. Estimates from den Heyer et al.'s Figure 1 yield the following values (+ is facilitation, – is inhibition): +12 ms and –3 ms for category/200 SOA; +6 ms and –26 ms for category/1000 SOA; +2 ms and –1 ms for associative/200 SOA; +14 ms andand –1 ms for associative/1000 SOA. These corrections do not substantially affect Neely's overall conclusions about facilitation and inhibition dominance.

6. Becker (1980) also found that priming became more facilitation dominant for category-exemplar pairs when a list containing such items followed a list containing antonyms (Exp. 3) or when category-exemplar pairs were intermixed with antonyms and semantic associates in a single list (Exp. 5). This result is an example of the phenomena discussed in Chapter 16 and will be discussed there.

[Chapter 14]

1. The literature on the relation between masked priming and retrospective priming (i.e., effects of prime-target relatedness on prime identification rate) is contradictory. Several studies indicate that masked priming and retrospective priming are positively correlated, whereas others indicate that the two are independent or negatively correlated (see text for references).

[Chapter 15]

1. The effect of judging the number syllables in the prime is apparently inconsistent. Parkin (1979) found that Stroop interference was eliminated when subjects judged the number of syllables in the prime, whereas Smith et al. (1983) obtained reliable semantic priming in lexical decision using a similar prime task. Friedrich, Henik, and Tzelgov (1991) cite unpublished results consistent with Parkin's findings.
2. As far as I can tell, all letter search tasks on the prime have involved visual presentation. If reading and hearing qualify as separate "domains," then letter/phoneme search on an auditorily presented prime should not interfere with semantic priming in a visual lexical decision task. Similarly, visual search for a letter in the prime should not interfere with auditory lexical decision on the target.
3. RP and nonword ratio (NR) were confounded in these experiments; therefore, we do not know which variable was responsible for moderating the prime-task effect.

[Chapter 17]

1. Norris (1984) and Wilding (1988) obtained an interaction between word frequency and stimulus quality when the interval between trials was long (3–4 s) and unfilled. This effect is probably caused by loss of vigilance during the empty interval (for discussion, see Wilding, 1988).
2. RP and NR were confounded in these experiments. In the RP = 0.50 condition, NR = 0.50; in the RP = 0.25 condition, NR = 0.39. Hence, we do not know which variable is moderating the context by stimulus quality interaction. For ease of exposition, I will follow Stolz and Neely's lead and assume that the crucial variable is RP.
3. For SOA = 200 ms and strong associates, 34 versus 46 was not statistically reliable, whereas 31 versus 52 was reliable. A power analysis indicated that the former result was probably not a Type II error.
4. Borowsky and Besner (1993, p. 816) have criticized the model's handling of word frequency effects. The foundation of their criticism is that the sensory set is really the set of orthographic neighbors of the stimulus. However, according to Becker (1980), the sensory set is not constructed using orthographic features (i.e., letters and their combinations) but, rather, primitive visual features (e.g., lines, curves).
5. To the extent that performance in the related prime condition is determined in part by trials in which verification of the semantic set fails and the sensory set must be verified, then it, too, will be affected by poor stimulus quality. Assuming that the proportion of such trials is small, effects of poor stimulus quality in the related prime condition will be small. The relative success rates of semantic verification in the related and the unrelated prime conditions determine the magnitudes of the semantic priming effect and the interaction between semantic context and stimulus quality. I cannot think of a reason why these relative success rates would be influenced by RP if the strategic process of expectancy was not operative, which seems to have been the case in Stolz and Neely's 200-ms SOA condition.
6. Plaut (1995; see also Plaut and Booth, 2000, footnote 4) claims to have demonstrated an additive relation between word frequency and stimulus quality. In fact, however, he demonstrated no interaction between word frequency, stimulus quality, and context (i.e., priming). This shows only that the stimulus quality by word frequency relation, which may or may not be additive, is the same for each level of context (related vs. unrelated primes).
7. To my knowledge, Oldfield and Wingfield (1965) published the first demonstration of stimulus repetition effects and their interaction with word frequency, albeit in naming of line drawings of objects.

[Chapter 18]

1. For reasons that are not clear to me, Deacon et al. (1998) concluded that the unrelated intervening item eliminated semantic priming. The data clearly show otherwise (see, e.g., Figure 2 and Table 1 of Deacon et al.).

2. Standard fMRI experiments use block designs, in which blood oxygen level dependent (BOLD) activity is averaged across trials within a block of trials of a particular type. In efMRI designs, BOLD activity is assessed for individual trials and then averaged across trials of a particular type.

[Chapter 19]

1. Attentionally controlled processes can be conscious or unconscious, and attention-free processes (to the extent they exist) presumably can be unconscious. The only empty cell contains conscious processes not under attentional control. Perhaps obsessive thoughts fall into this category.

References

Abernethy, M., & Coney, J. (1993). Associative priming in the hemispheres as a function of SOA. *Neuropsychologia, 31,* 1397–1409.

Abrams, R. L., & Greenwald, A. G. (2000). Parts outweigh the whole (word) in unconscious analysis of meaning. *Psychological Science, 11,* 118–124.

Abrams, R. L., Klinger, M. R., & Greenwald, A. G. (2002). Subliminal words activate semantic categories (not automated motor responses). *Psychonomic Bulletin & Review, 9,* 100–106.

Adams, J. K. (1957). Laboratory studies of behavior without awareness. *Psychological Bulletin, 54,* 383–405.

Agresti, A. (1990). *Categorical data analysis.* New York: John Wiley & Sons.

Anderson, J. R. (1976). *Language, memory, and thought.* Cambridge, MA: Harvard University Press.

Anderson, J. R. (1983a). *The architecture of cognition.* Cambridge, MA: Harvard University Press.

Anderson, J. R. (1983b). A spreading activation theory of memory. *Journal of Verbal Learning and Verbal Behavior, 22,* 261–295.

Anderson, J. R. (1993). *Rules of the mind.* Hillsdale, NJ: Erlbaum.

Antos, S. J. (1979). Processing facilitation in a lexical decision task. *Journal of Experimental Psychology: Human Perception and Performance, 5,* 527–545.

Balota, D. A. (1983). Automatic semantic activation and episodic memory encoding. *Journal of Verbal Learning and Verbal Behavior, 22,* 88–104.

Balota, D. A., Black, S. R., & Cheney, M. (1992). Automatic and attentional priming in young and older adults: Reevaluation of the two-process model. *Journal of Experimental Psychology: Human Perception and Performance, 18,* 485–502.

Balota, D. A., & Chumbley, J. I. (1984). Are lexical decisions a good measure of lexical access? The role of word frequency in the neglected decision stage. *Journal of Experimental Psychology: Human Perception and Performance, 10,* 340–357.

Balota, D. A., & Lorch, R. F., Jr. (1986). Depth of automatic spreading activation: Mediated priming effects in pronunciation but not in lexical decision. *Journal of Experimental Psychology: Learning, Memory, and Cognition, 12,* 336–345.

Balota, D. A., & Paul, S. T. (1996). Summation of activation: Evidence from multiple primes that converge and diverge within semantic memory. *Journal of Experimental Psychology: Learning, Memory, and Cognition, 22,* 827–845.

Battig, W. F., & Montague, W. E. (1969). Category norms for verbal items in 56 categories: A replication and extension of the Connecticut category norms. *Journal of Experimental Psychology Monograph, 80,* 1–46.

Becker, C. A. (1976). Allocation of attention during visual word recognition. *Journal of Experimental Psychology: Human Perception and Performance, 2,* 556–566.

Becker, C. A. (1979). Semantic context and word frequency effects in visual word recognition. *Journal of Experimental Psychology: Human Perception and Performance, 5,* 252–259.

Becker, C. A. (1980). Semantic context effects in visual word recognition: An analysis of semantic strategies. *Memory & Cognition, 8,* 493–512.

Becker, C. A. (1985). What do we really know about semantic context effects during reading? In D. Besner, T. G. Waller, & E. M. MacKinnon (Eds.), *Reading research: Advances in theory and practice* (Vol. 5, pp. 125–166). San Diego, CA: Academic Press.

Becker, C. A., & Killion, T. H. (1977). Interaction of visual and cognitive effects in word recognition. *Journal of Experimental Psychology: Human Perception and Performance, 3,* 389–401.

Becker, S., Moscovitch, M., Behrmann, M., & Joordens, S. (1997). Long-term semantic priming: A computational account and empirical evidence. *Journal of Experimental Psychology: Learning, Memory, and Cognition, 23,* 1059–1082.

Beeman, M., Friedman, R. B., Grafman, J., Perez, E., Diamond, S., & Lindsay, M. B. (1994). Summation priming and course semantic coding in the right hemisphere. *Journal of Cognitive Neuroscience, 6,* 26–45.

Bentin, S., McCarthy, G., & Wood, C. C. (1985). Event-related potentials associated with semantic priming. *Electroencephalography and Clinical Neurophysiology, 60,* 343–355.

Bernstein, I., Bissonnette, V., Vyas, A., & Barclay, P. (1989). Semantic priming: Subliminal perception or context? *Perception & Psychophysics, 45,* 153–161.

Besner, D., & Roberts, M. A. (2003). Reading nonwords aloud: Results requiring change in the dual route cascaded model. *Psychonomic Bulletin & Review, 10,* 398–404.

Besner, D., & Smith, M. C. (1992). Models of visual word recognition: When obscuring the stimulus yields a clearer view. *Journal of Experimental Psychology: Learning, Memory, and Cognition, 18,* 468–482.

Besner, D., & Swan, M. (1982). Models of lexical access in visual word recognition. *Quarterly Journal of Experimental Psychology, 34A,* 313–325.

Besner, D., Twilley, L., McCann, R. S., & Seergobin, K. (1990). On the association between connectionism and data: Are a few words necessary? *Psychological Review, 97,* 432–446.

Bjorkman, M., Juslin, P., & Winman, A. (1993). Realism of confidence in sensory discrimination: The underconfidence phenomenon. *Perception & Psychophysics, 54,* 75–81.

Blum, T. L., & Johnson, N. F. (1993). The effect of semantic priming on the detection of letters within words. *Memory & Cognition, 21,* 389–396.

Bodner, G. E., & Masson, M. E. J. (2003). Beyond spreading activation: An influence of relatedness proportion on masked semantic priming. *Psychonomic Bulletin & Review, 10,* 645–652.

Bodner, G. E., & Masson, M. E. J. (2004). Beyond binary judgments: Prime validity modulates masked repetition priming in the naming task. *Memory & Cognition, 32,* 1–11.

Borowsky, R., & Besner, D. (1993). Visual word recognition: A multistage activation model. *Journal of Experimental Psychology: Learning, Memory, and Cognition, 19,* 813–840.

Bourassa, D. C., & Besner, D. (1998). When do nonwords activate semantics? Implications for models of visual word recognition. *Memory & Cognition, 26,* 61–74.

Bracewell, R. (1978). *The Fourier transform and its applications* (2nd ed.). New York: McGraw-Hill.

Briand, K., den Heyer, K., & Dannenbring, G. L. (1988). Retroactive semantic priming in a lexical decision task. *Quarterly Journal of Experimental Psychology, 40A,* 341–359.

Brown, C. M., & Hagoort, P. (1993). The processing nature of the N400: Evidence from masked priming. *Journal of Cognitive Neuroscience, 5,* 34–44.

Brown, C. M., Hagoort, P., & Chwilla, D. J. (2000). An event-related brain potential analysis of visual word priming effects. *Brain and Language, 72,* 158–190.

Brown, M. S., Roberts, M. A., & Besner, D. (2001). Semantic processing in visual word recognition: Activation blocking and domain specificity. *Psychonomic Bulletin & Review, 8,* 778–784.

Burgess, C., & Lund, K. (2000). The dynamics of meaning in memory. In E. Dietrich & B. Arthur (Eds.), *Cognitive dynamics: Conceptual and representational change in humans and machines* (pp. 117-156). Mahwah, NJ: Erlbaum.

Burgess, C., & Simpson, G. B. (1988). Cerebral hemispheric mechanisms in the retrieval of ambiguous word meanings. *Brain and Language, 33,* 86–103.

Burke, D. M., White, H., & Diaz, D. L. (1987). Semantic priming in young and older adults: Evidence for age constancy in automatic and attentional processses. *Journal of Experimental Psychology: Human Perception and Performance, 13*, 79–88.

Bushell, C. M. (1996). Dissociated identity and semantic priming in Broca's aphasia: How controlled processing produces inhibitory semantic priming. *Brain and Language, 55*, 264–288.

Canas, J. J. (1990). Associative strength effects in the lexical decision task. *Quarterly Journal of Experimental Psychology, 42A*, 121–145.

Carr, T. H., McCauley, C., Sperber, R. D., & Parmelee, C. M. (1982). Words, pictures, and priming: On semantic activation, conscious identification, and the automaticity of information processing. *Journal of Experimental Psychology: Human Perception and Performance, 8*, 757–777.

Cheesman, J., & Merikle, P. M. (1984). Priming with and without awareness. *Perception & Psychophysics, 36*, 387–395.

Cheesman, J., & Merikle, P. M. (1986). Distinguishing conscious from unconscious perceptual processes. *Canadian Journal of Psychology, 40*, 343–367.

Chiappe, P. R., Smith, M. C., & Besner, D. (1996). Semantic priming in visual word recognition: Activation blocking and domains of processing. *Psychonomic Bulletin & Review, 3*, 249–253.

Chiarello, C. (1985). Hemisphere dynamics in lexical access: Automatic and controlled priming. *Brain and Language, 26*, 146–172.

Chiarello, C. (1998). On codes of meaning and the meaning of codes: Semantic access and retrieval within and between hemispheres. In M. Beeman & C. Chiarello (Eds.), *Right hemisphere language comprehension: Perspectives from cognitive neuroscience* (pp. 141–160). Mahwah, NJ: Erlbaum.

Chiarello, C. (2003). Parallel systems for processing language: Hemispheric complementarity in the normal brain. In M. T. Banich & M. Mack (Eds.), *Mind, brain, and language: Multidisciplinary perspectives*. Mahwah, NJ: Erlbaum.

Chiarello, C., Burgess, C., Richards, L., & Pollock, A. (1990). Semantic and associative priming in the cerebral hemispheres: Some words do, some words don't . . . sometimes, some places. *Brain and Language, 38*, 75–104.

Chiarello, C., Liu, S., Shears, C., Quan, N., & Kacinik, N. (2003). Priming of strong semantic relations in the left and right visual fields: a time-course investigation. *Neuropsychologia, 41*, 721–732.

Chiarello, C., & Richards, L. (1992). Another look at categorical priming in the cerebral hemispheres. *Neuropsychologia, 30*, 381–392.

Chiarello, C., Richards, L., & Pollock, A. (1992). Semantic additivity and semantic inhibition: Dissociable processes in the cerebral hemispheres? *Brain and Language, 42*, 52–76.

Chwilla, D. J., Hagoort, P., & Brown, C. M. (1998). The mechanism underlying backward priming in a lexical decision task: Spreading activation versus semantic matching. *Quarterly Journal of Experimental Psychology, 51A*, 531–560.

Chwilla, D. J., & Kolk, H. H. J. (2002). Three-step priming in lexical decision. *Memory & Cognition, 30*, 217–225.

Chwilla, D. J., Kolk, H. H. J., & Mulder, G. (2000). Mediated priming in the lexical decision task: Evidence from event-related potentials and reaction time. *Journal of Memory and Language, 42*, 314–341.

Clark, H. H. (1973). The language-as-fixed-effect fallacy: A critique of language statistics in psychological research. *Journal of Verbal Learning and Verbal Behavior, 12*, 335–359.

Cohen, J. (1976). Random means random. *Journal of Verbal Learning and Verbal Behavior, 15*, 261–262.

Cohen, J. (1977). *Statistical power analysis for the behavioral sciences*. New York: Academic Press.

Collins, A. M., & Loftus, E. F. (1975). A spreading-activation theory of semantic processing. *Psychological Review, 82*, 407–428.

Collins, M. (1999). Differences in semantic category priming in the left and right cerebral hemispheres under automatic and controlled processing conditions. *Neuropsychologia, 37*, 1071–1085.

Coltheart, M., Rastle, K., Perry, C., Langdon, R., & Ziegler, J. (2001). DRC: A dual route cascaded model of visual word recognition and reading aloud. *Psychological Review, 108,* 204–256.

Cree, G. S., McRae, K., & McNorgan, C. (1999). An attractor model of lexical conceptual processing: Simulating semantic priming. *Cognitive Science, 23,* 371–414.

Dagenbach, D., Carr, T. H., & Wilhelmsen, A. (1989). Task-induced strategies and near-threshold priming: Conscious influences on unconscious perception. *Journal of Memory and Language, 28,* 412–443.

Dalrymple-Alford, E. C., & Marmurek, H. H. C. (1999a). More on semantic priming in a fully recurrent network: A response to Masson (1999). *Journal of Experimental Psychology: Learning, Memory, and Cognition, 25,* 795–803.

Dalrymple-Alford, E. C., & Marmurek, H. H. C. (1999b). Semantic priming in fully recurrent network models of lexical knowledge. *Journal of Experimental Psychology: Learning, Memory, and Cognition, 25,* 758–775.

Damian, M. F. (2001). Congruity effects evoked by subliminally presented primes: Automaticity rather than semantic processing. *Journal of Experimental Psychology: Human Perception and Performance, 27,* 154–165.

Dark, V. J. (1988). Semantic priming, prime reportability, and retroactive priming are independent. *Memory & Cognition, 16,* 299–308.

Dark, V. J., & Benson, K. (1991). Semantic priming and identification of near threshold primes in a lexical decision task. *Quarterly Journal of Experimental Psychology, 43A,* 53–78.

de Groot, A. M. B. (1983). The range of automatic spreading activation in word priming. *Journal of Verbal Learning and Verbal Behavior, 22,* 417–436.

de Groot, A. M. B. (1984). Primed lexical decision: Combined effects of the proportion of related prime-target pairs and the stimulus-onset asynchrony of prime and target. *Quarterly Journal of Experimental Psychology, 36A,* 253–280.

de Groot, A. M. B., Thomassen, A. J. W. M., & Hudson, P. T. W. (1982). Associative facilitation of word recognition as measured from a neutral prime. *Memory & Cognition, 10,* 358–370.

De Houwer, J., Hermans, D., Rothermund, K., & Wentura, D. (2002). Affective priming of semantic categorization responses. *Cognition and Emotion, 16,* 643–666.

Deacon, D., Hewitt, S., & Tamny, T. (1998). Event-related potential indices of semantic priming following an unrelated intervening item. *Cognitive Brain Research, 6,* 219–225.

Deacon, D., Hewitt, S., Yang, C.-M., & Nagata, M. (2000). Event-related potential indices of semantic priming using masked and unmasked words: evidence that the N400 does not reflect a post-lexical process. *Cognitive Brain Research, 9,* 137–146.

Dehaene, S., Naccache, L., Le Clec'H, G., Koechlin, E., Mueller, M., Dehaene-Lambertz, G., van de Moortele, P.-F., & Le Bihan, D. (1998). Imaging unconscious semantic priming. *Nature, 395,* 597–600.

den Heyer, K., & Benson, K. (1988). Constraints on the additive relationship between semantic priming and word repetition and on the interactive relationship between semantic priming and stimulus clarity. *Canadian Journal of Psychology, 42,* 399–413.

den Heyer, K., Briand, K., & Dannenbring, G. L. (1983). Strategic factors in a lexical-decision task: Evidence for automatic and attention-driven processes. *Memory & Cognition, 11,* 374–381.

den Heyer, K., Briand, K., & Smith, L. (1985). Automatic and strategic effects in semantic priming: An examination of Becker's verification model. *Memory & Cognition, 13,* 228–232.

den Heyer, K., Goring, A., & Dannenbring, G. L. (1985). Semantic priming and word repetition: The two effects are additive. *Journal of Memory and Language, 24,* 699–716.

Donchin, E. (1981). Surprise! . . . Surprise? *Psychophysiology, 18,* 493–513.

Dosher, B. A. (1998). The response-window method—Some problematic assumptions: Comment on Draine and Greenwald. *Journal of Experimental Psychology: General, 127,* 311–317.

Dosher, B. A., & Rosedale, G. (1989). Integrated retrieval cues as a mechanism for priming in retrieval from memory. *Journal of Experimental Psychology: General, 118,* 191–211.

Draine, S. C., & Greenwald, A. G. (1998). Replicable unconscious semantic priming. *Journal of Experimental Psychology: General, 127,* 286–303.

Durante, R., & Hirshman, E. (1994). Retrospective priming and masked semantic priming: The interfering effects of prime activation. *Journal of Memory and Language, 33,* 112–127.

Durgunoglu, A. Y. (1988). Repetition, semantic priming, and stimulus quality: Implications for the interactive-compensatory reading model. *Journal of Experimental Psychology: Learning, Memory, and Cognition, 14,* 590–603.

Eisenberg, P., & Becker, C. A. (1982). Semantic context effects in visual word recognition, sentence processing, and reading: Evidence for semantic strategies. *Journal of Experimental Psychology: Human Perception and Performance, 8,* 739–756.

Eriksen, C. W. (1960). Discrimination and learning without awareness: A methodological survey and evaluation. *Psychological Review, 67,* 279–300.

Farah, M. J. (1989). Semantic and perceptual priming: How similar are the underlying mechanisms? *Journal of Experimental Psychology: Human Perception and Performance, 15,* 188–194.

Farah, M. J., & McClelland, J. L. (1991). A computational model of semantic memory impairment: Modality specificity and emergent category specificity. *Journal of Experimental Psychology: General, 120,* 339–357.

Faust, M., & Chiarello, C. (1998). Constraints on sentence priming in the cerebral hemispheres: Effects of intervening words in sentences and lists. *Brain and Language, 63,* 219–236.

Favreau, M., & Segalowitz, N. S. (1983). Automatic and controlled processes in first- and second-language reading of fluent bilinguals. *Memory & Cognition, 11,* 565–574.

Feldman, L. B., & Moskovljevic, J. (1987). Repetition priming is not purely episodic in origin. *Journal of Experimental Psychology: Learning, Memory, and Cognition, 13,* 573–581.

Feustel, T. C., Shiffrin, R. M., & Salasoo, A. (1983). Episodic and lexical contributions to the repetition effect in word identification. *Journal of Experimental Psychology: General, 112,* 309–346.

Fischler, I. (1977a). Associative facilitation without expectancy in a lexical decision task. *Journal of Experimental Psychology: Human Perception and Performance, 3,* 18–26.

Fischler, I. (1977b). Semantic facilitation without association in a lexical decision task. *Memory & Cognition, 5,* 335–339.

Fischler, I., & Goodman, G. O. (1978). Latency of associative activation in memory. *Journal of Experimental Psychology: Human Perception and Performance, 4,* 455–470.

Fodor, J. A., & Pylyshyn, Z. W. (1988). Connectionism and cognitive architecture: A critical analysis. *Cognition, 28,* 3–71.

Forbach, G. B., Stanners, R. F., & Hochhaus, L. (1974). Repetition and practice effects in a lexical decision task. *Memory & Cognition, 2,* 337–339.

Forster, K. I. (1976). Accessing the mental lexicon. In R. J. Wales & E. C. T. Walker (Eds.), *New approaches to language mechanisms.* Amsterdam: North-Holland.

Forster, K. I. (1979). Levels of processing and the structure of the language processor. In W. E. Cooper & E. C. T. Walker (Eds.), *Sentence processing: Psycholinguistic studies presented to Merrill Garrett.* Hillsdale, NJ: Erlbaum.

Forster, K. I. (1981). Priming and the effects of sentence and lexical contexts on naming time: Evidence for autonomous lexical processing. *Quarterly Journal of Experimental Psychology, 33A,* 465–495.

Forster, K. I. (1999). The microgenesis of priming effects in lexical access. *Brain and Language, 68,* 5–15.

Forster, K. I., & Davis, C. (1984). Repetition priming and frequency attenuation in lexical access. *Journal of Experimental Psychology: Learning, Memory, and Cognition, 10,* 680–698.

Fowler, C. A. (1986). An operational definition of conscious awareness must be responsible to subjective experience. *Behavioral and Brain Sciences, 9,* 33–34.

Fowler, C. A., Wolford, G., Slade, R., & Tassinary, L. (1981). Lexical access with and without awareness. *Journal of Experimental Psychology: General, 110,* 341–362.

Franks, J. J., Bilbrey, C. W., Lien, K. G., & McNamara, T. P. (2000). Transfer-appropriate processing (TAP) and repetition priming. *Memory & Cognition, 28,* 1140–1151.

Friedrich, F. J., Henik, A., & Tzelgov, J. (1991). Automatic processes in lexical access and spreading activation. *Journal of Experimental Psychology: Human Perception and Performance, 17,* 792–806.

Fuentes, L. J., Carmona, E., Agis, I. F., & Catena, A. (1994). The role of the anterior attention system in semantic processing of both foveal and parafoveal words. *Journal of Cognitive Neuroscience, 6,* 17–25.

Fuentes, L. J., & Tudela, P. (1992). Semantic processing of foveally and parafoveally presented words in a lexical decision task. *Quarterly Journal of Experimental Psychology, 45A,* 299–322.

Garner, W. R., Hake, H. W., & Eriksen, C. W. (1956). Operationism and the concept of perception. *Psychological Review, 63,* 149–159.

Gillund, G., & Shiffrin, R. M. (1984). A retrieval model for both recognition and recall. *Psychological Review, 91,* 1–67.

Grainger, J., & Jacobs, A. M. (1996). Orthographic processing in visual word recognition: A multiple read-out model. *Psychological Review, 103,* 518–565.

Greenwald, A. G., & Draine, S. C. (1998). Distinguishing unconscious from conscious cognition—Reasonable assumptions and replicable findings: Reply to Merikle and Reingold (1998) and Dosher (1998). *Journal of Experimental Psychology: General, 127,* 320–324.

Greenwald, A. G., Draine, S. C., & Abrams, R. L. (1996). Three cognitive markers of unconscious semantic activation. *Science, 273,* 1699–1702.

Greenwald, A. G., Klinger, M. R., & Schuh, E. S. (1995). Activation by marginally perceptible ("subliminal") stimuli: Dissociation of unconscious from conscious cognition. *Journal of Experimental Psychology: General, 124,* 22–42.

Hagoort, P., Brown, C. M., & Swaab, T. Y. (1996). Lexical-semantic event-related potential effects in patients with left hemisphere lesions with aphasia and patients with right-hemisphere lesions without aphasia. *Brain, 119,* 627–650.

Hebb, D. O. (1949). *The organization of behavior.* New York: Wiley.

Hellige, J. B. (1993). *Hemispheric asymmetry: What's right and what's left.* Cambridge: Harvard University Press.

Henik, A., Friedrich, F. J., & Kellogg, W. A. (1983). The dependence of semantic relatedness effects upon prime processing. *Memory & Cognition, 11,* 366–373.

Henik, A., Friedrich, F. J., Tzelgov, J., & Tramer, S. (1994). Capacity demands of automatic processes in semantic priming. *Memory & Cognition, 22,* 157–168.

Hess, D. J., Foss, D. J., & Carroll, P. (1995). Effects of global and local context on lexical processing during language comprehension. *Journal of Experimental Psychology: General, 124,* 62–82.

Hill, H., Strube, M., Roesch-Ely, D., & Weisbrod, M. (2002). Automatic vs. controlled processes in semantic priming—differentiation by even-related potentials. *International Journal of Psychophysiology, 44,* 197–218.

Hines, D., Czerwinski, M., Sawyer, P. K., & Dwyer, M. (1986). Automatic semantic priming: Effect of category exemplar level and word association level. *Journal of Experimental Psychology: Human Perception and Performance, 12,* 370–379.

Hino, Y., & Lupker, S. J. (1996). Effects of polysemy in lexical decision and naming: An alternative to lexical access accounts. *Journal of Experimental Psychology: Human Perception and Performance, 22,* 1331-1356.

Hinton, G. E., & Shallice, T. (1991). Lesioning an attractor network: Investigations of acquired dyslexia. *Psychological Review, 98,* 74–95.

Hintzman, D. L. (1986). "Schema abstraction" in a multiple-trace memory model. *Psychological Review, 93,* 411–428.

Hirshman, E., & Durante, R. (1992). Prime identification and semantic priming. *Journal of Experimental Psychology: Learning, Memory, and Cognition, 18,* 255–265.

Holcomb, P. J. (1988). Automatic and attentional processing: An event-related brain potential analysis of semantic priming. *Brain and Language, 35,* 66–85.

Holcomb, P. J. (1993). Semantic priming and stimulus degradation: Implications for the role of the N400 in language processing. *Psychophysiology, 30,* 47–61.

Holender, D. (1986). Semantic activation without conscious identification in dichotic listening, parafoveal vision, and visual masking: A survey and appraisal. *Behavioral and Brain Sciences, 9,* 1–66.

Holender, D., & Duscherer, K. (2004). Unconcious perception: The need for a paradigm shift. *Perception & Psychophysics, 66,* 872–881.

Hopfield, J. J. (1982). Neural networks and physical systems with emergent collective computational abilities. *Proceedings of the National Academy of Sciences, 79,* 2554–2558.

Hopfield, J. J., & Tank, D. W. (1986). Computing with neural circuits: A model. *Science, 233,* 625–633.

Huber, D. E., & O'Reilly, R. C. (2003). Persistence and accommodation in short-term priming and other perceptual paradigms: temporal segregation through synaptic depression. *Cognitive Science, 27,* 403–430.

Huber, D. E., Shiffrin, R. M., Lyle, K. B., & Quach, R. (2002). Mechanisms of source confusion and discounting in short-term priming 2: Effects of prime similarity and target duration. *Journal of Experimental Psychology: Learning, Memory, and Cognition, 28,* 1120–1136.

Huber, D. E., Shiffrin, R. M., Lyle, K. B., & Ruys, K. I. (2001). Perception and preference in short-term word priming. *Psychological Review, 108,* 149–182.

Huber, D. E., Shiffrin, R. M., Quach, R., & Lyle, K. B. (2002). Mechanisms of source confusion and discounting in short-term priming: 1. Effects of prime duration and prime recognition. *Memory & Cognition, 30,* 745–757.

Hughes, A. D., & Whittlesea, B. W. A. (2003). Long-term semantic transfer: An overlapping-operations account. *Memory & Cognition, 31,* 401–411.

Hutchison, K. A. (2002). The effect of asymmetrical association on positive and negative semantic priming. *Memory & Cognition, 30,* 1263–1276.

Hutchison, K. A. (2003). Is semantic priming due to association strength or featural overlap? A microanalytic review. *Psychonomic Bulletin & Review, 10,* 785–813.

Jobard, G., Crivello, F., & Tzourio-Mazoyer, N. (2003). Evaluation of the dual-route theory of reading: A meta-analysis of 35 neuroimaging studies. *NeuroImage, 20,* 693–712.

Jonides, J., & Mack, R. (1984). On the cost and benefit of cost and benefit. *Psychological Bulletin, 96,* 29–44.

Joordens, S., & Becker, S. (1997). The long and short of semantic priming effects in lexical decision. *Journal of Experimental Psychology: Learning, Memory, and Cognition, 23,* 1083–1105.

Joordens, S., & Besner, D. (1992). Priming effects that span an intervening unrelated word: Implications for models of memory representation and retrieval. *Journal of Experimental Psychology: Learning, Memory, and Cognition, 18,* 483–491.

Kahan, T. A., Neely, J. H., & Forsythe, W. J. (1999). Dissociated backward priming effects in lexical decision and pronunciation tasks. *Psychonomic Bulletin & Review, 6,* 105–110.

Kahana, M. J. (2002). Associative symmetry and memory theory. *Memory & Cognition, 30,* 823–840.

Kawamoto, A. H., Farrar, W. T., & Kello, C. T. (1994). When two meanings are better than one: Modeling the ambiguity advantage using a recurrent distributed network. *Journal of Experimental Psychology: Human Perception and Performance, 20,* 1233–1247.

Keefe, D. E., & Neely, J. H. (1990). Semantic priming in the pronunciation task: The role of prospective prime-generated expectancies. *Memory & Cognition, 18,* 289–298.

Kellenbach, M. L., Wijers, A. A., & Mulder, G. (2000). Visual semantic features are activated during the processing of concrete words: event-related potential evidence for perceptual semantic priming. *Cognitive Brain Research, 10,* 67–75.

Kiefer, M. (2002). The N400 is modulated by unconsciously perceived masked words: further evidence for an automatic spreading activation account of N400 priming effects. *Cognitive Brain Research, 13,* 27–39.

Kiefer, M., Weisbrod, M., Kern, I., Maier, S., & Spitzer, M. (1998). Right hemisphere activation during indirect semantic priming: Evidence from event-related potentials. *Brain and Language, 64,* 377–408.

Kintsch, W. (1988). The role of knowledge in discourse comprehension: A construction-integration model. *Psychological Review, 95,* 163–182.

Kirk, R. E. (1995). *Experimental design: Procedures for the behavioral sciences* (3rd ed.). Pacific Grove, CA: Brooks/Cole.

Kirsner, K., & Smith, M. C. (1974). Modality effects in word identification. *Memory & Cognition, 2,* 637–640.

Klauer, K. C., & Greenwald, A. G. (2000). Measurement error in subliminal perception experiments: Simulation analyses of two regression methods—Comment on Miller (2000). *Journal of Experimental Psychology: Human Perception and Performance, 26,* 1506–1508.

Klinger, M. R., Burton, P. C., & Pitts, G. S. (2000). Mechanisms of unconscious priming: I. Response competition, not spreading activation. *Journal of Experimental Psychology: Learning, Memory, and Cognition, 26,* 441–455.

Koivisto, M. (1997). Time course of semantic activation in the cerebral hemispheres. *Neuropsychologia, 35,* 497–504.

Koivisto, M. (1998). Categorical priming in the cerebral hemispheres: automatic in the left hemisphere, postlexical in the right hemisphere? *Neuropsychologia, 36,* 661–668.

Koivisto, M. (1999). Hemispheric dissociations in controlled lexical-semantic processing. *Neuropsychology, 13,* 488–497.

Koivisto, M., & Hämäläinen, H. (2002). Hemispheric semantic priming in the single word presentation task. *Neuropsychologia, 40,* 978–985.

Koivisto, M., & Laine, M. (2000). Hemispheric asymmetries in activation and integration of categorical information. *Laterality, 5,* 1–21.

Koivisto, M., & Revonsuo, A. (2001). Cognitive representations underlying the N400 priming effect. *Cognitive Brain Research, 12,* 487–490.

Kolers, P. A. (1973). Remembering operations. *Memory & Cognition, 1,* 347–355.

Kolers, P. A. (1976). Reading a year later. *Journal of Experimental Psychology: Learning, Memory, and Cognition, 2,* 554–565.

Koriat, A. (1981). Semantic facilitation in lexical decision as a function of prime-target association. *Memory & Cognition, 9,* 587–598.

Kouider, S., & Dupoux, E. (2004). Partial awareness creates the "illusion" of subliminal semantic priming. *Psychological Science, 15,* 75–81.

Kroll, J. F., & Potter, M. C. (1984). Recognizing words, pictures, and concepts: A comparison of lexical, object, and reality decisions. *Journal of Verbal Learning and Verbal Behavior, 23,* 39–66.

Kunimoto, C., Miller, J., & Pashler, H. (2001). Confidence and accuracy of near-threshold discrimination responses. *Consciousness and Cognition, 10,* 294–340.

Kutas, M., & Hillyard, S. A. (1980). Reading senseless sentences: Brain potentials reflect semantic incongruity. *Science, 207,* 203–205.

Kutas, M., & Van Petten, C. K. (1994). Psycholinguistics electrified: Event-related brain potential investigations. In M. A. Gernsbacher (Ed.), *Handbook of Psycholinguistics* (pp. 83–143). San Diego, CA: Academic Press.

Lachter, J., Forster, K. I., & Ruthruff, E. (2004). Forty-five years after Broadbent (1958): Still no identification without attention. *Psychological Review, 111,* 880–913.

Landauer, T. K. (1998). Learning and representing verbal meaning: The Latent Semantic Analysis Theory. *Current Directions in Psychological Science, 7,* 161–164.

Landauer, T. K., & Dumais, S. T. (1997). A solution to Plato's problem: The latent semantic analysis theory of acquisition, induction, and representation of knowledge. *Psychological Review, 104,* 211–240.

Latham, G. P., Erez, M., & Locke, E. A. (1988). Resolving scientific disputes by the joint design of crucial experiments by the antagonists: Application to the Erez-Latham dispute regarding participation in goal setting. *Journal of Applied Psychology, 73,* 753–772.

Livesay, K., & Burgess, C. (1998). Mediated priming in high-dimensional semantic space: No effect of direct semantic relationships or co-occurrence. *Brain and Cognition, 37,* 102–105.

Livesay, K., & Burgess, C. (2003). Mediated priming in the cerebral hemispheres. *Brain and Cognition, 53,* 283–286.

Logan, G. D. (1980). Attention and automaticity in Stroop and priming tasks: Theory and data. *Cognitive Psychology, 12,* 523–553.

Lorch, R. F., Jr. (1982). Priming and search processes in semantic memory: A test of three models of spreading activation. *Journal of Verbal Learning and Verbal Behavior, 21,* 468–492.

Lorch, R. F., Jr., Balota, D. A., & Stamm, E. G. (1986). Locus of inhibition effects in the priming of lexical decisions: pre- or postlexical access? *Memory & Cognition, 14,* 95–103.

Lucas, M. (2000). Semantic priming without association: A meta-analytic review. *Psychonomic Bulletin & Review, 7,* 618–630.

Luchins, A. S. (1942). Mechanization in problem solving. *Psychological Monographs, 54.*

Luck, S. J., Vogel, E. K., & Shapiro, K. L. (1996). Word meanings can be accessed but not reported during the attentional blink. *Nature, 383,* 616–618.

Lupker, S. J. (1984). Semantic priming without association: A second look. *Journal of Verbal Learning and Verbal Behavior, 23,* 709–733.

Lupker, S. J. (1986). Conscious identification: Where do you draw the line? *Behavioral and Brain Sciences, 9,* 37–38.

Lupker, S. J., Brown, P., & Colombo, L. (1997). Strategic control in a naming task: Changing routes or changing deadlines? *Journal of Experimental Psychology: Learning, Memory, and Cognition, 23,* 570-590.

MacLeod, C. M. (1991). Half a century of research on the Stroop effect: An integrative review. *Psychological Bulletin, 109,* 163–203.

Macmillan, N. A. (1986). The psychophysics of subliminal perception. *Behavioral and Brain Sciences, 9,* 38–39.

Macmillan, N. A., & Creelman, C. D. (2005). *Detection theory: A user's guide* (2nd ed.). Mahwah, NJ: Erlbaum.

MacNevin, C., & Besner, D. (2002). When are morphemic and semantic priming observed in visual word recognition? *Canadian Journal of Experimental Psychology, 56,* 112–119.

Marcel, A. J. (1983). Conscious and unconscious perception: Experiments on visual masking and word recognition. *Cognitive Psychology, 15,* 197–237.

Marí-Beffa, P., Fuentes, L. J., Catena, A., & Houghton, G. (2000). Semantic priming in the prime task effect: Evidence of automatic semantic processing of distractors. *Memory & Cognition, 28,* 635–647.

Marí-Beffa, P., Houghton, G., Estévez, A. F., & Fuentes, L. J. (2000). Word-based grouping affects the prime-task effect on semantic priming. *Journal of Experimental Psychology: Human Perception and Performance, 26,* 469–479.

Masson, M. E. J. (1991). A distributed memory model of context effects in word identification. In D. Besner & G. W. Humphreys (Eds.), *Basic processes in reading: Visual word recognition* (pp. 233–263). Hillsdale, NJ: Erlbaum.

Masson, M. E. J. (1995). A distributed memory model of semantic priming. *Journal of Experimental Psychology: Learning, Memory, and Cognition, 21,* 3–23.

Masson, M. E. J. (1999). Semantic priming in a recurrent network: Comment on Dalrymple-Alford and Marmurek (1999). *Journal of Experimental Psychology: Learning, Memory, and Cognition, 25,* 776–794.

Masson, M. E. J., & Borowsky, R. (1998). More than meets the eye: Context effects in word identification. *Memory & Cognition, 26,* 1245–1269.

Maxfield, L. (1997). Attention and semantic priming: A review of prime task effects. *Consciousness and Cognition, 6,* 204–218.

McCauley, C., Parmelee, C. M., Sperber, R. D., & Carr, T. H. (1980). Early extraction of meaning from pictures and its relation to conscious identification. *Journal of Experimental Psychology: Human Perception and Performance, 6,* 265–276.

McClelland, J. L. (1987). The case for interactionism in language processing. In M. Coltheart (Ed.), *Attention and performance XII: The psychology of reading* (pp. 3–35). Hillsdale, NJ: Elbaum.

McClelland, J. L., & Rumelhart, D. E. (1981). An interactive activation model of context effects in letter perception: Part 1. An account of basic findings. *Psychological Review, 88,* 375–407.

McClelland, J. L., & Rumelhart, D. E. (1985). Distributed memory and the representation of general and specific information. *Journal of Experimental Psychology: General, 114,* 159–188.

McClelland, J. L., & Rumelhart, D. E. (Eds.). (1986). *Parallel distributed processing: Explorations in the microstructure of cognition: Vol. 2. Psychological and biological models.* Cambridge, MA: MIT Press.

McKone, E. (1995). Short-term implicit memory for words and nonwords. *Journal of Experimental Psychology: Learning, Memory, and Cognition, 21,* 1108–1126.

McKoon, G., & Ratcliff, R. (1992). Spreading activation versus compound cue accounts of priming: Mediated priming revisited. *Journal of Experimental Psychology: Learning, Memory, and Cognition, 18,* 1155–1172.

McKoon, G., & Ratcliff, R. (1995). Conceptual combinations and relational contexts in free association and in priming in lexical decision and naming. *Psychonomic Bulletin & Review, 2,* 527–533.

McNamara, T. P. (1986). Mental representations of spatial relations. *Cognitive Psychology, 18,* 87–121.

McNamara, T. P. (1992a). Priming and constraints it places on theories of memory and retrieval. *Psychological Review, 99,* 650–662.

McNamara, T. P. (1992b). Theories of priming: I. Associative distance and lag. *Journal of Experimental Psychology: Learning, Memory, and Cognition, 18,* 1173–1190.

McNamara, T. P. (1994). Theories of priming: II. Types of primes. *Journal of Experimental Psychology: Learning, Memory, and Cognition, 20,* 507–520.

McNamara, T. P., & Altarriba, J. (1988). Depth of spreading activation revisited: Semantic mediated priming occurs in lexical decisions. *Journal of Memory and Language, 27,* 545–559.

McNamara, T. P., & Diwadkar, V. A. (1996). The context of memory retrieval. *Journal of Memory and Language, 35,* 877–892.

McNamara, T. P., & Healy, A. F. (1988). Semantic, phonological, and mediated priming in reading and lexical decisions. *Journal of Experimental Psychology: Learning, Memory, and Cognition, 14,* 398–409.

McNamara, T. P., & Holbrook, J. B. (2003). Semantic memory and priming. In A. F. Healy and R. W. Proctor (Eds.), *Experimental psychology* (pp. 447-474). Vol. 4 in I. B. Weiner (Editor-in-chief), *Handbook of psychology.* New York: Wiley.

McRae, K., & Boisvert, S. (1998). Automatic semantic similarity priming. *Journal of Experimental Psychology: Learning, Memory, and Cognition, 24,* 558–572.

McRae, K., de Sa, V. R., & Seidenberg, M. S. (1997). On the nature and scope of featural representations of word meaning. *Journal of Experimental Psychology: General, 126,* 99–130.

Mellers, B., Hertwig, R., & Kahneman, D. (2001). Do frequency representations eliminate conjunction effecs? An exercise in adversarial collaboration. *Psychological Science, 12,* 269–275.

Merikle, P. M., & Reingold, E. M. (1998). On demonstrating unconscious perception: Comment on Draine and Greenwald. *Journal of Experimental Psychology: General, 127,* 304–310.

Meyer, D. E., & Schvaneveldt, R. W. (1976). Meaning, memory structure, and mental processes. *Science, 192,* 27–33.

Meyer, D. E., Schvaneveldt, R. W., & Ruddy, M. G. (1975). Loci of contextual effects on visual word recognition. In P. M. A. Rabbitt & S. Dornic (Eds.), *Attention and performance V* (pp. 98–118). New York: Academic Press.

Miller, J. (2000). Measurement error in subliminal perception experiments: Simulation analyses of two regression methods. *Journal of Experimental Psychology: Human Perception and Performance, 26,* 1461–1477.

Morris, C. D., Bransford, J. D., & Franks, J. J. (1977). Levels of processing versus transfer appropriate processing. *Journal of Verbal Learning and Verbal Behavior, 16,* 519–533.

Morton, J. (1969). Interaction of information in word recognition. *Psychological Review, 76,* 165–178.

Moss, H. E., Ostrin, R. K., Tyler, L. K., & Marslen-Wilson, W. D. (1995). Accessing different types of lexical semantic information: Evidence from priming. *Journal of Experimental Psychology: Learning, Memory, and Cognition, 21,* 863–883.

Mummery, C. J., Shallice, T., & Price, C. J. (1999). Dual-process model in semantic priming: A functional imaging perspective. *NeuroImage, 9,* 516–525.

Murdock, B. B. (1982). A theory for the storage and retrieval of item and associative information. *Psychological Review, 89,* 609–626.

Naccache, L., Blandin, E., & Dehaene, S. (2002). Unconscious masked priming depends on temporal attention. *Psychological Science, 13,* 416–424.

Naccache, L., & Dehaene, S. (2001). Unconscious semantic priming extends to novel unseen stimuli. *Cognition, 80,* 223–237.

Nakagawa, A. (1991). Role of anterior and posterior attention networks in hemispheric asymmetries during lexical decisions. *Journal of Cognitive Neuroscience, 3,* 313–321.

Neely, J. H. (1976). Semantic priming and retrieval from lexical memory: Evidence for facilitatory and inhibitory processes. *Memory & Cognition, 4,* 648–654.

Neely, J. H. (1977). Semantic priming and retrieval from lexical memory: Roles of inhibitionless spreading activation and limited-capacity attention. *Journal of Experimental Psychology: General, 106,* 226–254.

Neely, J. H. (1991). Semantic priming effects in visual word recognition: A selective review of current findings and theories. In D. Besner & G. W. Humphreys (Eds.), *Basic processes in reading: Visual word recognition* (pp. 264–336). Hillsdale, NJ: Erlbaum.

Neely, J. H., & Kahan, T. A. (2001). Is semantic activation automatic? A critical re-evaluation. In H. L. Roediger, III, J. S. Nairne, I. Neath & A. M. Surprenant (Eds.), *The nature of remembering: Essays in honor of Robert G. Crowder* (pp. 69–93). Washington, DC: American Psychological Association.

Neely, J. H., & Keefe, D. E. (1989). Semantic context effects on visual word processing: A hybrid prospective-retrospective processing theory. In G. H. Bower (Ed.), *The psychology of learning and motivation: Advances in research and theory* (Vol. 24, pp. 207–248). New York: Academic Press.

Neely, J. H., Keefe, D. E., & Ross, K. L. (1989). Semantic priming in the lexical decision task: Roles of prospective prime-generated expectancies and retrospective semantic matching. *Journal of Experimental Psychology: Learning, Memory, and Cognition, 15,* 1003–1019.

Nelson, D. L., McEvoy, C. L., & Pointer, L. (2003). Spreading activation or spooky action at a distance? *Journal of Experimental Psychology: Learning, Memory, and Cognition, 29,* 42–52.

Nelson, D. L., McEvoy, C. L., & Schreiber, T. A. (1991). *The University of South Florida word association, rhyme, and word fragment norms.* Unpublished manuscript.

Nelson, D. L., & Zhang, N. (2000). The ties that bind what is known to the recall of what is new. *Psychonomic Bulletin & Review, 7,* 604–617.

Nelson, D. L., Zhang, N., & McKinney, V. M. (2001). The ties that bind what is known to the recognition of what is new. *Journal of Experimental Psychology: Learning, Memory, and Cognition, 27,* 1147–1159.

Newell, A. (1973). Production systems: Models of control structures. In W. G. Chase (Ed.), *Visual information processing.* New York: Academic Press.

Newell, A., & Simon, H. (1972). *Human problem solving.* Englewood Cliffs, NJ: Prentice Hall.

Norman, D. A., & Rumelhart, D. E. (1975). *Explorations in cognition.* San Francisco: Freeman.

Norris, D. (1984). The effects of frequency, repetition and stimulus quality in visual word recognition. *Quarterly Journal of Experimental Psychology, 36A,* 507–518.

Norris, D. (1986). Word recognition: Context effects without priming. *Cognition, 22,* 93–136.

Norris, D. (1995). Signal detection theory and modularity: On being sensitive to the power of bias models of semantic priming. *Journal of Experimental Psychology: Human Perception and Performance, 21,* 935–939.

Oldfield, R. C., & Wingfield, A. (1965). Response latencies in naming objects. *Quarterly Journal of Experimental Psychology, 17,* 273–281.

Ortells, J. J., Abad, M. J. F., Noguera, C., & Lupiáñez, J. (2001). Influence of prime-probe stimulus onset asynchrony and prime precuing manipulations on semantic priming effects with words in a lexical-decision task. *Journal of Experimental Psychology: Human Perception and Performance, 27,* 75–91.

Osterhout, L., & Holcomb, P. J. (1995). Event-related potentials and language comprehension. In M. D. Rugg & M. G. H. Coles (Eds.), *Electrophysiology of mind* (pp. 171–215). Oxford: Oxford University Press.

Paap, K. R. (1986). The pilfering of awareness and guilt by association. *Behavioral and Brain Sciences, 9,* 45–46.

Paap, K. R., Newsome, S. L., McDonald, J. E., & Schvaneveldt, R. W. (1982). An activation-verification model for letter and word recognition: The word superiority effect. *Psychological Review, 89*, 573–594.

Parkin, A. J. (1979). Specifying levels of processing. *Quarterly Journal of Experimental Psychology, 31*, 175–195.

Pastore, R. E., Crawley, E., Skelly, M. A., & Berens, M. S. (2003). Signal detection theory analyses of semantic priming in word recognition. *Journal of Experimental Psychology: Human Perception and Performance, 29*, 1251–1266.

Pastore, R. E., Crawley, E. J., Berens, M. S., & Skelly, M. A. (2003). "Nonparametric" *A'* and other modern misconceptions about signal detection theory. *Psychonomic Bulletin & Review, 10*, 556–569.

Pecher, D. (2001). Perception is a two-way junction: Feedback semantics in word recognition. *Psychonomic Bulletin & Review, 8*, 545–551.

Pecher, D., & Raaijmakers, J. G. W. (1999). Automatic priming effects for new associations in lexical decision and perceptual identification. *Quarterly Journal of Experimental Psychology, 52A*, 593–614.

Pecher, D., Zeelenberg, R., & Raaijmakers, J. G. W. (1998). Does pizza prime coin? Perceptual priming in lexical decision and pronunciation. *Journal of Memory and Language, 38*, 401–418.

Perea, M., & Lupker, S. J. (2003). Does *jugde* activate COURT? Transposed-letter similarity effects in masked associative priming. *Memory & Cognition, 31*, 829-841.

Perea, M., & Rosa, E. (2002). Does the proportion of associatively related pairs modulate the associative priming effect at very brief stimulus-onset asynchronies? *Acta Psychologica, 110*, 103–124.

Peterson, R. R., & Simpson, G. B. (1989). Effect of backward priming on word recognition in single-word and sentence contexts. *Journal of Experimental Psychology: Learning, Memory, and Cognition, 15*, 1020–1032.

Pexman, P. M., Lupker, S. J., & Hino, Y. (2002). The impact of feedback semantics in visual word recognition: Number-of-features effects in lexical decision and naming tasks. *Psychonomic Bulletin & Review, 9*, 542-549.

Plaut, D. C. (1995). Semantic and associative priming in a distributed attractor network. In *Proceedings of the 17th Annual Conference of the Cognitive Science Society* (pp. 37–42). Hillsdale, NJ: Erlbaum.

Plaut, D. C. (1997). Structure and function in the lexical system: Insights from distributed models of word reading and lexical decision. *Language and Cognitive Processes, 12*, 765–805.

Plaut, D. C., & Booth, J. R. (2000). Individual and developmental differences in semantic priming: Empirical and computational support for a single-mechanism account of lexical processing. *Psychological Review, 107*, 786–823.

Plaut, D. C., McClelland, J. L., Seidenberg, M. S., & Patterson, K. (1996). Understanding normal and impaired word reading: Computational principles in quasi-regular domains. *Psychological Review, 103*, 56–115.

Pollatsek, A., & Well, A. D. (1995). On the use of counterbalanced designs in cognitive research: A suggestion for a better and more powerful analysis. *Journal of Experimental Psychology: Learning, Memory, and Cognition, 21*, 785–794.

Posner, M. I., & Snyder, C. R. R. (1975a). Attention and cognitive control. In R. L. Solso (Ed.), *Information processing and cognition: The Loyola symposium* (pp. 55–85). Hillsdale, NJ: Erlbaum.

Posner, M. I., & Snyder, C. R. R. (1975b). Facilitation and inhibition in the processing of signals. In P. M. A. Rabbitt (Ed.), *Attention and performance V* (pp. 669–682). London: Academic Press.

Postman, L., & Keppel, G. (Eds.). (1970). *Norms of word association*. New York: Academic Press.

Protter, M. H., & Morrey, C. B., Jr. (1964). *Modern mathematical analysis*. Reading, MA: Addison-Wesley.

Quillian, M. R. (1967). Word concepts: A theory and simulation of some basic semantic capabilities. *Behavioral Science, 12*, 410–430.

Raaijmakers, J. G. W. (2003). A further look at the "Language-as-Fixed-Effect Fallacy". *Canadian Journal of Experimental Psychology, 57*, 141–151.

Raaijmakers, J. G. W., Schrijnemakers, J. M. C., & Gremmen, F. (1999). How to deal with "The Language-as-Fixed-Effect Fallacy": Common misconceptions and alternative solutions. *Journal of Memory and Language, 41*, 416–426.

Ratcliff, R. (1978). A theory of memory retrieval. *Psychological Review, 85*, 59–108.

Ratcliff, R., Hockley, W., & McKoon, G. (1985). Components of activation: Repetition and priming effects in lexical decision and recognition. *Journal of Experimental Psychology: General, 114*, 435–450.

Ratcliff, R., & McKoon, G. (1981). Does activation really spread? *Psychological Review, 88*, 454–462.

Ratcliff, R., & McKoon, G. (1988). A retrieval theory of priming in memory. *Psychological Review, 95*, 385–408.

Ratcliff, R., & McKoon, G. (1995). Sequential effects in lexical decision: Tests of compound cue retrieval theory. *Journal of Experimental Psychology: Learning, Memory, and Cognition, 21*, 1380–1388.

Ratcliff, R., & McKoon, G. (1996). Bias effects in implicit memory tasks. *Journal of Experimental Psychology: General, 125*, 403–421.

Ratcliff, R., & McKoon, G. (2001). A multinomial model for short-term priming in word identification. *Psychological Review, 108*, 835–846.

Reingold, E. M., & Merikle, P. M. (1988). Using direct and indirect measures to study perception without awareness. *Perception & Psychophysics, 44*, 563–575.

Reynolds, M., & Besner, D. (2002). Neighbourhood density effects in reading aloud: New insights from simulations with the DRC model. *Canadian Journal of Experimental Psychology, 56*, 310–318.

Reynolds, M., & Besner, D. (2004). Neighbourhood density, word frequency, and spelling-sound regularity effects in naming: Similiarities and differences between skilled readers and the dual route cascaded computational model. *Canadian Journal of Experimental Psychology, 58*, 13–31.

Rhodes, G., Parkin, A. J., & Tremewan, T. (1993). Semantic priming and sensitivity in lexical decision. *Journal of Experimental Psychology: Human Perception and Performance, 19*, 154–165.

Richards, L., & Chiarello, C. (1995). Depth of associated activation in the cerebral hemispheres: mediated versus direct priming. *Neuropsychologia, 33*, 171–179.

Rissman, J., Eliassen, J. C., & Blumstein, S. E. (2003). An event-related fMRI investigation of implicit semantic priming. *Journal of Cognitive Neuroscience, 15*, 1160–1175.

Rosenblatt, F. (1962). *Principles of neurodynamics*. New York: Spartan.

Rossell, S. L., Bullmore, E. T., Williams, S. C. R., & David, A. S. (2001). Brain activation during automatic and controlled processing of semantic relations: a priming experiment using lexical-decision. *Neuropsychologia, 39*, 1167–1176.

Rossell, S. L., Price, C. J., & Nobre, A. C. (2003). The anatomy and time course of semantic priming investigated by fMRI and ERPs. *Neuropsychologia, 41*, 550–564.

Rubenstein, H., Garfield, L., & Millikan, J. A. (1970). Homographic entries in the internal lexicon. *Journal of Verbal Learning and Verbal Behavior, 9*, 487–494.

Rugg, M. D. (1985). The effects of semantic priming and word repetition on event-related potentials. *Psychophysiology, 22*, 642–647.

Rumelhart, D. E., & McClelland, J. L. (1982). An interactive activation model of context effects in letter perception: Part 2. The contextual enhancement effect and some tests and extensions of the model. *Psychological Review, 89*, 60–94.

Rumelhart, D. E., & McClelland, J. L. (Eds.). (1986). *Parallel distributed processing: Explorations in the microstructure of cognition: Vol. 1. Foundations*. Cambridge, MA: MIT Press.

Ryle, G. (1949). *The concept of mind*. London: Hutchinson.

Scarborough, D. L., Cortese, C., & Scarborough, H. S. (1977). Frequency and repetition effects in lexical memory. *Journal of Experimental Psychology: Human Perception and Performance, 3*, 1–17.

Schneider, W., & Shiffrin, R. M. (1977). Controlled and automatic human information processing: I. Detection, search, and attention. *Psychological Review, 84*, 1–66.

Schvaneveldt, R. W., & McDonald, J. E. (1981). Semantic context and the encoding of words: Evidence for two modes of stimulus analysis. *Journal of Experimental Psychology: Human Perception and Performance, 7,* 673–687.

Seidenberg, M. S., & McClelland, J. L. (1989). A distributed, developmental model of word recognition and naming. *Psychological Review, 96,* 523–568.

Seidenberg, M. S., Waters, G. S., Sanders, M., & Langer, P. (1984). Pre- and postlexical loci of contextual effects on word recognition. *Memory & Cognition, 12,* 315–328.

Shears, C., & Chiarello, C. (2003). No go on neutrals? An interhemispheric account of semantic category priming. *Laterality, 8,* 1–23.

Shelton, J. R., & Martin, R. C. (1992). How semantic is automatic semantic priming? *Journal of Experimental Psychology: Learning, Memory, and Cognition, 18,* 1191–1210.

Shiffrin, R. M., & Schneider, W. (1977). Controlled and automatic human information processing: II. Perceptual learning, automatic attending, and a general theory. *Psychological Review, 84,* 127–190.

Silva-Pereyra, J., Harmony, T., Villanueva, G., Fernández, T., Rodríguez, M., Galán, L., Díaz-Comas, L., Bernal, J., Fernández-Bouzas, A., Marosi, E., & Reyes, A. (1999). N400 and lexical decisions: automatic or controlled processing? *Clinical Neurophysiology, 110,* 813–824.

Simpson, G. B. (1994). Context and the processing of ambiguous words. In M. A. Gernsbacher (Ed.), *Handbook of psycholinguistics* (pp. 359–374). San Diego, CA: Academic Press.

Smith, J. E. K. (1976). The assuming-will-make-it-so fallacy. *Journal of Verbal Learning and Verbal Behavior, 15,* 262–263.

Smith, L. C., Briand, K., Klein, R. M., & den Heyer, K. (1987). On the generality of Becker's verification model. *Canadian Journal of Psychology, 41,* 379–386.

Smith, M. C. (1979). Contextual facilitation in a letter search task depends on how the prime is processed. *Journal of Experimental Psychology: Human Perception and Performance, 5,* 239–251.

Smith, M. C., Bentin, S., & Spalek, T. M. (2001). Attentional constraints of semantic activation during visual word recognition. *Journal of Experimental Psychology: Learning, Memory, and Cognition, 27,* 1289–1298.

Smith, M. C., & Besner, D. (2001). Modulating semantic feedback in visual word recognition. *Psychonomic Bulletin & Review, 8,* 111–117.

Smith, M. C., Besner, D., & Miyoshi, H. (1994). New limits to automaticity: Context modulates semantic priming. *Journal of Experimental Psychology: Learning, Memory, and Cognition, 20,* 104–115.

Smith, M. C., Meiran, N., & Besner, D. (2000). On the interaction between linguistic and pictorial systems in the absence of semantic mediation: Evidence from a priming paradigm. *Memory & Cognition, 28,* 204–213.

Smith, M. C., Theodor, L., & Franklin, P. E. (1983). The relationship between contextual facilitation and depth of processing. *Journal of Experimental Psychology: Learning, Memory, and Cognition, 9,* 697–712.

Sperling, G. (1960). The information available in brief visual presentations. *Psychological Monographs, 74.*

Squire, L. R. (1987). *Memory and brain.* New York: Oxford University Press.

Stanovich, K. E., & West, R. F. (1983). On priming by a sentence context. *Journal of Experimental Psychology: General, 112,* 1–36.

Stenberg, G., Lindgren, M., Johansson, M., Olsson, A., & Rosen, I. (2000). Semantic processing without conscious identification: Evidence from event-related potentials. *Journal of Experimental Psychology: Learning, Memory, and Cognition, 26,* 973–1004.

Sternberg, S. (1969). The discovery of processing stages: Extensions of Donders' method. In W. G. Koster (Ed.), *Attention and performance II* (pp. 276–315). Amsterdam: North-Holland.

Stolz, J. A., & Besner, D. (1996). Role of set in visual word recognition: Activation and activation blocking as nonautomatic processes. *Journal of Experimental Psychology: Human Perception and Performance, 22,* 1166–1177.

Stolz, J. A., & Besner, D. (1997). Visual word recognition: Effort after meaning but not (necessarily) meaning after effort. *Journal of Experimental Psychology: Human Perception and Performance, 23,* 1314–1322.

Stolz, J. A., & Besner, D. (1998). Levels of representation in visual word recognition: A dissociation between morphological priming and semantic processing. *Journal of Experimental Psychology: Human Perception and Performance, 24,* 1642–1655.

Stolz, J. A., & Besner, D. (1999). On the myth of automatic semantic activation in reading. *Current Directions in Psychological Science, 8,* 61–65.

Stolz, J. A., & Neely, J. H. (1995). When target degradation does and does not enhance semantic context effects in word recognition. *Journal of Experimental Psychology: Learning, Memory, and Cognition, 21,* 596–611.

Stone, G. O., & Van Orden, G. C. (1992). Revolving empirical inconsistencies concerning priming, frequency, and nonword foils in lexical decision. *Language and Speech, 35,* 295–324.

Stroop, J. R. (1935). Studies of interference in serial verbal reactions. *Journal of Experimental Psychology, 18,* 643–662.

Swinney, D. A. (1979). Lexical access during sentence comprehension: (Re)consideration of context effects. *Journal of Verbal Learning and Verbal Behavior, 18,* 645–659.

Taylor, T. E., & Lupker, S. J. (2001). Sequential effects in naming: A time-criterion account. *Journal of Experimental Psychology: Learning, Memory, and Cognition, 27,* 117-138.

Thompson-Schill, S. L., Kurtz, K. J., & Gabrieli, J. D. E. (1998). Effects of semantic and associative relatedness on automatic priming. *Journal of Memory and Language, 38,* 440–458.

Tweedy, J. R., Lapinski, R. H., & Schvaneveldt, R. W. (1977). Semantic-context effects on word recognition: Influence of varying the proportion of items presented in an appropriate context. *Memory & Cognition, 5,* 84–89.

Tyler, L. K., & Moss, H. E. (1997). Functional properties of concepts: Studies of normal and brain-damaged patients. *Cognitive Neuropsychology, 14,* 511–545.

Usher, M., & McClelland, J. L. (2001). The time course of perceptual choice: The leaky, competing accumulator model. *Psychological Review, 108,* 550–592.

VanVoorhis, B. A., & Dark, V. J. (1995). Semantic matching, response mode, and response mapping as contributors to retroactive and proactive priming. *Journal of Experimental Psychology: Learning, Memory, and Cognition, 21,* 913–932.

Versace, R., & Nevers, B. (2003). Word frequency effect on repetition priming as a function of prime duration and delay between the prime and the target. *British Journal of Psychology, 94,* 389–408.

Weber, E. U. (1988). Expectation and variance of item resemblance distributions in a convolution-correlation model of distributed memory. *Journal of Mathematical Psychology, 32,* 1–43.

Wechsler, D. (1991). *Wechsler intelligence scale for children* (3rd ed.). San Antonio, TX: Harcourt Brace.

Weisbrod, M., Kiefer, M., Winkler, S., Maier, S., Hill, H., Roesch-Ely, D., & Spitzer, M. (1999). Electrophysiological correlates of direct versus indirect semantic priming in normal volunteers. *Cognitive Brain Research, 8,* 289–298.

Whitney, P. (1998). *The psychology of language.* Boston: Houghton Mifflin.

Whittlesea, B. W. A., & Jacoby, L. L. (1990). Interaction of prime representation with visual degradation: Is priming a retrieval phenomenon? *Journal of Memory and Language, 29,* 546–565.

Wickelgren, W. A. (1977). Speed-accuracy tradeoff and information processing dynamics. *Acta Psychologica, 41,* 67–85.

Wickens, T. D., & Keppel, G. (1983). On the choice of design and of test statistic in the analysis of experiments with sampled materials. *Journal of Verbal Learning and Verbal Behavior, 22,* 296–309.

Wilding, J. M. (1986). Joint effects of semantic priming and repetition in a lexical decision task: Implications for a model of lexical access. *Quarterly Journal of Experimental Psychology, 38A,* 213–228.

Wilding, J. M. (1988). The interaction of word frequency and stimulus quality in the lexical decision task: Now you see it, now you don't. *Quarterly Journal of Experimental Psychology, 40A,* 757–770.

Winer, B. J. (1971). *Statistical principles in experimental design* (2nd ed.). New York: McGraw-Hill.

Woltz, D. J. (1990). Repetition of semantic comparisons: Temporary and persistent priming effects. *Journal of Experimental Psychology: Learning, Memory, and Cognition, 16,* 392–403.

Woltz, D. J. (1996). Perceptual and conceptual priming in a semantic reprocessing task. *Memory & Cognition, 24,* 429–440.

Zeelenberg, R., & Pecher, D. (2002). False memories and lexical decision: Even twelve primes do not cause long-term semantic priming. *Acta Psychologica, 109,* 269–284.

Zeelenberg, R., Pecher, D., de Kok, D., & Raaijmakers, J. G. W. (1998). Inhibition from non-word primes in lexical decision reexamined: The critical influence of instructions. *Journal of Experimental Psychology: Learning, Memory, and Cognition, 24,* 1068–1079.

Index of Names

Subject Index